# Awkward Moments
## WITH MEN

# Awkward Moments
## WITH MEN

### STORIES ABOUT THE SEX
### WE CAN'T LIVE WITHOUT

by Shannon Lee Miller and Megan Leigh Byrd

# Dedication

*To our parents. All that stuff you mentioned about life not being easy? You were right. We get it now. We love you.*

# Table of Contents

## Editorial Disclaimer

This is a work of non-fiction. However, there has been slight fibbing when it comes to names and identifying characteristics so that we may protect both the innocent, as well as the legion of "men" we've attempted to date and who've screwed up so royally that we couldn't *not* write it down. Everything within these pages happened, though sometimes our recollection is more precise than at other times. If it makes you feel better, you may blame these less exact instances on any of the following: a) alcohol, b) denial, or c) Harry Potter.

*Introduction*

# ADMISSION OF GUILT

S omeone is going to be disappointed. That always happens when you publish a book. Not that we'd really know since this is our first foray into authordom, but people who have published books before have told us this. Okay, they didn't really tell us. They told Oprah while sitting on her couch indulging in public therapy. But they said it nevertheless: *Someone isn't going to like what you say.*

And they're right. This writing is already feeling flimsy. Give it four months and we'll probably traverse the continent, rounding up every copy out of sheer embarrassment that we ever thought this book was decent reading material. So, to make things efficient, instead of acknowledging everyone who helped us make this book, we figured we'd go ahead and apologize to everyone who will be disappointed by its release and mass distribution.

I. OURSELVES

It just occurred to us that Oprah quit, and now we have more of a reason to be disappointed than everyone else. We'll never get to sit on her couch and talk about all of our personal issues. Ellen, this means we're coming for you.

## 2. OUR PARENTS

We're not perfect, and this book makes that painfully clear. They did an excellent job rearing us and, in return, we have done embarrassing and inappropriate things. For instance, instead of acting like normal human beings or American politicians and lying about our transgressions, we are writing them down and selling them for cold, hard cash. They still love us, even though we didn't go to med school and are currently sending out press releases with the word "penis" in them. I bet they wish we had written about ponies.

## 3. OUR PAST AND PRESENT SIGNIFICANT OTHERS

We're making money off a lot of men. A rare few who are stand-up gentlemen, but mostly a hefty lot who deserve to be sent through a trash compactor with a skunk. We will not name names (but gee, would we ever like to) because that could incur highly volatile lawsuits, but we will raise our eyebrows suggestively at the guilty parties. You left us with heartbreak, sirs, and now we will wipe our tears with the millions of dollars we will make off your awkwardness. (Note to reader: The bit about the money could be a premature and inaccurate statement.)

## 4. MOST IMPORTANTLY, OUR READERS

When you bought this book, you probably assumed you were purchasing a book from real authors. People who have a chance at winning Pulitzer Prizes and having museums named after them where their frocks are hung up on display with signs that read something like, "Margaret Mitchell wore this dress every day while writing *Gone with the Wind*." But we don't wear frocks. And we don't even know what a Pulitzer Prize looks like—Is it a statue? A pen cast in gold? A large plaque purchased at Wal-Mart? We will never know. Truth is, you don't even have to really know what you're doing to make a book. Unlike Advanced Calculus, there are no prerequisites. No one even has to buy the bloody thing, but as long as you can slap a decent number of words on a page, you, too, can gain the title. So with this in mind, please be kind to us. We are new authors. Fledglings. And we're as vulnerable and sure to be swallowed up as those little baby birds you see on Animal Planet who fall out of the nest and then are immediately surrounded by wild, poultry-obsessed cheetahs. Please know that we tried and that, if you return the book, it is almost certain that we will die sad and alone, surrounded by a pile of awkward regrets.

# The Stories

"*Being a woman is a terribly difficult task, since it consists principally in dealing with men.*"

**—Joseph Conrad**

# One

# THE CATHOLIC
# OF THE ROUNDTABLE

*I*'m in a Catholic cafeteria drinking beer. I'm wearing heels and a form-fitting black dress, but I've already forgotten that by now because the menu of barbecue has forced me to bib a white Dixie napkin into my neckline like I am in a hotdog-eating contest. Only I'm not in a contest; I'm on a first date. I was told it was black tie, but it appears by the overwhelming number of Tommy Bahama shirts that The Catholic of the Roundtable has been misinformed.

I'm only a medium fan of barbecue, but no one would know that by looking at me. I have it piled on my plate. I could build a small castle with my pork. This is all part of my new strategy to harness inappropriate words from coming out of my mouth since discovering that when The Catholic of the Roundtable said, "black tie dinner party," what he really meant was, "casual swearing in ceremony for the Knights of Columbus."

I imagine some dates are supposed to be challenging. When you go mountain climbing, for instance. Or when you meet your boyfriend's ex-wife who can't go three sentences without mentioning the word "alimony." But this date was supposed to be easy. Cakewalk easy. We were supposed to do something like have a beer and talk about how much we both unexpectedly like wild geese. After all, The Catholic of the Roundtable was my rebound. And rebounds aren't supposed to take effort. Or social skills. Or an extensive knowledge of one of the world's great religions. Only the ability to consume adult beverages and the foresight to wax. But instead of partaking in overpriced Italian, I end up severely overdressed at a Catholic church being asked if I know the difference between "faithful navigators," "district deputies," and "supreme masters."

I can see cupid maliciously dancing off in the sidelines. Welcome back to dating.

When he picks me up, I know I'm not going to marry him. He's handsome, sure, but in a wax figurine kind of way. The type of person you observe, but never actually interact with. He's wearing a nice suit paired with some shined dress shoes. His smile takes up the entire driveway. When I open the door, I immediately regret my decision. I'm overwhelmed by him. And not in the good, swooning, Frank Sinatra kind of way, but in the way you get at the DMV when you realize there are no less than three hundred people in line and none of them speak English.

But I force a smile. I'm not here, after all, to get married. I'm here for the free food. I'm here so when my friends ask me how my weekend went, I don't have to say, "I knitted a sweater for my dog."

We get in his car to leave and he buckles my seatbelt for me. An odd gesture to be sure, but he's what you'd call a prepared person, the kind of guy who childproofed his cabinets even though he lives alone. *Just in case*, he says. And who can really argue with that? Toddlers appear at my apartment unexpectedly all the time.

I met him months back at some government building. He'd

been on duty at the fire station and came when some eight year old pulled the alarm and went running. He rode in on the large red truck and stepped out all six foot three of his inches onto the pavement. I was standing to the side just watching the lack of emergency unfold when he walked over to me. "Are you alright ma'am?" And just then, of course, I was. After all it's true what they say: every boy wants to be a firefighter, and every girl wants to kiss one.

He asked me out then, but I said no. I was taken. In love. But that was then and this is now.

When The Catholic of the Roundtable isn't a firefighter, he's something akin to an emergency responder. I don't really know what this means except to know that he has sirens on the top of his SUV and instead of listening to music, we listen about all the wrecks occurring within the city limits. When we drive past a fire station, he honks. He knows the numbers of all the ambulances that drive past us by heart. They are like his children. Only large and made of metal.

When we pull into the church, I get my first hint that something is off kilter. Black tie dinner parties normally occur at places like restaurants and well-decorated residences, not houses of God.

"I think the ceremony is in the chapel," he says, "and then dinner is in the gym afterward." He points to a brick structure that has a banner draped over the doorway: "Senior Bingo— Mondays at 6:00 P.M."

I try not to panic. Ceremony? I run through our list of text messages, none of which committed me to sitting through speeches or slideshows. What are we doing here? Has someone died? Are we championing the children's choir? Or a cure for leukemia in pets? All I can picture are malnourished puppies sitting in Colbie Caillat's lap. I look at him begging for an explanation. Or, better yet, a *Gotcha! Zing. How hilarious. Now here's what we're really doing*... But instead of laughing and pulling the wool off my terrified eyes, he says: "How much do you know about the Knights of Columbus?"

I pause. And then I pause again. The pause runs around the earth twelve times and then continues dancing in orbit. I have absolutely, positively nothing to say. I know nothing about the Knights of Columbus except that it sounds like a PBS special. And I don't know why they'd have anything to do with me. I must look mildly handicapped because The Catholic of the Roundtable puts his hand on my hand, like he's cradling a wounded duck.

"It's okay," he says. "I realize we can't all have the same background."

And then he launches into a pint-sized history of the Catholic Church and an explanation of the night's events, which include his induction ceremony into the Knights as Treasurer.

This all would have been helpful information, I think, *beforehand.*

We walk into the church, he does his Catholic bit, and I look around. There are about thirty people in the room, most of which are wearing khaki shorts and polos. A few of the women are wearing casual sundresses, but most have opted for jeans. I immediately feel like the woman who goes to a funeral wearing her cleavage. Inappropriate. Embarrassing. The walking scarlet letter.

"Don't worry," he says, rubbing my back. "Classic black is always appropriate."

Sure, and Bill Clinton didn't have sexual relations with that woman. I want to pull all the hair out of his nostrils.

We walk to the back of the chapel where other to-be-inducted Knights have accumulated. The guy who seems to be leading the ceremony is explaining how everything will work. I tune most of it out until the part where he mentions something about me putting a ribbon around The Catholic of the Roundtable's neck. My eyes perk up. Was he talking to me? I momentarily had nodded off to a land where people go to Olive Garden on the first date. "I'm sorry . . . what did you say? I couldn't quite hear you." I brush a strand of hair away from my face and lie directly to the man of God.

"Yes, and that's when you can walk to the front and put the ribbon around his neck . . ."

A healthy pause fills the air. Pregnant even. I consider my options. Most roads end with me married and not allowed to use birth control. I look at The Catholic of the Roundtable. He has very large eyes. Eyes that beg me to treat him like Seabiscuit. He angles his neck to demonstrate how perfect it is for ribboning. I feel bad, truly. Perhaps he thought rebounding was something only Lebron James did. Perhaps he wanted more. Perhaps he's already told his mother about me and she's started researching florists for our wedding. He grabs my hand, and I wiggle my fingers. This is too much. I've known the ribbon as long as I've known him. And I'm certain if I put a ribbon around his neck, I'll have to put a kiss on his lips, and a ring on his finger. We'll be married tomorrow and have children on Thursday.

Moments like these are meant for families. Wives who grew up doing Catholicky things and who genuinely want to crown ribbons around their husbands' heads like they just won the Kentucky Derby of religion. I'm proud of him. But only in that kind of way you get proud of strangers when you see them holding open doors for the elderly. *Good human being*, you clap in your head, but you certainly don't go over and pin a medal on their collar and take pictures that will sit framed for years on the mantle place next to Grandma's ashes.

"I think it's best if I sit this round out," I joke seriously.

He smiles, but I can tell he wants a divorce.

Despite my lack of involvement, the ceremony is short and sweet and full of traditions I am completely unfamiliar with. I take pictures of him putting his ribbon on his own neck, applaud at a reasonable decibel, and stand and sit according to my neighbors. At one point The Catholic of the Roundtable puts his hand on my knee as if to say he has forgiven me for my non-ribboning and that we can still have triplets. I try to make my knee feel as indifferent and stubborn as possible.

After all the ribbons have been hung and all blessings have been blessed, we walk with the newly-minted Knights to the cafeteria where barbecue is served on Styrofoam plates, and I sit at a table listening to bad ideas for Catholic t-shirt slogans. I make it a goal to not stop eating. Ever. The only words I utter are, "Make that two please," when a Supreme Master asks if I would like a beer.

Inevitably, finally, the dinner is over and we emerge from the church into fresh, protestant air. It's through, I think. It's done. I'm only ten miles away from a place where the only kind of robe is terrycloth. I will shake his hand, delete his number, and then submerge myself in more bubbles than a preschooler's birthday party.

But he learned his lesson with the ribbon. People can only really say no when you ask them a question. So he holds the door open for me and says, "Coffee next." He's decisive and firm. No one before has ever made me dread dark roast from Kenya. I grimace, but all the same climb into his emergency response vehicle in time to hear the tail end of a pile up on Briley Parkway. Then we head to a coffee shop on the other side of town to figure out how many other things we don't have in common.

The Catholic of the Roundtable takes me to his spot. The kind of coffee shop where none of the chairs match, all of the tables wobble, and every regular has taken a personal oath to boycott Starbucks, those "savages." He knows all the baristas.

He leans on the counter, laughs, and tries to make me believe that everyone wants to drink shots of vanilla off his firefighting nipples. I ignore it. I order a small coffee and head for a chair with its back to the wall, but he intervenes.

"Do you mind if I sit there? If an assailant comes in, that seat will better prepare me to protect you."

I stand very still. I'm afraid if I move, I will slap him in the face. No one's used the word assailant since 1857, except for maybe John Grisham. Someone really needs to tell him he isn't an actual knight, and I'm not an actual damsel in distress. A man with an AK-47 is not going to come in here and demand all the almond croissants. But I save my breath, and we settle into our respective leather seats.

It doesn't take me very long to figure out that The Catholic of the Roundtable isn't very interested in me. My sole purpose for the next hour is to sip coffee and listen to his successful resume of life accomplishments. He starts, as most people do, with war stories. He's a hero. Shot in the Middle East. I find this impressive and admirable and consider briefly that the Knights of Columbus catastrophe might be overlooked as he once spent a year in a wheelchair, six months on crutches, and has a skin graft to prove it. But my admiration quickly dilapidates as he proceeds to tell me everything that's happened in his life since he was circumcised.

He speaks five languages fluently. Polish (how useful can that possibly be?), German, Italian, French, and English. I hear a snippet of each so I can perform my own polygraph. He once even tried to teach himself to speak Old English, and he recites the prologue to the *Canterbury Tales* while I gulp my dark roast. He is a statistician, runs a nonprofit for children with cancer, has sailboats in the Pacific and Atlantic, owns a culinary kitchen and a salt water pool, is a certified vet tech who has performed surgeries on tiny puppies, is a fireman in his spare time, and once helped uncover a lost submarine. He is also, did I mention, a Knight of Columbus.

I finish my coffee before he takes a sip of his, and I wonder if he's going to start pulling out family photos. I hope he doesn't have one of those wallets that extend into an accordion of pictures of five year olds at Olan Mills. I fumble the empty cup in my hand and wait (naïvely) for him to ask me about me because, well, that's what kind, considerate, just plain decent human beings do. But instead he says, "I don't like to talk about myself because it makes people feel overwhelmed with how much I've accomplished."

And that's when I know, even if he is a war hero, firefighting, five-language speaker, I don't ever want to take shots of vanilla off his chest. I only want to drown him in a vat of eggnog.

We wait for him to finish his coffee, and then get back in the car so he can drive me home. He comes inside, uninvited, and tells me how to do things like potty train my dog and ensure the lifespan of my ferns. He puts his hands around my waist and asks what movie we're going to watch—an unfortunate question as I've had far too many storylines for the evening. I rub my eyes, dawn an egregious yawn, and tell him the day (or did I mean his life?) has been far too eventful, and I need some shuteye. He looks at me with his large eyes that say, "I'm disappointed you don't want to take my accomplished clothes off." My eyes look back at him and say, "Your accomplished clothes have far too many personalities for a pair of slacks."

I tell him I will call him, but what I really mean is I will call him if I have a fire, if my dog needs surgery, or if I have an unexpected urge to translate the Bible into Old English. Those items aside, my phone will practice doing something he never does: absolutely, positively nothing.

## Two

# THE BOY IN PUPPY LOVE

*T*he only benefit to having sex at sixteen is saving yourself the ridicule of not having sex when everybody else with a learner's permit is shagging like a puppy mill stud. Having sex with The Boy in Puppy Love was a strategic move—he was in college, he'd bought me a locket for my birthday, and he had a snowboard. He was, in any self-indulgent sixteen-year-old's opinion, the ideal candidate.

A product of the public school system, I was never really discouraged from having sex. In fact, it's safe to say that the Board of Education expected a good fraction of the class of '02 to have first-hand experience with gonorrhea before the eleventh grade. Sure, they gave us a few half-assed lectures, but nothing that truly struck fear into our hearts. So, instead of dwelling on things like the "meaning" of sex, they taught us how to put a condom on a banana, where to get an abortion, and sent us off into the world.

The Boy in Puppy Love's bedroom was in a dark corner of his family's basement. It had a double bed and a stereo. His parents rarely ventured to this part of the house so we weren't afraid of being caught with our pants down trying to assemble our junk properly. His father was a busy man. He was deeply involved in the Lions Club and spent most of his time organizing rummage sales and attending adult line-dancing classes. His mother was an insomniac who spent most of her time upstairs playing solitaire with a bottle of Friexenet.

Fortunately for our girded loins, they didn't seem to know we existed. Nevertheless, we opted to err on the side of paranoia since we were completely uncertain of what good sex exactly entailed. In my misguided adolescent mind, I expected there was a very good chance that I would end up moaning and screaming in ecstasy like they did on *Melrose Place* for an extended period of time, so I made him wait until his folks left for their Sunday drive. After all, I couldn't be sure what kind of racket my pleasure center was capable of producing.

Mere seconds after Mr. and Mrs. Puppy Love departed, I lit a candle that smelled like spoiled apple cider and was, to my delight, immediately ravaged. It went something like this: Off with the shirt, on with the Puff Daddy CD, down with the horribly uncomfortable cheetah underpants, away with the innocence. In three and a half thrusts and two verses, I became a woman. I was not sure if I had liked the sex, but I was glad to have gotten that chore out of the way, and I felt honored that my second favorite rapper could be a part of it. Not only had I been able to check a crucial item off my bucket list, but I was certain now that the girls at school would stop making fun of my sweater sets and invite me to a party or two. After all, I was having sex—college sex—not the peon sex of public high schools, but the sex of institutions of higher learning. Surely that had to count for something.

We lay in bed spooning stiffly for a few moments. The room stank horribly of a grandmother's kitchen, and pink wax was threatening to jump from the votive to the carpet. Then The Boy in Puppy Love got an idea. "I'll be right back," he said jumping back into his boxers. He returned about a minute later with a package of Lucky Strikes that his brother had picked up in Mexico several months ago. We lit one up and passed it back and forth, neither of us inhaling, both of us worrying that the smell would stick to our fingers, but ultimately feeling terribly adult and important.

That is, until White Fang walked in.

White Fang was the family dachshund. He was neither white nor adequately fanged, but if you let a little boy name his first dog, it will either be called White Fang or Optimus Prime. Fang was fat, hostile, and he smelled of canned ham. I hated that dog. Of course, my boyfriend and his family were able to look past this cylindrical beast's mange and general ill will toward the world. To them, the musty pile of canine was Benji incarnate, so I pretended to be amused rather than hopeful when they made me watch him play dead for table scraps. He waddled over to the bed and growled, staring directly into my eyes. The boy who moments ago had ripped the button off my Levis began to shriek like a little girl.

"Get him out of here! He'll smell like cigarettes!"

*So much for feeling like an adult*, I thought.

I understood why he might prefer that his dog not smell of tobacco, yet I would have rather done a line of cocaine off his stomach in front of his mother than risk losing my arm trying to remove the snarling little shit.

"It'll be fine," I said, rolling over and reaching for my special tacky panties that were the most perfect shade of jungle cat. I slipped them on and we began to make out which is what all teenagers do when they run out of things to say.

As it happens, things weren't going to be fine.

Things were going to be catastrophic.

Seconds later, holding his cigarette daintily like Audrey

Hepburn, he let out a blood-curdling screech. Fang had eaten the condom.

Oftentimes I had fantasized about this animal's demise, but it was not supposed to end like this. It was supposed to be dog cancer or, better yet, dog suicide. I began to panic. I wasn't a murderer; I was practically still a virgin. We had no idea what to do. We didn't even pay for our cellular phones; how the fuck were we going to afford a replacement dog? The Boy in Puppy Love had his tube of a pup wrapped in a used towel and was rocking him back and forth, sputtering apologies through his tears. I wanted to slap him and tell him to pull himself together like they did before a cavalry charge in the old war movies, but, the truth was, I was equally terrified and the beginnings of a fairly impressive sob were beginning to fill my eyes.

I raced up the stairs, raided his mother's address book, which was mostly filled with doodles of flowers and dried splashes of liquor, and began to dial the vet's home number.

He picked up on the third ring, which wasn't bad for a Sunday.

"Hello?" a doctorly voice bellowed into my ear.

I paused. What does one say when they have inadvertently fed used prophylactics to a wiener dog? I was going to have to dig deep and handle this maturely.

"White Fang Mitchell swallowed a water balloon," I wept into the receiver.

A water balloon. This was the best I could do.

I was far too guilty about the sex to even acknowledge it.

His father's community service connections coaxed the doctor away from his eggs Benedict and into the office.

We arrived at the vet and introduced ourselves. I had suggested that The Boy in Puppy Love go in alone. Surely the vet would not have believed that a young couple had been having a water balloon fight in the dead of winter. My college boyfriend, however, had a different plan; he went rogue.

"I didn't know Mr. Puppy Love had a daughter," the vet remarked and shook my hand enthusiastically.

My boyfriend had introduced me as his sister.

Not only had we refused to acknowledge the sex, but we had made it illegal in all fifty states.

Unruffled by our very troubling story of brother-sister balloon fights, the vet, who happened to look a bit like a bespectacled Ghostbuster, pumped Fang full of doggy ipecac and placed him outside where he began to wretch. We were terrified. Fang was staggering along the curb dizzily pausing to look up at us with his hateful dachshund eyes. The Boy in Puppy Love began to sweat onto his thick, Mediterranean brow, and I could see the questions rolling around in his university-educated skull: "Would they have to operate?" "Could the vet see through our brilliant scheme?" "What would we do when the good doctor saw that our water balloon was a used, chocolate-raspberry flavored condom?" And, most frightening of all, "Were we going to lose our car privileges for this?"

After a few minutes of watching Fang stumble around like a rehab movie star on Santa Monica, the vet went inside to take a call. Within seconds, the dog let out a thunderous belch and floating in a pile of dog vomit, the condom appeared. The heavens had shone upon us. My boyfriend sprang into action, plucked up the condom, and threw it over the chain link fence. It landed next to a Blockbuster. He grabbed me, kissed me on the mouth, and told me he loved me. If we weren't crying and trying to wipe the dog yak from our hands onto each other's jeans in front of a video store, it would have been a beautiful photograph. We were home free.

The doctor returned, I'm sure very disturbed to see his client's children tongue kissing and, also, unsatisfied with Fang's prognosis. As far as he was concerned, the dog still had a water balloon lodged in his esophagus so the beloved family pet spent the next hour eating medicine from a syringe and barfing in an empty parking lot. We never said a thing. I was sure that Fang would spend the next years of his life trying to get rabies and then attack me.

The drive back to the house was silent. The Boy in Puppy Love sat shotgun, still trembling, swaddling his dog up like the baby Jesus, and holding him close to his chest. I shook my head, hair still tangled and wooly from the pillow burn. I imagined we would break up, the psychological consequences of this day would surely haunt both of us for our entire adult lives, and neither of us would likely be interested in having sex with the other ever, ever again. I had already concluded that I was going to marry a goldfish owner.

As we rolled slowly past my high school, with its crab grass and its crumbling faded mural, I became overcome with anger. Mrs. Anderson was a fucking idiot, standing up there with her giant plastic science uterus and her complimentary rubbers. If she wanted to eradicate teen pregnancy, I was pretty sure she could go ahead and skip the gonorrhea bullshit, and go straight to the puppy killing.

*Three*

# THE MAN WHO JOHNNY
# WALKERED AT THE WHEEL

*I* first met his family at the McDonalds in Harmon, Illinois. Right off the interstate, convenient to truckers and people who can't seem to make it all the way home without a giant diet soda. Always tire deep in corn and Wrangler jeans, there is nothing in Harmon except the people who decide to live there. And they're just as tragic as you might think.

My boyfriend, let's call him James, tried to prepare me.

"There are a few things you should know before you meet them," he said, prefacing me for the worst:

- His dad, who lived somewhere in the great slab of Texas, was a former pastor who cheated on all of the four wives he'd married . . . and consequently divorced. Now in his spare time, when he wasn't investing in continually failing business opportunities, he was a billboard model for hair transplants.

- His sister, Vanessa, was known for chronic bouts of pain and living out of wedlock with her boyfriend. Terrified of her grandfather who was approximately five feet tall, she lied and told everyone she had eloped with her boyfriend in

Cancun. She was in her late twenties, had once mistakenly married a gay man, and at some point had undergone gastric bypass surgery, though I was never, under any circumstances, to admit I knew this.

• His mother, a single woman in her early fifties, was the least colorful. He defined her as "the sweetest woman in the world," if not slightly "dim." She had been on one date in the past twenty years, and that was with the state governor who had briefly separated from his wife, then thought better of it.

At some point I had been excited to meet these people. Getting to know the family, however dysfunctional, is step one toward saying yes to the dress. But I hadn't planned on meeting them like this. I thought a traditional dinner would do. Throw a pound of turkey on the table and then we could all exchange small talk about dressing. Moreover, I had pictured him there, at my side, so when someone wanted to talk about our marriageability or how I was in my "peak nesting period" —whatever that means—I could squeeze his hand under the table like it were a giant stress ball.

But my boyfriend wasn't there. He couldn't be. He was in prison.

Something's definitely going on. This is what my friend said as I sprawled on my living room hardwood floors, gulping small Titanics of Chardonnay. When you're upset, it's impossible to sit in a chair. The height and the width are inordinately confining for how you want your arms and legs and complete and utter melancholy to spill out around you.

Telling the first person was going to be the hardest. The rest would all hear through the nosey grapevine, greedily pick pocketing the knowledge from one another like they were discussing

Kim Kardashian's thirty-seventh divorce. And then, when I saw them in public, both of us just standing there in the produce aisle, we wouldn't have to talk about it or even so much as mention his name, but they would know and I would know that I was dating a convict. We would stand there, staring, talking about the wind chill factor, and I would fondle the squash, trying not to look embarrassed.

You want to be proud of your significant other. You want to bubble over with excitement that he has just been promoted to VP or adopted a small infant from Swaziland. But my boy-friend's biggest accomplishment was that he had the same housing arrangements as TI.

I pulled into the McDonalds to wait. I was twenty minutes early, so I went inside and grabbed some fries. When I get nervous, I munch. And fidget. And check the weather on my iPhone a minimum of seventy-seven times.

The Man Who Johnny Walkered at the Wheel told me to look for a red Corolla and two women, which had seemed like plenty of information at the time. But Harmon is the type of place where everyone looks like everyone else. It's a giant DMV amassing in public where full cousin-on-cousin matrimony is allowed.

"It won't be a big deal," he said. "Just say hi, grab the key, and you'll be done."

But he knew, like I knew, that this wasn't just a big deal. It was the deal. It was meeting the family, and it could only happen once.

I checked my watch, peering out the window, and practiced what I would say. I wanted them to like me. I wanted to say imaginative, witty things they would quote later on to friends and extended family. "Yes, she's so delightful. Do you know that when she was only ten years old..." and then they'd go on to tell a story about how I saved a penguin. Or started the

Internet. But I had never rescued an animal or revolutionized the technology industry. My best quality was that I'd never received a traffic violation. And now, considering the present location of their immediate family member, it would be impossible to talk about how awesome my driving skills were. It would seem like I was rubbing it in.

Ever since it happened, I started acting like one of those people in self-help seminars who say everything out loud. Except instead of saying uplifting things like, "I'm a winner," or "Yes, I can!" I said things like, "My boyfriend is incarcerated."

True, it wasn't really a morale booster, but I found unless I said it often and repeatedly, I wouldn't really believe it. I would text him and wait for him to text me back. I would get reservations for dinner on Friday nights and be entirely disappointed when he didn't show up. After all, it's not easy going from saying, "My boyfriend is a financial analyst," to, "My boyfriend is an inmate." There are some things in life Girl Scouts just doesn't prepare you for.

I sat in the car, shoving fries in my mouth, repeating my new mantra to my steering wheel. *This is probably just the beginning*, I mused, fishing deeper into my happy meal and self-pity. *After this, I'll get knocked up on a conjugal visit, end up working at the Waffle House, and live at the Super 8 Motel.*

I don't know how they appeared there. So quickly. Two Leslie Knope sized angels hovering at my car door. They weren't very tall really. Perhaps five foot two at best. Both round and grinning, like retirees turned Wal-Mart greeters. I stepped out of the car and extended my hand, but instead of taking it, they smashed their biscuit arms around me, forcing me into a group hug.

"How was the drive?"

"We're so glad you're here."

"We figured it had to be you."

"But how awkward if it hadn't been!"

The conversation ping-ponged back and forth between the two, while I tried to keep a smile plastered to my face. I nodded, laughed, and finally managed an, "It's nice to meet you both. I've heard so much about you." And despite my urge, I did not, at any point, use the term gastric bypass surgery.

It was awkward really. Just standing there. And we all knew it. We weren't supposed to meet like this. We weren't supposed to be stranded at a McDonalds exchanging small talk. Small talk is for people waiting to get their hair cut. Not for people who might some day be related. I leaned back on my heels and thought about checking the weather.

"Here," his sister said, shoving a package in my hands. "It's just a little something to welcome you."

It was a small bag covered in bright stripes, complete with a hand-penned note. Her penmanship was perfect. Wedding invitation perfect. I wanted to extract her cursive and make it a font.

"That's so sweet of you," I said, thumbing the crease of the bag. I felt bad. I hadn't brought anything for them. Should I have made them a casserole? Or picked a bouquet of flowers? What do you do on occasions like this? Touch them lightly on the shoulder and say I'm sorry one of your immediate family members is in the can?

"Are you sure you don't want us to go with you?" they asked.

And I looked quietly back and forth between the two of them. Really, they were more like sisters than mother and daughter. They were dressed in sweat pants and holding drinks as large as Christian Slater's forehead. They were in no shape to go to a prison. And I certainly had no desire to go with them. This was awkward enough without accidently sobbing snot onto their shoulders.

"No, really. I'll be fine. No point of you all making the drive if you can't even see him."

"Alright then," his mother said, patting me on the back. "Well, here's the key to his apartment. There should be new sheets on the bed. And call if you need anything at all. The prison is only about a forty-five minute drive from here, so you should get there in plenty of time.

"Thank you," I said, reaching out and giving them both tremendously awkward hugs. "It was so nice to meet you all."

And then I climbed in my car and waited for them to pull away.

Inside there was a bottle of hand sanitizer, some tissues, and a bag of popcorn that I would most certainly burn in the microwave later. The note was short and simple:

> *I can't tell you how much I appreciate what you're doing for my brother. I can't wait to get to know you better! Enjoy your time with James. I've packed a little hand sanitizer in your goody bag… prison isn't exactly the cleanest place. Call if you need anything! – Vanessa*

I sat the bag in the passenger seat and pulled out of the driveway. I had exactly an hour and a half to get to "not the cleanest place," but even still I drove ninety. Prison isn't like a restaurant. You can't call and bump your reservation back thirty minutes because there was bad traffic on the interstate. You get there or you don't. And if you don't, no amount of sobbing or apologizing will make a difference. They're not exactly in the business of second chances.

I guess you could say I was new to this whole thing. That would be fair. It isn't every day you drive five hours to a federal facility because your boyfriend thought it would be fun to get not one, not two, but three DUIs. And, in turn, the judge thought it would be sensible to give him not one, not two, but three months in prison. Plus a handful of things like parole for two years, one hundred hours of community service, three mandatory AA meetings a week, and one of those blowy things in your car that starts wailing if the guy sitting next to you has had so much as a sip of Mike's Hard Lemonade.

I got there forty-five minutes early and drove around the outside gates. I had never seen so much barbed wire in my life. It could trace around the U.S. border seven times and still have enough left over to gift-wrap illegal immigrants.

There were a handful of buildings inside. Seven as far as I could count. All shaped like rather large, run-down elementary school cafeterias. I sat in my car and eyed the facility from the road. The closest I'd ever been to a prison was watching *Shawshank Redemption* on my couch in the tenth grade.

I wondered what it was like in there. Did he do laundry all day? Did he go out in the yard? Did they call it the yard? Were there gangs where everyone called everyone else chico? Did they carry shanks? What were shanks anyway? Did the fact that he looked remotely like a J.Crew catalog encourage male-on-male bonding? Should I write him letters in code? If I wore a black dress and pearls, would people think I was Holly Golightly?

His mother had given me the rundown earlier. At Camdenville, each prisoner was allowed one fifteen-minute time slot a day for visitation. And it wasn't in person. None of that sitting across the lunch table from one another business you see in the movies. No, all the visitors sat in a lobby together and were assigned stations. The stations were all lined up on one wall, a video screen, a stool, and a phone for each. When it hit the hour, your TV would turn on and your prisoner of choice would show up on the other end. When you had a minute left, a voice would come on—in Spanish no less—and count down until the screen went blank.

About twenty minutes before my appointment, I pulled in and parked. I walked inside, past the hoard of regulars, and went up to the front counter. I slid my ID into a metal slot. A police officer was there behind what I could only assume was 300,000 pounds of bullet proof glass. She leaned down and talked into the speaker.

"And who are you here to see?"

I looked from left to right and whispered into the mic, "James Haverson."

"And what relationship do you have with James Haverson?" Her voice reverberated across the entire waiting room.

I had no idea if she had any right to know. Or if she was simply amused. Here I was, a girl in Michael Kors, surrounded by men and women who were wearing more cigarette smoke than clothing.

"I'm his girlfriend," I said quietly, more embarrassed than I had expected.

Her eyebrows lifted, but she didn't ask me to elaborate. For a moment there, I was sure she could see my life going down the toilet, spinning into a future where I only drank Bud Light and shopped at Wal-Mart.

"You're stall thirty-two," she said, and slid my ID back through the metal slot. "Next!"

Most days I feel like my life is pretty normal. It consists of laundry, paperclips, and buying two pounds of ground beef at the grocery store. But sitting there, with my hand gripping a sweaty telephone that was 100 percent likely covered in some form of STD, I felt like a character in one of those Hallmark movies they play around Christmas. The one where the town donkey dies and everyone wears black and goes to the funeral. It's sad sure. But it's also just a twinge too dramatic. It's a donkey after all. Not a person.

I checked my watch. I had three minutes until The Man

Who Johnny Walkered at the Wheel showed up on the TV screen. I didn't really know if I wanted to see him. What could I possibly say? What would he say? Once I saw him like that, I'd never be able to take that image of out of my mind. Would they have him in handcuffs? Would he have lost thirty pounds from only eating spoonfuls of lentils and misery? Would the orange jumpsuit clash with his pretty face?

I took a deep breath. The Man Who Johnny Walkered at the Wheel had been stupid, yes. Incredibly stupid. But it wasn't like I was never going to see him again. There were guys in there serving life sentences who had murdered people and put guns in inappropriate places. But he was going to get out. And soon, relatively speaking. Only three months. Sort of like an extended summer vacation. As an adult. In a place nothing at all like the Hamptons, except for that it, too, was extremely exclusive.

The girl sitting next to me leaned over. There was no such thing as "personal space" in prison. I could smell the Kit Kat on her breath as she held out her hand and introduced herself as Shamiqua. She came so often she pranced around the place like it was her living room. Her shorts covered a fraction of her ass, and I complemented her on her neon green bra.

"You new here?" she asked. "I can tell." And she swiveled back around to talk to her friend whose husband had been busted for armed robbery.

I wanted a drink. This wasn't the correct reaction, I know. He was in prison for consuming enough Patron to drown all of Barnum and Bailey's elephants, but it was unfair. Just because he insisted on sucking back all of Napa Valley, shouldn't mean that I couldn't responsibly participate in a healthy but not illegal amount of adult beverages.

I went to the grocery store and got a bottle of pinot, and then

I drove to his apartment. His neighbors were outside laughing. I was carrying a black duffel bag and wearing sunglasses at eight p.m. Did they wonder where he was? Did they wonder why I sounded like I was choking on a baguette while mascara ran down my face in black, clumpy avalanches? I put the key in the door quickly and walked inside before they could ask.

I set my stuff on his counter and got out a glass. I opened the top drawer and rustled through his utensils. Then the next drawer. Then the next.

No wine opener.

Classic.

I got out a knife and hacked my way in, then poured half the bottle into a plastic cup. I sat on the ground. "I am 100 percent classy," I said, and then I took a swig.

I sat on the floor until I had enough wine to stop crying, then I went through his desk. There were pictures of him shirtless with ex-girlfriends and a letter from a girl named Brandy who asked him not to break her heart. I had met Brandy before. She looked like a squirrel. I threw the letter in the trash and only felt 10 percent bad.

I went into his closet. I put on a pair of his gym shorts and one of his t-shirts. They swallowed me whole. I stared in the mirror. It was like a really bad night at the Jersey Shore. There I was, a twenty-three year old woman, drinking alone on a Friday night, wearing the oversized gym clothes of her convict boyfriend. Why couldn't I have fallen in love with someone else?

I went back to his desk and took the letter out of the trash.

I climbed in his bed and turned out the lights, but it felt terrible to be sleeping there in his bed without him, so I went to the living room and turned on *Braveheart*. I fell asleep at one a.m., while Mel Gibson cut somebody's head off.

*Four*

# THE CAPTAIN OF THE
# WHORIENT EXPRESS

The most exciting thing that has ever happened to me is my brother's wife. She was born in Laos and, before he met her, I had positively no idea what the devil a "Laos" was. My family made meatloaf from a box and lived in a suburb where nearly everybody was called "Smith," so her addition to our lot was positively exhilarating, exotic even. I came to think of my brother as a hero of sorts for bringing this beautiful creature, along with her fascinating cultural heritage, into our sheltered, provincial lives. It's not as though we all sat around debating the virtues of the great eastern mystics, or carving shit out of jade, but every time I overheard her on the telephone drifting into her native tongue, I would feel delightfully cosmopolitan.

While it was wonderful when my brother, The Captain of the Whorient Express, and his wife would drop-in, it was my own visits to their sparkling city abode that I found to be the real, absolute treat. Not only did they feed me as many Hot Pockets as I wanted, but I was allowed to put my grubby hands on whatever was under their roof, including their state-of-the-art Hewlett Packard. As a technologically advanced woman of the twenty-first century with a penchant for buying discounted sweaters online and Googling myself, my relationship with the PC was vital on these brief sojourns to the condominium of my kinfolk. While they were off working during the day, the asthmatic whir of the desktop warmed my heart and beckoned to my VISA card.

It had been almost a year since my brother and Mrs. Brother had married, and I decided it was time, once again, to bless them with my familial presence. I rapped on the door musically, the way everybody raps on the door when they know they are the guest of honor, and Mr. and Mrs. Brother greeted me with very adult hugs and asked me very adult questions about the flight and work and my friends (whose names they even remembered). It was a glorious evening that left me wondering if perhaps marriage would one day make me mature, attentive, and in the possession of proper stemware, too.

I was relieved the following morning to find the apartment empty. The L.L.Bean online store was having a sale on over-sized cable knits in inoffensive colors at 11:00 a.m. EST, and I was certain it would require my full attention. My hosts had scampered off to work, and the HP was cooing at me from the other end of the room.

I heated up a Hot Pocket, flicked on the screen, and immediately logged into my Hotmail. I began scrolling through the numerous electronic communications I had received in the past seven hours. An electro-pop quintet from Cartagena wanted to be MySpace friends, and three separate business networking sites implored me to create a profile, which had I acquiesced would simply state, "Unemployed and kind of sad, really." My eyes ricocheted from message to message until they settled on something they liked: a mass email with "LOL" in the headline. It was serendipitous. I had exactly fourteen minutes until my mock turtleneck buying frenzy was to commence, and "LOL" seemed like a fabulous way to spend them.

"Oh! A fwd! An impersonal fwd addressed to hundreds of people with a picture attached!"

I salivated over the thought.

Was it a joke? A survey? An image of an amusing, misspelled street sign?

I clicked on the paperclip icon and waited patiently for the attachment to appear on the screen. Appear it did, in one of my dear brother's existing download folders. It was called "downloads2." But there were no games, or airline ticket receipts, or documents in downloads2; there were only Asians. So many Asians. Thousands of them on top of each other, behind each other, upside down, in boxes, with foxes, drinking vodkas on the rockses.

I leapt backward in horror, my hydraulic chair catching several inches of air before rolling to a halt on the plastic mat beneath it. I had logged into my brother's email on accident and witnessed the less Disney version of Mulan. The Hot Pocket, I'm sure equally scandalized, somersaulted to its death and now lay lifeless on a dusty patch of carpet under the desk, bleeding marinara.

I couldn't believe it. My brother was supposed have a large collection of video games. A drawer full of mismatched socks, perhaps. But not *The HooChie Minh Trail*, volumes one through three thousand!

Shocking. Disgusting.

I retrieved the derelict Hot Pocket from the floor, and the Hewlett Packard and I sat in silence. The screen was full of Asian characters and assholes. We would not be ordering fried rice from "Ho Lee Chow" later that night. We would not be ordering it ever again.

My grieving was interrupted by the jangling keys of Marco Porno and his wife.

Fuck. Really? Who comes home for lunch? I began to sweat.

"Honey, I'm hoooome," they sang jokingly to me in unison. If there were ever a time for a *Leave it to Beaver* reference, this was not it.

The computer spat a cautionary beep at me as I furiously tapped the mouse, attempting to quash each filthy image that had popped up in "downloads2." For every girl-on-girl tryst I erased, five more appeared in its place, then twenty-five. It could not be contained; it was an epidemic; it was all out yellow fever!

I could hear them giggling and unzipping their coats. I cringed. I had seen too many bare asses in the past few minutes to deal with the sound of a zipper. Their shadows dampened the glow of the HP's porn-filled visage as they rounded the coffee table and walked toward me. The terrible urgency of the situation became evident.

If Ward Cleaver had an electronic den of sin, Asian June Cleaver would not have known about it. She probably would have assumed that "downloads2" was just plain "downloads2," a folder of good ole wholesome computer things. Slowly through the fog of Japanese schoolgirls spanking each other with yardsticks, it dawned on me: I was about to reveal my brother's secret stash of vaguely racist pornography to his wife.

I dropped to the ground with such speed that my ergonomic seat was left spinning behind me. I shuddered as I grabbed the box of tissues from the desk, and I began furiously mopping up the pizza entrails from their carpet. Artfully, I also ripped the power cord out of the wall. It was located conveniently close to a glob of synthetic provolone. With a "tick," the machine powered down and the monitor turned a calming shade of blue.

"I'm so sorry! I'm an idiot! It was too hot! The cheese!" I sputtered through misappropriated tears as I scrubbed the orange-y grease stain, still shaking from the adrenaline.

"Don't worry about it!" My new sister-in-law cooed as she

trotted up to me in all of her perky glory, scooping me up in a hearty embrace.

"We're getting hardwoods."

I didn't care if they were getting fucking gravel.

The Captain of the Whorient Express seemed genuinely touched by this display of sister-by-marriagely bonding, which meant it was impossible for me to pull him aside and promptly discuss the ways in which I would blackmail him in the future. Drat.

Instead I offered him the half-eaten Hot Pocket, and he asked, "Can I seriously have this?"

"Absolutely," I answered as I stared at the flecks of lint still peeking out of its cavity.

I won't say I was vindicated by watching my older brother eat the heavily soiled pizza-in-a-blanket, but it was a start. I left the next morning, a couple of days early, with my lips tightly sealed. It'd have been gloriously vengeful to call him out. I might have even gotten a few bucks for my silence, but I couldn't. I love my brother. Not as much as he loves Asian porn perhaps, but I love him all the same.

*Five*

# THE OFFICER WHO
# STAMPED MY PASSPORT

*I* don't know what to do, so I ask for another bottle of wine. I tell myself this is okay because they're miniature and my conscience permits multiples of anything smaller than a foosball man. The flight attendant brings me another single serving chardonnay, and I make fists with my toes. I click the map on the TV embedded in the headrest in front of me. The little white plane hovers somewhere over the Pacific Ocean, no land in sight except for a small island or two that appear to be the size of toasted pine nuts. Six hours down. Four to go. Temperature outside: -60 degrees.

The lights are dim. It's three in the afternoon on the west coast, but we're all trying to trick our bodies into believing it's the middle of the night. My neighbor, an elderly Japanese woman, sits quietly, switching back and forth between her crossword puzzle and clicking her overhead light on and off. She speaks no discernible English and is curled up in her complimentary blanket, looking at me suspiciously out of the corner of her eye, as though at any moment I'm going to rouse my strength and run to the cockpit, revealing a minuscule, homemade bomb built into my shoelace. But I can hardly blame her. A white girl in her mid-twenties has no business being on a flight to Southeast Asia where the unifying characteristics of all passengers on board are consumption of noodles, briefcases, and stunted growth. Weren't there more reasonable destinations for someone of my height? Like the Florida Keys? Or Omaha?

The worst thing about planes is their ability to sequester you. When you're 30,000 feet in the air, you can't pretend like life isn't happening. You don't have a hamper of clothes to fold or an armoire that needs dusting. There's nothing to distract you but the man who walks to the bathroom in his holey socks, contracting herpes through the pores in his feet. So once you've leafed through Sky Mall seven times, considered investing in a dog house shaped like Versailles, and then given up on the half filled out Sudoku puzzle, the only thing you're left with is hours to sit in the same spot while trying not to disturb your neighbor who has commandeered the armrest.

Sitting there, it doesn't take long for me to begin considering the inevitable. The fact that this plane will land. And not back in Seattle. Or even somewhere relatively familiar. Or for that matter English. But in some foreign city where there are more drug lords per capita than day cares. By my third glass of wine, I'm nearly certain that within a mere handful of weeks my kidneys will be found on the black market, sold for a small but reasonable mark up to a clan of men in Bangladesh. Or perhaps I'll become the victim of the next legendary serial killer, an Asian version of Jack the Ripper who yanks unsuspecting victims' tonsils out with chopsticks. Or, of course, there is scenario most likely: he simply won't show up. He will let me fly around the world and then simply not appear, leaving me to fend for myself in a country where the only English word they know is McDonalds. This option, the being stood up option, is the worst. Someone will literally have spent thousands of dollars to fly me around the world so they can demonstrate how pathetic I am. I want to pass out. Or tackle the sleeping forty-year-old man who's hogging the emergency exit, swing open the door, and plummet to my death. Am I really this desperate? Couldn't I have met my potential betrothed somewhere more convenient? Like the supermarket? Or the DMV? Anywhere else, really, than the sex trafficking capitol of the planet?

I take another chug. My plan is to drink so much Chardonnay that I will think this is hilarious rather than what it really is: stupid. I've done a number of less than intelligent things in my life but this tops them all. I am flying fourteen hours to go on a blind date.

In Indonesia.

Dear.

Lord.

This never would have happened if I hadn't moved to Seattle. I didn't know a lot of people there. In fact, I only knew two. But that didn't deter me. I'd lived in plenty of places where I knew absolutely no one, and had become extremely skilled in the art of sitting in a corner, looking mysterious and sullen. Moreover, I thought living in the Northwest would do me well. It has lots of trees, granola, and enough coffee to power a rocket ship, I reasoned. What can possibly go wrong with that?

But my friend, let's call him Morty, disagreed.

"Listen," Morty said, "I have a friend. He doesn't exactly live in Seattle right now, but he will soon. He's been in Japan the past four years, but he's moving back in a couple months. You two should grab a beer. I'm sure he'll be glad to have some company, too."

I raised my eyebrows. This was intriguing, but not too intriguing. After all, the man could have a third nipple. Or an oriental lisp. Or a bumper sticker on the back of his minivan that says, "My other ride is your mom." Besides, most people are really bad at setting their friends up. They put needles with balloons and are appalled when it doesn't work out. This would probably end up no different. He'd order a porter, I'd order an ale, and by sip three we'd be arguing about how many WMD's Hillary Clinton is hiding in her bra.

Morty took the hint.

"He's a great guy. He's getting out of the military . . . It'll be harmless, promise. I'll just feel better if you know someone . . . He could be like your big brother."

"Fine," I said, reluctantly. "Give me his email, and I'll say hi. Maybe we can meet up."

I pretended to be put out. I mean, no one wants to look like what they actually are: desperate. And I didn't want to say out loud what I actually think every time I come across a new member of the opposite sex who doesn't have a snaggletooth or a rap sheet: *He could be the one.*

But, and this can't be overstated enough, when you're a woman and you're past the "supposed to be married" benchmark, every man you see on the street, on the Internet, or in the produce aisle has the potential to make the largest dream of your life come true. Men aren't just men anymore. They're all contestants in a game they never signed up to play. Walking around in a plaid shirts or dungarees, they might look like "Steves" or "Roberts," but underneath all their sale rack clothing, they showcase their true identities: husbands, future spouses, inevitable proposers.

I knew when I got off the phone with Morty that I should let this one go. This new guy, this friend of a friend, was a military man. His job entailed shooting people and living in countries that require the frequent use of accent marks. He probably hated literature and had a tattoo of the Constitution under his left nipple. Men like that don't want to get married; they want to get laid before going to another country and getting laid in another language. And then, when they're bored of getting laid, they shoot something. The only thing he'd likely do with my heart is water board it for two hours before shocking it with 75,000 volts of electricity.

I knew if I was going to write The Officer Who Stamped My Passport and get out of it without bolstering the stock of Kleenex, I was going to have to have the most toddler of expectations. I'd be brief and kind, but not overly kind. I'd assume he wouldn't respond, but, on the off chance he did, I'd assume he'd have the intelligence of a Chechnyan five year old. Moreover, he would have terrible grammar, a complete lack of charm, and an inability to recall my first name. He'd only be writing me back because he was in a foreign country, utterly bored, and unable to locate any other people he could correspond with about *The Biggest Loser*.

I took a deep breath and sat down at the computer, armed with my complete lack of hopes. I cracked my knuckles, took a large gulp of Chardonnay, and spent the better part of my Saturday evening parceling together a few sentences.

*Our mutual friend, Morty, passed along your email. I'm moving out to Seattle in a few weeks and he mentioned you were doing the same. If you have some spare time when you get in town, we should grab a beer. Would be great to have a friend on the West coast.*

I reread the email no less than fifty-three times before pressing send.

It doesn't matter what you say because he's not going to say anything back, I reassured myself. This isn't a big deal. In fact, it's such a small deal you wouldn't even find it in the bargain bin at the Dollar Store. I sat down on the couch and put in a movie, then managed to only casually check my inbox every three to six minutes.

When it came, it was the morning. I was standing in the kitchen, wearing a pair of flannel pants. My hair looked like it had been at a rave with the Muppets, and I was trying not to check my email before the coffee brewed. I was certain there was nothing in there. I was certain he was sleeping with twelve beauty queens from Thailand and that the only thing he was transmitting was STDs. But nevertheless, I settled into my chair, popped open the screen, and logged onto my mail. And despite my doubts, there it was. Right there between The *Huffington Post* Daily and a Groupon for 25 percent off plastic surgery.

I could not possibly read it fast enough.

I was nervous immediately.

Iraq? Really?

It turns out Morty hadn't lied. The Officer Who Stamped My Passport really was in the military. He was a Green Beret deployed in Iraq. I didn't really know what "Green Beret" meant, but since I'd seen *Rambo* at least once, my imagination was permitted to see him jumping from helicopters onto moving trains, saving small children from exploding bombs and miscellaneous catastrophes.

I sat hunched over my computer, enthralled. I had imagined something much shorter. Words that could easily fold and fit in a fortune cookie. Words that would make me think he was more interested in taking a Lamaze class than any sort of dialogue with a stranger. But he had John Grishamed a response. And in a war zone no less. Within thirty seconds, my imagination had built a small tent outside Baghdad where he penned a note from an armored laptop, while sand swirled about him in miniature funnel clouds.

It had taken him three days to respond, and it had taken me approximately three days and five minutes to forget the age-old adage, "Guard your heart for it is the wellspring of life." My expectations were no longer the size of toddlers, crawling about at a very slow pace. They were the size of Macy's Day Parade balloons, inflated far beyond their intended capacity. It's simply sinful for Snoopy to be that big. He couldn't even fit inside the Chrysler Building, much less a dog crate. In the end though, rationality can't win out. Not with women. Not with me. Because there's something my gender always wants more than truth: love. And could there possibly be anyone better to love than Rambo?

The Officer Who Stamped My Passport, as it were, was twenty-nine years old and had gone to the University of Alaska. He had been in the military for the past eight years, could speak Chinese, and had some sort of medical credentials that allowed him to wear scrubs and participate in open-heart surgery. He was well travelled and well spoken. I imagined if someone kidnapped me, he could find me with as little as a compass and piece of red twine.

I wanted to write him back immediately. I had so many questions. Ones vital to national security and my heart. Had he ever shot a man? Could he survive solely off leaves and berries? Did he have a six-pack or an eight-pack? A picture would suffice. But instead, I snapped my laptop shut. There are rules after all. Rules like you can't let a guy know the best thing you have to do on a Saturday night is sit at home alone, drinking white wine while scanning Pinterest and refreshing your inbox.

The quickness is always surprising. Even if you suspect it. Even if you can feel it itching up your fingertips to your shoulders. Still, somehow, it catches you off guard. You find yourself in the shower. Or sitting at a restaurant. Or in a parking lot. And then, out of nowhere, something reminds you of him and you smile. You actually get giddy. Even though you've wanted this feeling for so long, even though you practically harassed it to come and storm your castle, you didn't know how *real* it could be. And how *quickly* it could get here.

The Officer Who Stamped My Passport and I began writing each other daily. Pithy, long, intimate correspondence. By day three, I knew his middle name, blood type, and his feelings about long underwear. But despite the frequency and length, I wanted more. It felt like every email was traveling by Pony Express, tediously forging through the Grand Canyon and Rocky Mountains to make it to my doorstep by dinnertime. I hadn't known this man a week. And to be fair, I really didn't know him *still*. But somehow he mattered to me immensely. I wanted to know how he was doing. That he was okay. I watched the nightly news and shuddered slightly when they'd report the tolls from Iraq. Was he in that truck? Was he on that base? My mind would hopscotch through a thousand "what ifs" until his next email arrived and I knew he was all right.

After a week of back and forths, he finally asked me for my phone number. I did a victory dance on my bathroom tile.

I would like to say from that point on we were rational. After all, we should have been. Our rather successful parents had raised us well. We knew not to run red lights, rob gas stations, or get into cars with strangers who have candy. But apparently no one ever talked to us about planes.

By the time it happened, I had known him for two weeks. We talked constantly. Even when we weren't on the phone, we were sending each other messages via heart palpitations and carrier pigeons. I had never liked someone so much. And even though two weeks is really a rather paltry amount of time—hell, it's shorter than Ramadan—I knew I didn't want to wait another two months for him to move to Seattle so we could sit across from each other and have that infamous beer Morty had cornered us into. Apparently, he didn't either.

We were on the phone one night, talking like usual, and a little out of the blue he paused.

"You there?" I said.

And he sighed, "Yeah."

"Something on your mind?"

"I know this is going to sound crazy, but I leave Iraq in two weeks to head back to Japan and can go on leave . . ." he paused, taking an audible deep breath. I had no idea where he was going with this.

"So . . . I want you to pick anywhere in the world, and I'll fly you there and meet you."

The line went quiet. Deathly quiet. You could hear crickets having babies. The whole rainforest was going frolicking mad. My jaw didn't even have the energy to drop. Could he be serious? Was this real? Didn't only people like Hugh Grant say this to thin, blonde actresses in B-grade movies?

But instead of saying no, or maybe this isn't the best idea, I told him the truth.

"I've always wanted someone to ask me that."

And I had.

Next thing I knew, I had a ticket to Bali.

I almost missed my flight. I stood in line for an hour and a half behind a group of tourists who spoke no discernible American, while flocking around a petite woman who hoisted an umbrella in the air. The girls all wore Dolce and Gabbana knock-off sweatpants with "D" printed on their left cheek, "G" on their right, and an ampersand right up their crack. They couldn't figure out how to use the self check-in machines and were all gawking about like a herd of sheep.

I was being anxious. And judgmental. I mean, what was I doing? Was everyone in Asia like this? Did they all have to walk around in clusters, having directions spouted at them from anorexic rain gear holders?

I should probably leave, I thought. This is a sign. This traffic jam of small Orientals is a definite indicator that I'm making the worst choice in my life. But instead of leaving, I checked my watch. And I sighed audibly so the United staff would know that I was a) unhappy, or b) constipated.

Part of me expected to get up to the counter, hand over my passport, and have the man with the squinty eyes and polyester shirt look back and just laugh. Laugh for hours. "This ticket is a counterfeit. Did you really expect to get on this flight with a forged confirmation number? SECURITY!" Then large men with muscles the size of Farah Fawcett's hair would come and put me in prison for at least a week. But instead, a woman with bright red lipstick smiled at me.

"Bali. That will be fun." She even gave me an exit row, window seat.

I need a brown paper lunch sack. In the movies, when everyone gets nervous and is about to hyperventilate, they have a brown paper bag at their immediate disposal so they can inhale and exhale at loud, frequent intervals. This would come in handy, just in case, I think.

I have stolen a stack of custom cards from the flight attendants and am writing a list of pros and cons.

- Pro: I've wanted to expand my friend circle. Even if he has cankles, I still have someone I can add to my Christmas card list.

- Con: No one looks worse than me when they get off an international flight. I'm going to meet the man of my dreams, and I'm going to smell like an airplane urinal.

- Pro: I am going to Bali. For free.

- Con: Wait, is the new-age way of paying for sex? Did I voluntarily become a prostitute? Or indentured servant?

- Pro: I will undoubtedly get a tan.

- Con: Unless he kills me first.

I press the call button. Wine please.

I watch the bags circle around the carousal. Everyone in Asia carries miniature luggage, tic-tac sized hard cases that could fit, on their best days, a toothbrush and a pair of tighty whities. Part of me wants this moment to last forever. If my bags never come out, if I never exit through the gates, I'll never have to find out if The Officer Who Stamped My Passport was a figment of my imagination. I could keep those weeks of perfect conversation sealed in a Ziploc bag, and I could return to Seattle to date a man who wears flannel and takes his Labrador to the dog park. Everything would be preserved, including my dignity and life. But the carousal churns and, five minutes later, out pops my suitcase, baggage so large it could house all the residents of Taiwan.

I come out of the doors and look around. I don't think my heart has ever beat this fast. My palms are sweating pools. Small children could wade in them with their floaties.

Part of me expects him to be standing there in the front. I pray he isn't holding a sign. Or balloons. Or anything that would indicate he could be a participant in the Ringling Brothers Circus. But as I walk out, all I see are a hoard of Asians, people babbling on in an indiscernible language I assume to be Chinese. I pause at the exit, flicking my eyes back and forth. I probably just didn't see him, I think. But another scan of the crowd reveals that I am the only American in the whole joint.

I try not to look desperate or anxious and keep walking, but my eyes dart over the crowd at colossally high speeds. It's the real life Where's Waldo? and it's a terrible game to play in a foreign country when you haven't slept in twenty-four hours and can speak approximately zero words of the native language. I begin to panic and my brain rattles off hysterically.

Maybe he took one look at the large bags under my weary eyes and decided he'd be better off without me? I am alone in the South Pacific. Where will I stay? How will I get there? I picture myself in an Indonesian sewer, eating leftover noodles people have thrown in the garbage. While I don't exactly relish the thought of being murdered by street urchins and then tossed in the jungle, I hate the idea of being stood up even more.

Just as I'm about to go looking for a cab, or a mule, or a rickshaw and depart for the embassy, I see him. He's leaning against a row of chairs, arms folded across his chest. He looks calm, a gentle smirk pressed across his face, a kind observant look like he's watching someone wake up in the morning.

I stop, mid luggage pull. He appears to have all limbs, all digits. A handsome face that would serve him well in an REI catalog. Or on *Survivor*. The lump that has risen in my throat shoots down to my chest and begins throbbing wildly. I let a small smile escape my lips and he smiles back. The woman on the plane was right to be concerned about me; I'm a total goner.

*Six*

# THE MAN ON MY
# ICE BUCKET LIST

The wedding night is sacred for many reasons—you've had your makeup done professionally, you've received an assload of small home appliances, and even if you've had sex a billion times prior, as my husband and I had, the wedding night sex is the supposed to be the best sex of the rest of your life. Unfortunately for me, it doesn't always work out that way.

I first questioned my level of sobriety after our reception. I was prepared for this night, maybe even over-prepared. I had purchased a teddy online, I had less body hair than a newborn baby, and I was packing enough Altoids to disarm a skunk. What I wasn't prepared for was the open bar. The Man on My Ice Bucket List and I were cuddled together in the corner of an elevator slowly gliding its way up to our hotel room when, suddenly, a cold vodka-scented sweat rushed over me.

Concerning.

I looked up at my new husband and smiled. I brushed it off as a bout of post-nuptial euphoria, a mere wave of excitement for the evening of acrobatic lovemaking before us.

But then I felt an incredible urge to dance and invite people over.

Very concerning.

Before I knew it, I had removed my shoes, my strapless bra had sunk around my waist underneath my dress, and I began to skip clumsily down the carpeted corridor—hallmarks of absolute inebriation. At this point, the best day of my life was beginning to turn into the worst hangover of the twenty-first century.

I can blame nothing on the room. The room did its job. We arrived to champagne and little strawberries dressed in little chocolate tuxedos. There was a roaring ocean and a television the size of my windshield. It was more than romantic; it was frightfully expensive. And I was about to ruin the whole thing.

We walked in and began to make out. As soon as we untangled ourselves, my husband uncorked and tended to the champagne. The lack of things to lean on sent me tumbling backward. With a mighty plop, I landed on the bed. Things were even worse than I thought.

*Think, think, think*, I begged myself.

The floral wallpaper began to swell, ebbing and flowing, crocuses and primroses rushing toward me and then sinking back.

I was not a tigress in the bedroom. On a good day, I was an aggressive cocker spaniel. There was no way I could perform my way past the lump of sea sickness in my belly, but it was our wedding night, our one and only wedding night, so even in my condition, I'd have been a fool not to try.

My husband dimmed the lights and kicked his boots into a corner. He was still hopped up on adrenaline and crudités, and it was clear he had no idea that I was positively shit-housed. I knew that if we were going to have sex, it needed to happen immediately, before my liver jumped out of my body and clubbed me on the head.

*Lingerie!* I thought.

All I needed to do was get into the lingerie, lie down, and

not vomit for at least fifteen minutes.

To the bathroom!

Sadly, nobody told me that putting on lingerie was like building a fucking pipe bomb.

There were straps. And buttons. And wiring. And an alarming amount of pink.

"Babe, are you okay?" I heard from the other room.

I teetered sideways, colliding with the bidet.

No, Babe was not okay. Babe was about to experience asphyxiation by lace and sateen.

I decided the best option was to lie on the ground and work from the legs up. The cold tile made me feel slightly less deathly and there wasn't as much for me to bang into whilst trying to navigate this promiscuous bundle of fuchsia. Each time I tried to yank on my negligee, bracing my feet against the granite and grunting like a sow in heat, my body rotated forty-five infuriating degrees and I was forced to start all over again.

Twenty minutes later, I emerged—dehydrated and panting—looking like a Valentine's Day card from 1983. Ring a ding-ding.

The Man On My Ice Bucket List was perched expectantly on the edge of the bed, collar unbuttoned, eyes wide. I flung open the door, briefly fumbling with the lock. I couldn't figure out how to fasten the garters, but through the fog of merlot and too little food, I was optimistic. The little black straps that I'd failed to attach slapped me encouragingly on the bottom as I wobbled over to him.

Maybe this will turn out okay? I thought, grinning through the nausea and trying to locate the bed.

He laid over me, his blue eyes twinkling brilliantly. I swear there were at least six of them, spinning in circles and multiplying at an alarming rate.

"We're married," he cooed kissing me on the forehead.

I was definitely going to throw up. His freckles were making me dizzy, and I all I could think about was stuffed-crust pizza.

Staring up at my newly-minted husband, I prayed for my shit to stay together, at least for the sex. It was not to be.

"I think I need a bucket."

Within seconds, the ice and bubbly were evicted from their silver cask, and I began to wretch. There I sat, in high heels and those slutty, thigh-high nylons, regurgitating. My eyes were burning, and it looked like I'd tried to OD on Children's Tylenol. That is all I remember.

The distended slits that used to be my eyes creaked open at 8:36 the next morning.

What the fuck had happened? And why was I in a bed that was worth more than my car? The room presented very few clues.

Flat champagne.

A shoe.

A half-eaten cracker.

A blazer.

An ice bucket . . . ICE BUCKET!

I vomited in the stainless steel ice bucket of a five-star hotel.

My marriage was doomed!

I did not have sex on my wedding night. I had half of a cracker.

I would probably never have sex again.

The down-covered mound that was my husband snored through the high thread count. This was definitely worse than forgetting his birthday. This was even worse than remembering his birthday and buying him those slacks with the front pleats. In an ideal world, I would have gone down on him instead of throwing up on him. In an ideal world, I would have looked more like Bridgette Bardot and less like a Pussy Cat Doll that had been run down by a Jack Daniels truck, but there was no turning back. There would never be another wedding night, and there was no way that housekeeping would ever be able to salvage the bed sheets. As I tried to calculate exactly how many acts of oral copulation it would take to redeem myself, a searing pain began between my eyebrows.

I stumbled over to the sink to brush the purple off my teeth. And then came the mirror.

Sweet Jesus.

Wrapped beneath layers of nylon rosettes and tattered Chantilly lace was a bloated orca, perhaps with some developmental disorder. The apparatus in which I had drunkenly packaged myself even groaned in disgust. But I knew the task that lay before me.

I pushed my tits as close to my chin as possible, stumbled in the direction of the sleeping pile of husband, and I leapt upon him. A small tuft of red hair emerged from beneath the plush duvet, and then, eventually, a face. He looked scared, he looked irritated, but he said nothing. So I grabbed his junk. I grabbed it like it was the Olympic torch.

We did not have great sex, but we did consummate the marriage. Afterward, we laid in bed muttering sentimental things to each other. He never mentioned the fact that I had hurled a bit on his right arm, or the fact that I didn't even know what the fuck a garter was. He just handed me a glass of water, some Advil, and listened to me apologize profusely until I fell into a clammy, nauseous sleep. Love does not conquer all—namely alcohol poisoning, sheer stupidity, or tricky under things—but it does know where you keep the Advil the next morning.

*Seven*

# THE YOUNG DOG WITH

# OLD TRICKS

ave you ever wondered at exactly what age a man becomes a conniving, panty-collecting Lothario? It happens at about nine. They don't spend their grade school recesses incinerating grasshoppers with magnifying glasses and playing Red Rover as they would have women across the world believe; they spend it practicing the dark art of seduction.

When The Young Dog with Old Tricks hunted me down, I was in a dog park with a broken foot. I was miserable. I was doing my American Society for the Prevention of Cruelty to Animals duty, filling the community water bowl so the various drooling fur balls didn't keel over and die in the summer heat, while their owners sat on benches gossiping with each other and playing Angry Birds. The rusted tap groaned between my fingers but it wouldn't shut off. I was hopping around a gushing spigot, surrounded by yapping terriers, and seriously contemplating drowning the place, puppies and all.

Most people go to the dog park to meet dog people. I go to the dog park to do a crossword puzzle, let Bob the dog sniff other dogs, and go home as soon as I'm convinced he's expelled enough energy that he can go twelve hours without eating a piece of my living room. It's not fun for me to watch other people's dogs behave better than mine. I don't want to talk to people about how badly I fucked up my pet and or what particular brand of organic kibble he seems to be really into lately. Furthermore, the very prospect of having a serious conversation while holding a bag of shit and tossing a slobbery tennis ball whose origins are unknown is not entirely appetizing. So there Bob and I stood: embarrassed, frustrated, soaking wet, ready for home, and not in the mood to make friends.

"Somebody looks like they've got a hitch in their giddy up."

The tiny voice startled me.

There was only one kind of person who referred to the human gait as a "giddy up." I looked up expecting to find myself face-to-face with an old man in a cardigan accompanied by an equally old schnauzer nipping at his Keds, but there was no one. My crippled leg and I were relieved to have avoided socializing with the elderly. I carried on, pitying myself.

But then it spoke again.

"No more high heels for you. Now that's a crying shame."

I looked up once more, mostly irritated, but slightly terrified that a very forward ghost was haunting me.

But again, there was no one. That is, until I looked down.

There, poking holes in the ground with a stick for no apparent reason, was a boy about four feet tall sporting a very small pair of Crocs and a disturbing expression that said, "I'd sure like to see you on a seesaw."

I gave him a look that registered somewhere between, "Run along, youngster," and, "Fuck off and die."

Like the majority of attempts to communicate with simple body language, it was ineffective. He cocked his little head and stared at me, blinking. I was flustered. Surely this kid had better

things to do than hang around with me. He was fucking surrounded by puppies. The place was one Tickle Me Elmo away
from being kid heaven. Did he want to sign my cast? Was he
trying to sell me Boy Scout cookies? Do Boy Scout cookies exist?
Did he think I had an unmarked van around the corner full of
candy corn?

This made absolutely no sense.

Neither a fan of children nor sexual harassment, I continued
fumbling and wishing Peter Pan would go back to whatever
jungle gym he'd fallen out of. He resumed irrigating the dog park
and leering over my shoulder.

And just then, as I felt all was in the clear, I felt a tiny,
clammy palm on the small of my back. I leapt backward almost
knocking the little tyke on his ass.

"Somebody could use a little help, couldn't they?" he asked.

I righted myself and quickly explained that I was fine.

My life was fine, my foot was fine, and I certainly didn't
need help from a kid who probably couldn't ride a two-wheeler.

"You don't look fine," he chuckled, striding over to the
streaming water.

"Allow me."

He raised an eyebrow.

A very familiar eyebrow.

An eyebrow that boys his age weren't supposed to know
existed.

He had to be a changeling.

With remarkable ease he coaxed the faucet into submission.
I thanked him, grabbed my Sudoku, and hobbled away. But he
was not to be satisfied and followed after me, and in three words
it went from mildly cute to all kinds of wrong.

"You here alone?" he asked.

Oh no.

Oh shit.

I knew what those three words meant to a man in a bar, and it turned out they meant the same thing to a boy in a park. The Young Dog With Old Tricks not only wanted to go to second base with me, but he believed this was a very reasonable possibility. He looked me up and down like I was a life-sized Tonka Truck filled with GI Joes and ice cream sandwiches.

In my bachelorette days, I had often imagined that I would take up with a younger man when I was an old classy dame, but he was at least forty years early. Something had to be done, but unfortunately my experience in blowing men off is severely limited.

I immediately began flashing my engagement ring at him, waving it wildly like it was a rape whistle at a homeless person. I was hoping the little fella would get the picture, but of course he didn't. It wasn't spelled out in Crayolas.

It was definitely time to leave.

I looked around for Bob the dog, but he was nowhere to be found, so the boy continued. "I'm here with my grandpa. We're just catching up. I'm only in town for a couple days."

The only thing they could have been catching up on was their mutual love of Hunt's Pudding Packs and an 8:00 p.m. bedtime. I followed his little pointer to a bench under a tree. There sat the oldest man I had ever seen, snoring into his beard.

*Jesus Christ*, I thought. *That man might have a faint pulse, but there is no way he is in possession of a valid driver's license.* I began to feel terrible. The poor kid's parents had probably dumped him off at Gandalf's place and high tailed it to Biloxi. And they left him wearing Crocs. Abomination.

As annoyed as I truly was by this miniature Don Juan, perhaps I had taken his advances the wrong way. He sat on a large rock and patted the spot next to him insistently. I had no choice but to join him. Bob the dog had abandoned me, and I was wounded.

The second my ass landed beside his, he was practically in my lap. He was good, real good. Thank God he wasn't old enough to be too obnoxious and patronizing. Thank God he wasn't old enough to buy me a drink.

"I was in a music video once," he said out of nowhere.

*Adorable*, I thought. *The little guy's grasping at straws; he's trying to impress me.*

"But," he continued, "You probably wouldn't know it. It's a real new cool band, for young people; it's kind of like rock."

He called me old.

That dick.

I could like music. I could know about music. Hell, I did know about music. I was more than a pair of legs with a wet T-shirt. Who was he to assume what I did and didn't know about?

I'd had conversations like these before. He was just like any other dude, only smaller, whittling away at my self-esteem until I felt vulnerable and desperate and had unlocked any "daddy issues" I had long forgotten about.

I looked down at his bucked teeth and his rubber clogs. I wanted to tell him I hated his stupid Crocs. But then I remembered: he was nine.

I decided I was overreacting. He probably didn't mean anything by it. After all, to him I was old. I was practically Mrs. Claus. I was sure he didn't mean to be condescending. *I should just be nice to the kid*, I thought. He was visiting his grandfather, and he probably didn't have cable.

He liked music, so I told him I could play the guitar and piano. He seemed unimpressed. "People give me their CDs all the time. I tell them how to be better at singing and stuff," he quipped, shrugging his bony shoulders.

Okay. Show off. He was definitely trying to make me feel bad about myself; this was very clear. He thought he was better at life than I was and I needed to regain the power in the conversation. Just because I was crippled and didn't know how to operate running water did not mean I wasn't a strong, successful, charming woman.

I needed to teach that kid a lesson. There were lots of things I'd done that Pee Wee couldn't trump me on, but I needed something good, something that would make him want to run away and weep into his Grandfather's tobacco-stained facial hair.

"Did you know I'm getting married?" I asked, certain that this would be the nail in the coffin. But this only made him laugh hysterically. Diabolically even. *If I were getting married then where was my boyfriend?* he wanted to know. *Why was I at the park all by myself?* For a moment my throat closed up a bit, and my eyes began to sting. I twisted my Sudoku in my hands.

Kids can be so mean.

My fiancé was at home, in bed. I didn't know why he wasn't at the dog park with me. My heart sank. Junior obviously thought I was a loser, a misfit, incapable of true happiness, and about to have a piss poor marriage. Maybe he was right? I did kind of want my fiancé there, especially so he could tell Alfalfa to suck it. The Young Dog With Old Tricks enjoyed taking a dig at my relationship. He became aware that he was winning our battle of egos, and he was eating it up like a bowl of Cocoa Puffs.

"Did I tell you I'm published?" he countered. "I wrote an article . . . about science . . . for a magazine."

I wasn't published. I would probably never be published. When he was in diapers, I was in a Chevy Suburban with unreliable brakes and still he'd beat me to the printing press. What exactly had I done with the past twenty years? I began to feel rather ashamed. I was never going to be the white Oprah; I was never going to be anything.

He seemed pleased by my lack of retort and resumed poking the ground with his tree branch. Gandalf lumbered over to the rock hocking a big wad of wizardly phlegm onto the grass, narrowly missing the German Shepherd beside him. "Time to go, dear," he motioned to his grandson.

He obediently hopped off the rock and grabbed his grandfather's hand.

"I'm coming back tomorrow," he said. "We could talk again if you want."

*Like Hell*, I thought.

But he was staring at me hopefully from underneath his shaggy bowl cut.

"Sure," I replied. "Sounds fun."

With all kinds of age-inappropriate swagger, he told me to take care of my leg, and wandered off staring back at me for one final wave. I smiled back, knowing very well I would never see him again. After all, it's never too soon for a boy to learn that a girl can stand him up.

## Eight

# THE MAN WHO FRIED
# THE NEST EGG

"Wait, there's more . . ."

Unless those words come from Bob Barker and you're a confident estimate away from a Showcase Showdown victory, they are almost always about to shatter your heart.

He is flat broke. He told me yesterday in the parking lot of a Traders Joe's. That was supposed to be the near devastating shocker. But today we are on the porch of our love nest, and I am terrified. What could "more" be? I am certain that my husband is about to reveal his addiction to methamphetamines and online blackjack, things much more expensive than Trader Joe's frozen tamales. Things that we, certainly, cannot afford.

What is he going to tell me? *Please don't let him be gay.*

He stands, wobbling the little teak bench we inherited from his design savvy mother. He is clearing his throat and holding my hand; for a moment I think he's about to propose again. The tears in his eyes begin to seize violently and my heart—which like most newlyweds' is overfed and bloated—stalls, rumbles, and struggles to turn over. I know the admission hiding in his cheeks is going to hurt.

I brace myself against the window, pushing the back of my skull so hard against the pane, I'm afraid it might break. He begins to speak in a tone that's detached, clinical, and unrecognizable.

He hasn't filed his taxes . . . in three years.

He has spent $24,000 of savings in a matter of months.

He owes the government almost $15,000.

We are broke.

We are broken.

My eyes are large and dry; his are still flooding and dripping onto his t-shirt. We have been married for almost a year and lived together for two before that, building a life together with an upward and onward trajectory. How could this have happened?

He is red-faced and sullen, looking like he wants some sort of reassurance. I want to hate him but I can't. I feel like an idiot and all of my energy is currently directed toward the dwarfing mountain of "should haves" being erected in my brain

We never joined bank accounts before we got married. We really fucking should have. I had been handling the monthly living expenses while he was getting his business off the ground. I never should have agreed to that. Our savings were kept in an account at his bank where I had imagined they were "accruing interest" or whatever it is that large sums of money do when they sit around for a long time. I should have asked more questions. I really should have grown up and grown out of the assumption that all banks looked like Uncle Scrooge's vault from *Duck Tales*.

I'm such an idiot. I don't believe it. I'm not shocked, disgusted, or furious. I actually can't believe it. We're married. Married people don't do this. Husbands don't do this. *Especially husbands with finance degrees.*

I cringe as I remember this wildly unfortunate fact.

How had he managed to fry our nest egg while I was bringing

home the bacon?

All I can do is stare through him blankly.

He stammers and I jolt to attention. Then the explanation begins. He was in far over his head with work expenses like rent and fancy equipment. He expected that business would turn around and that he'd come up with the money. He was afraid of hurting me, which, of course, he did anyway.

I don't believe him; I don't know if I'll ever believe him again. It wasn't an accident—this took calculation and masterful avoidance.

I can feel him watching me, hunching his shoulders, and silently apologizing. I want him to feel hurt, I want him to atone, I want him to regret. But more than anything, I just want it to go away. I get up and curl my body over the railing, forcing the air out of my lungs in an effort to regulate my shallow breathing. I'm having a panic attack. My arms feel weak and my heart is throbbing against my ribs, blind spots start to cloud my vision, and I remember . . .

We got married on the end of dock. Part of me wishes I'd jumped in the lake. That day, I grew up. I swallowed my ego and I became a wife. I settled into the adequately monotonous employment of an adult. It was horrible and humbling at times, but I did it because I had a family now.

My mind begins to wander. I knew what I had given up for us, but what sacrifices other than suffering through a few unfortunate casseroles had he made?

Fuck marriage.

"Everything will be okay. I'm so proud of you for telling me," is all I can manage.

I hug him, not because I want to, but because it's mechanical and mechanics are all I have left. Then, the fear takes over.

He's smoking a cigarette and sobbing at the same time, sending erratic puffs of smoke out of his nostrils like an old-fashioned steam engine laboring to leave the station. I quickly shift away from him, no longer comforted by the softness of his gray T-shirt under my chin and his patchy red beard on my cheek. It doesn't feel right. He's become a stranger with new smells and a new touch. I don't know him and it scares me. He wants me to look him in the eye but I can't. He wants me to kiss him but I can't. When his figure does find its way into my salt-stained periphery, all I see is a villainous lump of shadow fighting with the moths for a taste of the porch light. Then I lie to him and myself.

"We're going to get through this," I state assuredly.

His face softens and he gently grabs my hand as though it were made of glass.

"Really?" he whispers, his voice quiet and shaky.

But everything will *not* be okay.

"Why did you do this to us?" I stammer, the first signs of anger crawling into my sinuses and scratching at my eyes.

He doesn't know why.

Our relationship has lost something. It will never get it back. It will never be new. It will never be safe.

At bedtime, I tell him I love him and I mean it, but I don't know why. I don't know the man in front of me. We will sleep in the same bed, we will share a tube of toothpaste, and our last name will stay the same, but I don't recognize him. He is not the man who promised to love and protect me.

I go to the bathroom, seeking solace in routine, in flossing and scrubbing. I look like a stranger too, gaunt and steely. This isn't who I was supposed to be.

I turn the tap off and wonder if he'll love this anesthetized, rigid person, and if this person will be capable of loving him.

The television is left on. He turns the fans on, first the ceiling, and then the bathroom, knowing that white noise of late-night baseball and circulating air are the only stillness we'll find tonight. We crawl into the bed and not even our legs touch as I beg for a thoughtless sleep. I turn my back to him and curl into a ball, resigned to the fact that I will now have to protect myself, and him, too. He clearly isn't capable.

The anger will come tomorrow, I am certain. Viscous and sour, it will cling ruthlessly to the walls of our home and steal the soft open spaces that had lived freely in my mind; it will take me somewhere new and it may not give me back. I prepare myself to wake up to his face in the morning and hope that I can hold on to that groggy moment when he is just asleep and beautiful, before I remember just how badly he can hurt me.

*Nine*

# THE LAD WHO
# PEES SITTING DOWN

*I* should have known how it would end the first time he came to my door. He was freshly shaven, and smelled like he'd fallen in a relentlessly deep vat of Polo Blue by Ralph Lauren. His shirt was perfectly pressed, and he was wearing loafers that cost more than my mattress.

I opened the door and stared at him. I had never seen someone who looked so much like a wax figurine. Everything about his body was moisturized and plucked until it had the appearance of a Mattel doll. And yet, somehow, he was attractive. Startlingly so.

This was certainly going to be interesting.

It's a universal truth acknowledged that men who wear designer shoes lost a portion of their manhood in a shopping galleria. They don't pee standing up, and they carry hand moisturizer in their man bags. And all women know that unless you want to spend the rest of your life debating whether you or your spouse is prettier, you politely decline to hold hands with any male of this sort.

But I'm not very good at dating. I say yes to men who are unemployed and live in their parents' basement, so a little facial moisturizer wasn't going to scare me away. Even though he looked like he was the kind of man to hang a self-portrait over the family mantle, he might not be. The least I could do was let him buy me an overly priced dinner at a dimly lit Italian restaurant and then ignore his calls a week later. Plus, it would be fun to be seen in public with someone so attractive. People could only assume that: A) I was on my way to a Nobel Prize, or B) my nether regions tasted like mint chocolate chip ice cream. Either would have been acceptable.

The Man Who Wore Loafers was not the absolute worst first date I've had in my life. He took me to the kind of place where the tables are white and the walls are white and the waiters are white and everything you order sounds like it was made in Europe by a family that only drinks merlot with 60 percent alcohol. By the second glass of wine, I forgot how self-absorbed he was and how he cared more about money than Donald Trump's wife. He was surprisingly nice. Baby kitten nice. And he asked more questions than my mother, which seemed impossible.

"What do you do for a living?"

"Where do you go to school?"

"Do you want children?"

"Are you opposed to Botox?"

At the end of the night, we made out on my couch, and I had to bite my wine-induced tongue so I would refrain from telling him how much his face reminded me of a baby's butt.

The first rule in life is: never do anything because you're lonely. The second rule in life is: never date anyone who cares more about hygiene than Eva Longoria. Unfortunately when you're lonely, you don't really care about rules. You care about un-lonelying yourself. And so when a guy who looks like a slightly taller Tom Cruise wants to suck face and buy you cannoli, you throw the rules in the trash compactor and put on a dress two times two small and pray it doesn't rip when you're squatting to sexily pick up a dropped fork.

Truthfully, I didn't mean to date him for such a long time. It was supposed to be a month or two. A harmless fraction of a year where I could build up my capacity to be lonely again, and then plop him on the side of the road like a half-eaten Pop Tart. But once you start doing something, AA is right: it's very hard to stop. Before I knew it, he started calling me babe and leaving me voicemails where he only said, "Hey, it's me." I ate Thanksgiving dinner with every relative he's ever acquired, and we named our future children while we slept under the same silk sheets. We were going to have a Harper and a Lincoln, and they were going to be exquisitely well-rounded children who could play soccer and the harmonica. When he bought me a pair of loafers, I knew the deal was sealed.

How could this happen, you're wondering. How could an intelligent, decent, extremely good looking girl like yourself get to the point of having fake offspring with a knock-off Calvin Klein model?

And I'll tell you, dear reader, it's quite simple. Women end up with the wrong men the same way children end up eating broccoli. You start off life hating it—two things could not possibly be less made for each other—but your parents and your friends and your sales lady at Lane Bryant say, "Try it; it gets better." And so you do. You eat it again and again until, finally, you begin to see the redeeming qualities in broccoli, and the taste isn't so much like dusty cardboard anymore, but, instead, something fresh and healthy. "I like this," you say, and so you begin eating it with all your meals. And just like that, the thing that was horrible is now the thing you can't do without.

I was entirely, 100 percent prepared to walk down the aisle

with The Man Who Wore Loafers; I no longer cared that he had more beauty products than me, that he wouldn't let me touch his face because he was afraid my oily fingers would give him acne, or that every time before we kissed, he insisted on brushing his teeth. I loved him. Or, more accurately, I loved how he'd un-lonelyed me. The only thing that saved me from utter matrimonial hell was the toilet.

It was a Saturday, and I had just gotten out of the shower when he walked in. He was so casual about it all. Opening the door, sauntering through, smiling at me. It felt like we were at a Ponderosa in the buffet line—yes, I would like the lasagna! But there were no family-sized jellos here. No quiches or mildly burnt pot roasts. Only a toilet, some tile, and an open invitation to completely ruin our relationship.

I tried not to panic, but pit stains developed rapidly on my towel. What was he doing in here? He knew how I felt. He knew that a closed door meant that absolutely, positively, under no circumstances—even if Hillary Clinton were in the living room sucking George Bush's pinkie finger—should he enter.

I have a large problem watching people urinate. It makes me extremely uncomfortable and full of hot sweats. I know a number of people who are comfortable with the whole bit. They pee as openly in their houses as they cook chicken in their kitchens. One second we'll be talking about the state of Egypt and the value of homeschooling, and the next thing I know they'll be entering the bathroom, continuing our conversation with the door ajar and their pants around their ankles.

*You're not just grabbing a Bud Light,* I want to say. *We can wait to finish this later.* But despite my look of absolute horror, they continue whizzing, standing up to wipe, snap, and—dear God let's pray—wash their hands.

Of course, I'm just as terrified of being caught in the act as I am of catching others. I'm one of those people who performs acrobatics in public bathrooms, squatting with elaborate dexterity over the john, reaching across the cavernous stall while holding the flimsy lock in place so no female intruders can come in and try to decide by the color of my watery offspring whether I've downed a coke or eaten asparagus.

I'm sure a psychologist would trace this all back to my bed-wetter heroics as a child or my inability to pee in a cup on command in later years when doctors and employers required it.

"Can I have sample?" they'd say, extending the peace offering of a Dixie cup in my direction. And I would walk into the public lavatory with its mauve-colored tile and sanitary lotion, armed with a survival pack of bottled water. But no matter how much I squatted and thrust and pictured the watery deluge of a slip-n-slide, I'd come out with a mere yellow droplet. A tiny yellow tear that would scream into the doctor's head that I was a drug addict with a handicapped bladder.

So you can understand how I have an equal and almost unhealthy caginess when it comes to urine's abode, and how The Man Who Wore Loafers' entrance into my private lair caused me to nearly regurgitate that morning's coffee.

After all, *he knew better.*

I swallowed deeply and turned toward the mirror. The only adult way to handle this was to ignore him. But The Man Who Wore Loafers was humming. His voice was ricocheting off the tub and the tile directly toward my ears, making it all but impossible to ignore his rainforest moment to the side. I glanced at him out of my peripheral vision in an effort to shush him, but instead of seeing my then-boyfriend's back and the reassuring display of a slight jingle, I saw him sitting there, perched rather pleasantly on the toilet seat like a tremendously agile cat. I began to hyperventilate. This was horrible. Catastrophic even. I wasn't dating The Man Who Wore Loafers after all; I was dating The Lad Who Pees Sitting Down.

For women, the little droplets of urine on the toilet seat, however stain inducing and smelly, remind us that we are dating men. *Real men.* Sweaty, muscle-bearing, penis-wearing men who can do things like carry steel bookcases up two flights of stairs and arm wrestle strangers in public. While walking into the bathroom to find the toilet seat flexed up and scattered with a mosaic of man droppings can be annoying, it's also a peculiarly reassuring pat on the back. While he might have piss-poor aim when it comes to relieving himself in the bathroom, there's a large chance his thrust is better elsewhere.

When you date a man who pees sitting down, you begin to question his ability to hit a home intruder with a baseball bat. Rather than fighting to the death, he might, as it were, opt for the coward corner and start crying tears while sucking his thumb.

As I stood in the bathroom blow-drying my hair into a hot, frizz-less mess, I began to wonder if The Lad Who Pees Sitting Down had other secrets to share. Did he, perhaps, dry-clean his socks? Did he think me a savage when I put my elbows on the dinner table? Would he consider it amoral if I suggested a camping trip into the wilderness where we would be shower-less for a week, equipped only with leaves to wipe our private parts?

Inevitably, The Lad Who Pees Sitting Down stood up from the toilet seat and began washing his hands to a Brawny-man-clean. While we had been dating for a full-fledged year, I had stopped noticing how his stubble was embarrassingly puny and how his smile gave off a wax-and-polish glow. No part of him was out of place. No fly undone. No shoe untied. No armpit stained. No skin untanned. He was, in a sense, perfect. And this piss-sitting-down perfection made me want to upchuck on his

Cole Haan shoes.

As I watched his soap-and-scrub, I felt compelled to interrupt him and ask for a show of manhood. I wanted to send him out into the wild yonder to shoot me a deer or perhaps venture into the garage and build something like a picket fence. Or Noah's ark. I was the border patrol of Gentlemen-R-Us and I wanted to make sure he had all his man parts intact. After all, whom was I dating? This was all very new information. Very disturbing information. In a matter of minutes, he had become The Lad Who Pees Sitting Down. And if I was to venture any further down relationship row, I wanted to know if he planned to teach our future sons how to pee sitting down as well. Maybe he planned on starting a colony of hygienic friendly men who spent their afternoons making baskets of potpourri, followed by a night of Colin Firth romantic comedies. I wanted my yet-to-be-born sons to know more than a life of tanning salons and teeth whitener. I wanted them to roll around in the mud and know how to tether an ox.

It goes without saying that my relationship with The Lad Who Pees Sitting Down deteriorated at a very rapid speed from that point on. While he might attribute our decline to things like communication or differing taste in loafers, I know the truth: When you pee sitting down, you can never quite get up.

*Ten*

# THE MAN WITH A CLAN

*I*s this better or worse than having diarrhea in Buckingham Palace?

This is the only question I can seem to ask myself as we step off the plane, onto the tarmac, and everyone's waiting there. Standing in a clump, twiddling their thumbs, and rocking on their heels. There are three of them, perched specifically at different heights as if they were the real Russian nesting dolls, one built to fit inside another. The father being the largest. Beard full and generously tall, I picture the first words out of his mouth: "Only you can prevent wildfires."

Everything in San Luis Obispo is small—infinitesimally small. I assume this is because everything is infinitesimally more expensive. The runway is the size of a fruit roll-up stretched thinly in the hand of a five year old. The tiny planes have pet names instead of numbers. There is no baggage claim, no lobby of overpriced restaurants to get lost in, and no screening area. Apparently people who aerate their wine don't pose a security threat. But more terrifying than any bomber getting on a Boeing, is my complete inability to run. In San Luis Obispo, the airport is all conflated into one happy room where people pad through the airport in eleven pairs of sunglasses and Lacoste shirts giving each other high fives. Wealthy, weathered white folk who carry organic granola around in their Coach purses.

I'm not ready for this, clearly. As the space between his parents and me begins to collapse, I squeeze The Man with a Clan's hand and try to suck the residual airline pretzel off my teeth. This is all his fault, of course. Or, more accurately, it's his eyes' fault. Those manipulative green irises that downplay everything. It's no wonder that when he asked me to visit his parents three states away, I hardly realized I was agreeing to meet the Vanderbilts. If I'd known, I probably wouldn't have worn sandals I'd showered in.

I've pictured this moment before, but I didn't envision them like this. All standing in a line, smiling, showing a conservative amount of tooth, and cupping their hands into tiny half moons, rotating them in the most cordial of waves. They look as though they were lifted from a Royal Wedding commemorative plate, the kind that comes from Royal Dalton, not QVC.

The Man with a Clan is calm. Completely unfettered. But that's natural, I suppose, for an Army man. Introducing the girlfriend, no matter how intense, has to be slightly less traumatic than war. I can feel his family sizing me up already. While their son was off serving our country, I was uploading photos to Facebook. I desperately ransack my memory for any moments of personal achievement or valor, and can't help but wince. I knew I should have gotten a rescue dog.

As he steps toward his height appropriate spot in line, I begin to sweat and wonder if there will ever be a place for me to stand. The odd thing about meeting the parents is that you've had your whole life to think about what their son will be like. You piece him together like a Mr. Potato Head, only slightly less heavy in the abdomen. You know his height and build. How he makes his money and how he takes his coffee. But the parents? They've always just been these obscure inkblots. Sure, you assumed they were there. And that there'd be one of each. But beyond that, they didn't have faces or allergies, stock portfolios or baubles stored in the Tower Bridge.

I shimmy my sunglasses to the top of my head and stare at them, entirely forgetting everything I learned about manners in sixth grade cotillion. I search my mind, desperate for something to say, but nothing comes out. The Man with a Clan gives them each a brief hug with the requisite, "Hi Mom, Hi Dad," and then breaks away to the baggage carousal to get our belongings, leaving me standing there, exposed and un-introduced.

I look around. Everyone else in a fifty-foot vicinity is having outstanding conversations. They're talking about lobster and Dostoyevsky. They're reciting the Magna Carta. In French. I focus in on another twenty-something woman to my left. She's wearing black linen pants and a silk blouse. She is breathtakingly put together. I bet her closet looks like the Container Store. She's shaking hands. Like them, she is positively regal. And all of a sudden, just like that, I understand what's going on. The Royal Nesting Dolls aren't always this mute. They're disappointed. They saw her getting off the plane, thought it was me, and then became entirely lackluster when they realized I wasn't Tory Burch.

I am not the daughter in law they wanted.

But then his mother, God bless her, breaks the silence.

"You must be Megan. We've heard so much about you."

"Hi! It's so nice to finally meet you all."

I'm overly conscious of my inflection. Every exclamation point. Every flat line. If I pronounce one vowel without the appropriate amount of enthusiasm, I imagine I'll immediately be re-boarded on the plane and sent to Libya where I will be sold as a bride to the highest bidding goat farmer. I smile as loudly as I can, emitting a tiny squeak as though the hinges of my jaw have rusted, and then silence returns.

The only thing that makes the situation bearable is the woman who is standing slightly off to the side, Julie. While the rest of us are all awkwardly hugging at the hips and trying to make small talk about the legroom in planes these days, she's off in her own world, enthralled by a palm tree and wearing large pink sunglasses from the 1960s. Julie is The Man with a Clan's aunt. She's seventy and has Alzheimer's. Or dementia. Or some mix breed of the two that makes her face contort like Dustin Hoffman's. This trip to the airport is the most exciting thing that has happened to her in the past three years.

The Man with a Clan returns and we take our hulking slab of luggage and puzzle it into the Subaru, driving by vineyards and orchards filled with fruit I can't afford, only stopping on the way back to the house to buy fresh picked strawberries from the recovering drug addicts at Sunny Acres. The scenery flicks past the window in bolts. The grass is burnt white, starched and dry as my mouth. It rolls and rolls until, thirty minutes later, the wagon pulls into the driveway of a pristine teal ranch house.

Once we arrive, we are skirted in for the tour. Despite the fact they've only been there a year, the house feels lived in, like it had hosted a thousand Thanksgivings, most of which, I can only assume, were covered by a special *Town and Country* correspondent. I think of my own apartment with its dusty windows and sofa perpetually occupied by my unemployed roommate as Aunt Julie and I follow behind the trio, both of us staring at the walls in awe. Each room is tagged with its appropriate label: Kitchen, Bathroom, Den. Julie has no concept of spatial orientation, his mom quietly explains. A layer of plaque on her brain makes her forget, from one moment to the next, where to pee and where to sleep. So they use nametags.

We set my luggage down in what will be my room for the next week. The Man with a Clan will be sleeping down the hall. His parents are right next-door. They will hear me every time I undo my zipper or write cries for help in my Moleskine.

I guess you could say I was nervous. That would be reasonable. And only a marginal understatement from the real truth that I was mentally peeing my pants with every passing second. Most women spend their whole lives wanting to get married. They've planned their wedding since they got Barbie's Dream House under the Christmas tree at age five and they never looked back, hoarding *Martha Stewart Wedding* editions under the box springs like it were moonshine. So in moments like this—when they've met "The One" and "The One" has invited them home to meet the family—they rejoice at a decibel level only discernible to cats and women who own crock-pots. Meeting the parents is the Nobel Prize in relationships. It's the most certain sign that the next thing they'll meet is a man on bended-knee, cracking open a shiny, aqua colored box. But I don't own a crock-pot. And the only thing I've ever learned from Martha Stewart is not to obstruct justice.

Excusing myself, I walk down the carpeted hallway and into the bathroom. I lock the door so Julie doesn't walk in, accidentally thinking it's the closet or the grocery store. I peel off my shirt and jeans and turn on the shower. There's a handsome orange tree peeking through the window, and an assortment of half used luxury shampoos and conditioners on the ledge. I step inside the marble sarcophagus and begin, very unreasonably, to cry.

The thing is, I like the Man with a Clan. In fact, I like him a lot. We haven't said the L word yet, but I know its just playing hopscotch on our tongue until the right time. Our relationship is simply no longer as disposable as a camera in the 1990s. We're working toward forever. And despite what the Vegas chapels might say, forever doesn't mean, "Until you get dysentery," or "Until I meet someone whose ass sags less than yours." It means always. Regardless. No matter if you get a widow's peak. Or cancer. Or a constant desire to watch the movie *Lethal Weapon*.

I've never wanted to be married before. I've never been apprehensive about meeting the parents or curious if I have child bearing hips. But now, with him, in the promenade of San Luis Obispo, I find that my kitchen would be quite happy to have a crock-pot. That it, in fact, would be all sorts of thrilled to acquire an entire family of kitchen utensils. The only question is if the Royal Nesting Dolls will have me.

I turn on the fan and can hear his family's voices bouncing off the twelve-foot ceilings in the hallway, but I refuse to listen. They're probably telling The Man With the Clan that things between us are moving too fast. I don't want to know if I'm what they'd always hoped for. Or if they'd pictured someone entirely different. Perhaps a teacher. Or a lawyer. Or a veterinarian who can set a dog's broken leg. They've been dreaming about marrying their son off for ages. Enough grandbabies to start an orphanage. So surely, after all this time, after all this hope, they expect something.

I crank the faucet and step, big toe pointed, onto the plush mat lazing on the marble. The towels are folded into perfect white squares and feel like they're made of baby bunny ears. Just as I turn down the fan and begin to wipe the fog from the impossibly large mirror, I hear them.

"She's nice."

"Where did you meet her again?"

"Do you think she liked us?"

"What about the house?"

"And Julie?"

They sound nervous.

They sound self-conscious.

They sound exactly like me. Only richer.

By the time I've gotten out of the shower, blow-dried my hair, and put on something slightly more presentable, they're all standing outside the bedroom in their perfect nesting doll line. His mother is smiling widely, his father is smoothing the bristles of his beard, and Julie, in her giant pink sunglasses, is standing by the door holding Albert by the clump of his neck and extending him in the air toward me as if he were dry cleaning. The Man with a Clan is standing beside her. He doesn't look like he's having a midlife crisis. Or like he's considering extradition to Albania. Instead he's thinking about something much more practical: dinner.

"How do you feel about barbecue?" he asks me as he leans in the closet and pulls his fleece off the hanger.

The Royal Nesting Dolls stare at me as though their son has just proposed. They're clearly apprehensive about my response, terrified I might be vegan.

"I like coleslaw with my barbecue," Julie says before I can answer. To which, of course, I can only agree.

Julie starts toward the door muttering on about smoked meat, and the Man With The Clan finds my palm and we file out the door in a flawlessly jumbled procession behind Julie, his mother slightly patting me on the shoulder as I walk across the threshold.

It's not quite a coronation, but it's close.

*Eleven*

# THE MAN WHO PARTED
# THE RED SEA

*I*f I'm going to blame anyone, I'm going to blame Jessica Landol. We were all in the fourth grade, about nine or ten years old, but Jessica knew more than any of us because she had something the rest of us didn't have: a sister in middle school. Miranda Landol, who was thirteen and therefore knew everything there was about being an adult, had passed her wisdom along to her younger sister, sneaking her tidbits of what she called "grown up stuff." We were led to believe sixth through eighth grades were the upper echelon of society where people wildly kissed with tongues and exposed their midriffs. Huddled over chocolate milk in the cafeteria, Jessica would splurge on her vast knowledge of spin the bottle and seven minutes in heaven. She even created a dictionary of all the bases so we'd be certain to know when we'd "hit a homerun."

Jessica Landol, of course, had no more of an idea what a homerun was than any of us did, but since she had a pink trapper keeper, miraculously glossy blonde hair, and spoke with authority, we chose to believe her. More importantly, if any of us doubted or questioned her theories, she would look at us pityingly across the table and say, "I figured you wouldn't understand."

To be truthful, I didn't really like Jessica Landol. I can't imagine many people did. But I was terrified that without her I'd be left behind. That I would miss something. Some solitaire diamond of knowledge that would forever leave me on the outside of an inside joke. The great fear of abandonment consumed me, so I loyally followed her jelly shoes around, a lost elementary puppy. She became my voice of reason. My personal *Encyclopedia Britannica*. Unfortunately for me, she was only nine years old and entirely incorrect. Particularly when it came to tampons.

During my formative years, my family really didn't talk much about "being a woman." We never bought makeup or designer jeans. Instead we played softball and knew far too much about the PGA. So it's not surprising that Jessica Landol was the foremost authority in my life on the subject of sexual development. I would sit rapt, mouth agape, Oreo clenched in hand, as the great orator twirled her ponytail and delivered, chapter by chapter, milestone by milestone, what I deemed to be the Popular Girl's Guide to Puberty. While much of this new and terribly confusing information disappeared between spelling bee words and state capitals, I managed to absorb the following counsel: Only shave your legs with a pink razor; don't wear a sports bra unless you're a lesbian; and, most importantly, you should never ever use a tampon because once you do, you've officially lost your virginity. *Officially.*

My formal education on womanhood continued for many years down this windy, misleading path. As the lunch table rumors compiled, it wasn't just my virginity that was at stake; it was my health. I heard horror stories of the "small missiles" that caused the female gender to detonate or die from fungus. After one conversation during PE, I was entirely convinced they'd grow to the size of an enflamed octopus while I was in the swimming pool, and I'd forever be walking around with a bloated inanimate object in my interiors.

If only someone had bothered to stop and tell me the truth about how glorious and safe these small objects really were. How, once utilized, you could stop using words like "spotting" unless referring to a celebrity or an empty parking space. If only the PTA had organized and handed out something useful for Halloween. "Ladies, here's a kind of stick you can use," the mothers would say, forgoing the traditional Pixies of sugar for plastic blood blockers. I would have hated them then, of course, but thanked them later. So many things could have been prevented. Things no amount of prayer or bleach can ever take back.

How did I get there?

I'm not really sure.

Fate.

Boldness.

The interstate.

It didn't really matter. The only thing that mattered was that I was there, standing on his doorstep. Not borrowing an egg or a cup of sugar. Not ringing the wrong doorbell. But there. Wanted. Asked. Needed. *By him.* I felt like I'd been invited to the Grammys.

I took a deep breath and put my finger to the doorbell. I really didn't want to mess this up. I'd spent the better part of my life being forgettable. I'm never the object of attention. I'm the one who stands next to the object. Or in front of the object.

"No, not that one. The one behind the gangly brunette."

Yes, right.

In a high school of three hundred people, I was known to half the student body as the "funny girl's sister" who styled my hair the wrong way and whose most colorful attribute was the corn that was perpetually stuck in my teeth. I was not the girl who got the guy. Especially this one.

The Man Who Parted the Red Sea wasn't sort of good looking. He wasn't just for the kind of girls who liked athletes or the kind of girls who liked blondes. He was as universal as the Euro. Only less controversial. I fell in love with him the first day of PE in sixth grade when he ran a mile in five minutes flat, lapping me two times and downing a full Gatorade before I passed out on the track, acquiring grass stains and palpitations. I spent the better part of my juvenile years watching him play tonsil hockey with hoards of private school girls who could lift their plaid skirts higher than Bob Marley, while I tried, very unsuccessfully, to dissect the art of the push-up bra. He never noticed me, never talked to me. I was as invisible as Canada's military.

Inevitably we graduated from high school, parted our clearly inseparable ways, and I didn't see him again for three years until we ran into each other at a taco stand over the holidays. We exchanged a few pleasantries and then he said something I never would have imagined in a thousand million years: "You know, you should really come visit."

After a brief moment of squeal-filled inner-hysteria, I decided that indeed I would. It was an opportunity to rewrite my gangly, brunette history, to transform what was once a frizzy-haired, club-footed tragedy into a shining epic. I could be the object of affection instead of the skinny, awkward thing blocking it from view. Or so I thought.

The door opened and there he was standing in front of me. His cut jaw line had remained intact. He was wearing a t-shirt, a pair of jeans, and a five o'clock shadow. And surprisingly, he was smiling. Like he was happy to see me.

My expectations, admittedly, were large. Too large. Impractical. They were bigger than the man who has to buy two seats on the plane. I had dreamt about this moment for years, and, in my fantasies, it all ended at our high school reunion where we walk into the streamer-covered gymnasium, and I'm wearing a dress that cost more than an adopted child. People won't believe it. They won't believe *me*. They will be uncomfortably jealous, and they will talk about us in hushed tones over the fruit punch while I glow from the enormous amounts of married sex we just had in our five-star hotel room.

I stared at him, taking it all in.

*Can you believe it?* I wanted to scream. *Can you really believe it?*

But when I opened up my mouth to say something—anything—the hello caught on my tongue. And the hug, which I rehearsed more than children do their Christmas pageants, refused to wrap itself firmly but kindly around his chest. In my head, when this moment happened, I knew I would be charming. I would be witty. I would be captivating. We'd known each other for years, but had only amassed a total life conversation of approximately twenty words, mostly containing the phrase "I'm sorry," which I used when I klutzily bumped into him by the lockers. But just then, when I had the opportunity to do something other than apologize for my presence, I bore a striking and unfortunate resemblance to the stoic Queen's Guards at Buckingham Palace.

Still being the suave, popular one, he reached for my suitcase with his left hand and pulled me into him with his right arm.

"How was the trip? It's good to see you."

And at that moment, as I hung there nestled close to his chest, everything was perfect. I was Grace Kelly. I was Audrey Hepburn. I was Marilyn Monroe. I was all three blended together and shot out with a dash of Kate Middleton. Settled there ever so briefly in his nook, the Duchess of Happy Endings, I wouldn't have believed what would happen next. And if I had, I most certainly would have run. But instead I thought, *This is really going to happen.*

We went inside and he set my bag in the guest room, and a familiar cramping began to creep across my abdomen. I excused myself quickly to the bathroom. I told him I needed to freshen up before dinner, but that was a lie. What I really needed to do was check *down there.*

*Shit,* I thought, staring at the toilet.

*Shit, shit, shit, shit, shit.*

It's not a lady-like thing to think, I know. But generally speaking, the whole act of menstruation doesn't seem lady-like at all.

*How is this possible?* I screamed at my nether regions.

I went to my bag and rustled through for what I needed. And since some part of me still believed Jessica Landol was right when she said tampons were directly linked to cancer and blindness, what I needed was a pad.

We went to dinner at a place with burgers and beers and college students who were discovering, for the first time, what "binge drinking" means. I tried extra hard to make engaging, intelligent conversation, but the night was going steeply downhill. The dinner was undercooked. The conversation was bland. The saltshakers had more chemistry than we did.

I looked at him looking at me across the table, and I knew I no longer looked royal. The maxi pad in my underwear felt like an over-sized canoe. It could have easily held Boy Scout Troop 615, and its cooler of salami sandwiches. The ecstasy I felt for that 2.5 seconds standing on his threshold had come crashing down. No part of me looked sexy. No part of me looked like I was worth a long-distance relationship or even a modest over-the-clothes feel up. I'm pretty sure we could have been sequestered in a fully stocked brewery, and the only thing The Man Who Parted the Red Sea would have made out with is a hangover the size of Bangladesh.

The worst feeling in life is that you haven't made any progress. That somewhere between the ages of twelve and twenty, the only thing you've been able to gain is a dorm room and a questionably used credit card with high interest rates. Somewhere along the way, I was certain my chest was supposed to stop looking like stale Lays potato chips and more like the Twin Peaks. Or at least a pair of venerable hills. But I was still thirty-two acres of grade-A flatland. I looked average. Boring. The type of girl who always draws the fortune cookies that are facts. Things like, "You have a deep appreciation for arts and music." No cookie has ever promised me wealth. Or success. Or a meaningful new relationship just around the corner.

He was poking at his fries with his fork looking more bored than he ever did in algebra, and a simple truth dawned on me that I should have realized a month before: He didn't really want me to come visit; he was just trying to be nice.

We ended up back at his house by 10:00 p.m. and by 10:30 he'd fallen asleep on the couch watching a marathon of *Road Rules*. I headed to the guestroom, turned out the light, and fell asleep. *This can't possibly get any worse*, I thought. But of course it possibly could.

Some people are really good in panic situations. These people are not related to me. They own fire extinguishers, are CPR certified, and know where to go in case a nuclear bomb lands on their two-car suburban garage. But Composure is not my middle name, my last name, or even my grandfather's name. I am Lady Panic—heiress to a long and fruitful line of cold sweats, nervous shaking, and pants pissing.

For me, panic is one of those feelings that consumes your whole body. Creeping, sucking, bending, imploding. When I find myself overcome with intense worry, I am unable to function proactively and instead pluck myself down in the offending puddle of panic and listen to how fast my heart can beat.

Only this time it wasn't a puddle of panic. I was lying, quite literally, in a pool of my own blood. An inexcusable fact considering I had not starred in the movie *Braveheart* or taken boxing lessons from Muhammad Ali. It was 9:30 the next morning. I was at the apartment of the best looking man I had ever seen, and it looked as though I was hands down guilty of murdering a small dog in his bed.

I took a deep breath.

*This could be worse*, I considered. And then I tried to consider how because nothing seems worse than a can of Porter Paint canvassing cotton.

*Well, he could have been in the bed with me.*

I considered this.

Could have been in bed with me.

Large muscles.

Beautiful face of scruff and glory.

Long arms wrapped around me, spooning like we were high schoolers who still weren't entirely sure what the word period meant.

I smiled briefly.

And then I remembered the blood. The tidal wave of my insides that had made the entire guest bedroom look like it was cheering for the Alabama Crimson Tide. If he had been in bed with me, he would have been drenched in a Tsunami of far-too-much-too-quickly. Having your period *on someone* would be mortifying even if you were married. But doing so on a first date would be unforgivable. I would probably have to endure intense counseling for the next decade and banish the color red from my life forever for fear that it would induce seizures and bad memories.

I closed my eyes. This had to be a dream. Things like this didn't happen to real people. Real people wake up in the mornings, make their coffee, and eat waffles. They don't wake up feeling like they slept in maple syrup.

I counted to ten and then opened my eyes.

It was still there. All over. And my face officially turned the color of the bed sheets when I heard the only thing that could have made this situation terrifyingly worse: the doorknob.

As I braced myself and the door creaked open, I remembered the gawky, invisible fifteen year old who stood under the bleachers to watch the game, wandered the halls alone, and faded into the bubbling adolescent landscape. Wide-eyed, I stared at the crimson sheet set. I had no doubt the boy who ignored me for so many years would remember me quite well from now on.

As he appeared in the doorframe, I yanked the covers up to the pillow, confidently strode toward him, overnight bag under my arm. I left, telling him that regrettably I must get back home, and I thanked him for the bloody good time. I ran out the door and wished immediately that I could forget the whole thing. I wished I could bury it in a large wooden trunk and give it to the Russians to toss off the coast of Siberia. I wanted to go back a solid ten years and give a PowerPoint presentation on tampons to every girl who ever took Jessica Landol at her word. But in life there are embarrassing moments. And then there are the things you will never, ever forgive yourself for, no matter how much therapy and hypnosis you endure. Some things, after all, just leave a stain.

# Twelve

# THE MAN ENGAGED
# TO THE FAINTING GOAT

*H*e told me I had to come. This was his only instruction, which was a good instruction because had I not received it, I would have stayed home and watched *Flight of the Conchords* while knitting. I am not good at meeting people in large groups. More simply, I'm not good at meeting people. Everyone stands around, wearing more makeup than usual, and tries to see how many hands they can shake without getting laryngitis. Then inevitably, between sentences two and five, someone pulls the politics card, and all of a sudden there's tension by the cheese platter.

But my best friend was insistent.

"She is going to be there," he said, emphasis on the *she*. And that is when I knew that my attendance was no longer optional. My best friend had acquired, for the first time since I had known him, a full-fledged girlfriend. An odd truth as he was one of those very solitary, withdrawn people. The Lone Cyprus of humanity. And he seemed to like it there, out on his ledge, with no one to tell him he was drinking too much whiskey or putting in too many hours at the office. So this girlfriend bit—commitment to another human being—was a tremendous accomplishment, and I had to acknowledge it by going out in public and shaking her hand.

The group met at Bongo Java, a coffee shop downtown full of mismatched tables and tattooed baristas. People don't just go to Bongo; they gather there. They hole up at a table for hours, consuming 50 cent coffee refills until ulcers start appearing on their foreheads. By the time I made it to that part of town, they had gone through most of Costa Rica and were on their way through Ecuador. My best friend saw me out of the corner of his eye and stood up, hoisting his hands in the air as though he were signaling a touchdown.

"You made it! ... Come over and meet everyone."

This unnerved me slightly. My friend wasn't the type to hoist anything, much less his hands. He was cynical. Unanimated. Blessed with two wrong sides of the bed. The only thing I'd seen him affectionate about was Yankee baseball and me. I walked over to the table, and he gave me a peculiar pat on the shoulder. Like I were a small child or an estranged cousin. *I don't have Lyme's disease*, I wanted to say. *You can hug me.* But instead I smiled politely and passed my hand around the table.

"So nice to meet you."

"Yes, I've heard so much about you, too."

"Indeed, they do let me out in public."

Until, finally, I reached her. Though there were a dozen or so people at the table, it was easy to pick her out. I had one of those déjà vu feelings. Like I had seen her before in a past life or a Dove skin commercial. She was in her early thirties, rather pretty, and I imagined she enjoyed doing things like sitting on her couch and being picky about sushi. She was at the end of the table drinking a vanilla latte, a slightly dehydrated wildflower. She had a tattoo on her lower back, a fedora on her head, and change-purse bags under her eyes. She smiled at me, stuck her string-beanish hand out, and we shook on our newly cemented friendship.

My best friend cleared out a spot beside her and told me to sit down.

"There's plenty of room here," he said and waited for me to pick my way around the table and into the three inches of space.

My best friend was excited. Ralphie Red Ryder BB gun excited. I had never seen him wear such a preposterously large smile. It hadn't occurred to me until then that this could be real. Important. That he could even love her. I had just assumed she was a girl. Who would come and then go. The equivalent of a qualifying lap in NASCAR. I dug deep and endeavored to be as charming as possible. I made excessive amounts of eye contact and tried to appear extremely interested in her job as a paralegal. I knew this was an important moment, and I should ask her about all sorts of things like what kind of cul-de-sac she lived on and how she liked her stir-fry. Everyone knows the two-word girl friend meeting the one-word girlfriend is a critical event. If it goes poorly, the repercussions are far more costly than Dolly's implants.

But something was wrong. Off. I could feel the tension on my fingernails and in my kneecaps. It reverberated off the mismatched chairs. Every time I turned her direction in hopes of forming a kindred bond over Woody Allen, her eyes were staring at me glassed over. Her aura didn't feel like roses; it felt like airport security—I was entirely certain I wasn't carrying a homemade bomb, but her face told me otherwise. She was the puppy dog who refused to run when released in the backyard. I sat there, stunned for a minute, until I finally realized what was happening. The likeness was uncanny. She was the human equivalent of a fainting goat.

Now, admittedly, I've never seen a fainting goat before, but I've heard about them in reliable places like *National Geographic*. They're mystical creatures like unicorns. Or gnomes. Only less beautiful, less useful, and not featured on Saturday morning cartoon shows. Fainting goats are terribly dorky creatures. When they're startled or put in a very awkward situation, instead of reacting like normal, spine-filled animals, they stiffen their whole body and immediately stop functioning. The extreme ones keel completely over, weighted down, I imagine, by the emotional exhaustion of the moment. Then a bit later, the frozen fainters come to and proceed briefly through life with a stiff-legged scuffle. A drunken bumble without the benefit of beer. Having read so much about them I thought I knew what to expect, but Wikipedia doesn't do the terror and authenticity of the freezing act justice. It was more impressive than the life-size displays of dinosaurs you see off interstate exits in the Midwest.

I knew immediately this was a large misunderstanding. She had me pegged all wrong. It wasn't that I wasn't her type; it was that she thought I was her boyfriend's type—she suspected me. I might not be as good at socializing as Jackie Kennedy, but that certainly didn't make me a Marilyn Monroe. I wanted to set the record straight. I wanted to tell her that my best friend and I were as platonic as Will and Grace. We didn't have drinks in hotel bars followed by intimate rendezvous on the thirty-third floor. We never kissed, never held hands, and never so much as thought about uploading our portraits on MakeMeBabies.com just to see what might happen. I would never in a million years, even if offered ownership of Italy, contemplate doing the no-pants dance with a taken man. But she just started at me, her eyes judging what she could only assume were my lethal intentions.

I looked at my best friend hoping to see some recognition. *Are you witnessing this?* I wanted to say, raising my eyebrows suggestively in his direction (which, on later evaluation, probably didn't help). But my best friend seemed unaffected. Happy even.

I left that night with a palpable feeling of failure in my

stomach, along with a very awkward side hug from The Fainting Goat. I had met the girlfriend and had not succeeded in securing a follow-up date, complete with friendship bracelet making and laughing about the state of Nebraska. I returned home to my *Conchords* and knitting, with the naive assumption that women can, on occasion, be practical. She'll come around, I told myself. She has to. And I tried very hard to believe it.

As it turns out, The Fainting Goat had her heart broken. And not just a little roughed up, but thrown out a Jetta going ninety miles per hour, then obliterated by an eighteen-wheeler driving to Montague. She had been married, cheated on, and then divorced. All by the age of twenty-seven. She had cried about it with herself, with her friends, and then with him. And my best friend—who really is the best kind of friend—took to comforting her. He became a very sturdy, reliable shoulder. He hoisted her, held her, and then gave her a kiss.

After hearing that, I should have known how this would end. I should have seen my own semi coming. I felt bad for her, sure, but I also believed that by the time you hit your thirties, you're supposed to stop worrying about who takes who to the prom. You're supposed to realize that even though you have personal issues, everyone's got their own Samsonite full of insecurity.

For a while I tried hard to sympathize with her. I asked her over for wine and invited her to my birthday parties. I smiled at her and gave her warm hugs even when she turned me down. But it wasn't enough. She never could get comfortable with me. She always suspected me of things like treason and malpractice. Over the course of the next several months, she would repeatedly freeze and do the stiff-legged scuffle, then bumble off to my best friend to tell him all the horrible things I'd done. She would cry and nag until he bandaged up her insecure Achilles heel and then come lecture me.

"Why aren't you trying with her? Why don't you like her? Do you want to ruin this?"

I would purse my lips, unsure of what to say. After all, it's hard to like people who call you things that can be censored with asterisks.

Before this all began, when we were all at Bongo getting ulcers, I had wanted very much to like The Fainting Goat. My best friend's happiness was monumentally important to me. And because she was significant to him, she automatically became significant to me. I pictured us being like sisters, braiding each other's hair and having slumber parties on Saturday nights. But no matter what I did, the Fainting Goat didn't want to braid my hair. She wanted to shave it. Since I was female and did not require gastric bypass surgery, I was not welcome in her very small circle of acquaintances.

After a spell of feeling more unwelcome than smallpox, I gave up being nice and began hoping she would age into Fainting Goat Cheese. I crossed my fingers excessively that my best friend would realize her deeply ingrained flaws and put her out to pasture. But instead he did something entirely man-like and regrettable: he bought her a ring.

I should have known something was wrong from the moment he asked. He invited me out for a double cheeseburger at six o'clock in the evening, and when somebody invites you to eat dinner before its dark out, it's fair to assume you're a social appetizer, the palate cleanser for the real conversation that is to take place later. With my best friend, I was accustomed to being the main event, so naturally I was confused by his suspicious proposition. *We must be going somewhere fabulous afterward*, I assured myself, hoping it was a pool hall as my shot had improved tremendously since our last game. But it was clear when he sat down, checking his watch and tugging at the ends of his shirt, that he wasn't staying long. Something had changed.

"I'm getting married, and . . . " his voice trailed off, "I don't think I can see you anymore." The tone was stiff and learned, probably rehearsed several times in the parking lot by the light of his car mirror.

Surely, he couldn't be serious.

I laughed. This was funny. Hilarious. No one actually broke up with their friends.

"I mean it," he implored, trying to make me understand, but I still didn't believe him, rolling my eyes and pretending to duck under the table.

"There, you can't see me. Problem solved!"

But my best friend did not find my antics amusing. Over a few bites of a medium-rare burger, it became clear to everyone in the restaurant but me that he was serious indeed. He was really getting married to a woman who detested me, and he really didn't plan on seeing me ever again. But the very idea seemed so foolish that I refused to give it even a morsel of space. The perky waitresses with their bouncing breasts and hot pants trotted by our table, avoiding our eyes and empty bottles. The happy hour regulars ignored the empty booths around us, opting to drink their 2-for-1s perched atop wobbly bar stools, far away from the seething tension emanating from table five where my now ex-best friend had begun to explain his decision.

The Man Engaged to the Fainting Goat went on and on about how our relationship had become inappropriate and how he needed to focus his energy on the important woman in his life. I listened, craning my neck and nodding, all the while assuming that The Fainting Goat had just gotten her barnyard britches in a twist and that by next week my pal and I would be back to eating Buffalo wings and throwing darts. Then, when he had exhausted all of his most rational, adult words, he gave me a hug and the reality began to envelop my body. He grabbed the back of my head and placed it under his chin, cradling the back of my skull like it was a Faberge egg. I could hear the air squeaking down his windpipe as he swallowed uneasily and felt his pulse fluttering quickly down the side of his neck. He wasn't kidding after all.

My best friend and The Fainting Goat did indeed marry. The wedding was in November. It drizzled all morning for the small crowd in the downtown church, but it was delightful. They looked happy and full of promise. She wore a long, form-fitting white dress, and he wore a perfectly tailored suit, and afterward they jetsetted off to Italy where they christened their matrimony with European cheese and wine. At least that's what I heard; I wasn't invited.

For a long time I absolutely hated The Fainting Goat. It's so rare in life that you make true friends, and to have one taken from you prematurely for reasons that seem unfair is quite paralyzing. But after a while, I began to understand. He had promised to love and protect her. He had promised to guard her heart. And intentionally or not, I had been causing it to rupture.

I read once that in order to write a great book, you have to be willing to kill your darlings. Everything, simply, can't fit in. And I suppose it's the same in all things of life. In order to have the best things, sometimes, along the way, we have to be willing to set some really good things aside.

When I walk past Bongo Java now with its ulcer-inducing coffees, or walk into the bar with the best cheeseburger in town, my heart stiffens in my chest and I can't help but think about the best friend I once had and how much I still miss him. And in times like those, I kind of understand what she must have felt like those many, many months ago. In life's tougher moments, after all, we can all be a bit of a fainting goat.

*Thirteen*

# THE PHANTOM OF
# THE BUNGALOW

The good news is I'm not dead. The bad news is the man whose bedroom is but a thin sheet of drywall away from mine can't seem to remember my last name. We are platonic roommates, friends even, but he has yet to absorb that one easy-to-form syllable that has shown up on the year's worth of Victoria's Secret catalogues that have graced our mailbox.

Let's be honest here: living with somebody is extremely intimate. You pick up the maverick underpants that heroically eject themselves from your roomie's hamper; you share the same Windex to clean the bug massacre after-gunk off your shared windows; and you rearrange the phrases they've created with the juvenile word magnets on the Frigidaire into slightly dirty ones and never discuss it.

And so you can understand why I was shocked when we were gathered in our kitchen and he was trying to write me a check for some Home Depot-y items I had purchased on his behalf, and he paused right at $205.6 . . . He panicked and hung onto that last decimal like it was monkey bars over a pool full of poisonous blowfish.

He couldn't remember my last name. After the eleven punctual rent checks I had forked over, after meeting my parents and my friends, he was actually drawing a blank. And to think, I let that silky haired bastard use my shampoo. His lapse of brainpower kind of hurt my feelings. And by hurt I mean if it were medieval times, I would have spat in his face. Alas, it wasn't medieval times, so I didn't. Instead, my eyes grew about twelve sizes and my lower lip started seizing.

What I now know and should have known then is that before you move in with anybody, you should sit down and have the "Where is this going?" chat. Figure out whether it's going to be weekly poker games and morning coffee, or nothing but polite nods in the kitchen and skulking around like the Phantom of the Opera.

I found The Phantom of the Bungalow's ad on Craigslist when I first moved to town. I was reading the "Missed Connections" section from the comfort of my Marriot Courtyard like I would do on any other day. It's good, cheap entertainment, and it pleases me to think that people fall desperately in love while scooping cold pasta from across the salad bar or riding on stationary bikes at the gym. My eyes eventually wandered to the real estate page where I stumbled upon an overly detailed rental ad that captured my heart. It was filled with BUTS and THOUGHS, apologizing for appliances being "new but not brand new" and defending the second bedroom, which was "smaller, though very livable."

He sounded like a rambler, and I like ramblers because I am one. The clincher for me was at the bottom: "PS: No pets allowed, poodles considered . . . severe allergies."

How could I not get along with somebody who puts a poodle stipulation in his or her advertisement? That's like the most adorable proviso in want-ad history. Within one week, I'd signed a lease.

During the first few weeks of our cohabitation, The Phantom

of the Bungalow seemed like he would be fun and a little bit bonkers. He'd introduced me to a couple of his friends and his very loud Georgian girlfriend who liked to French kiss him in the living room while we were all watching Jeopardy. He was a very straight-laced fellow so naturally he appeared terrified every time this happened.

In the beginning, I thought I might find that conservative, tightly wound insanity endearing. And in the beginning it was. But it didn't take long for hairline cracks to appear in our roommate-tionship, cracks that one day would lead to the forgetting of certain last names and the hurting of certain feelings. We didn't take enough time to get to know each other, and if we'd discussed the following items, I suspect we never would have ended up under the same badly-shingled roof.

FOOD. The Phantom of the Bungalow mainly eats three foods: Pasta Roni Parmesan Herb Instant Spaghetti, Delissio Rising Crust Pizza with Feta Cheese, and strawberry Pop-Tarts. There are no alternatives. He has no interest in pears or ham sandwiches at all. This diet results in high toaster traffic and a house that smells like rancid cheese all the time. The aroma of Mediterranean cheese is similar to that of working out, so our house smells like a running shoe made of Fontina. The Phantom of the Bungalow *loves* to keep food years after it expires; he's strangely sentimental about half-consumed preserves with spore farms on top of them. This means our refrigerator is overcrowded, like a Southwest flight to Vegas. My pears, hammy stuffs, and other delights are confined to the little drawers near the floor. It's the only place I know they're safe.

SEX. Some of us 1) Are NOT familiar with the "sock on the door" method of ensuring privacy because we didn't spend four years of college playing beer pong and wearing togas, 2) Can't be held responsible for said sock falling off the door and exposing incredibly quiet sex in the missionary position, and 3) Will remain forever scarred by the quiet sex and the even greater silence that followed it. If we had discussed what a tube sock on the door meant, then there is a good chance that I would have understood what the tube sock on the ground directly below the door was trying to tell me. Had I known this, I would not have poked my head into a very plaid bedroom full of the most polite intercourse the world has ever known.

SHARING. When you've seen somebody make mediocre love and they've seen you in your embarrassing shower cap, it's fairly safe to assume you're friends. Friends share, right? Wrong. So very wrong. The Phantom of the Bungalow forgot to mention on Craigslist that he is a little bit weird about germs, and by a little bit weird I mean he won't let anybody use even the same spatula as him. Once I mixed up our respective pancake flipping devices, and I thought he was going to beat me to death with the bloody thing. He spotted his spatula from two rooms away and sputtered accusingly: "What do you think you're doing?"

Dead serious.

It was very clear what I was doing. I was making the best grilled cheese sandwich a frying pan has ever seen. Still, he needed clarification. He actually threw out the cooking instrument after I was done with it because washing it would not sufficiently remove the essence of me, and I, apparently, was toxic.

CLEANLINESS. My organization and spic-and-spanness have never been complimented, *ever*. This is due to the undeniable fact that I am a complete disaster of a human being. But if I am a complete disaster, The Phantom of The Bungalow is mother-fucking doomsday. In a sick way, my self-esteem loves that he's a derailed train of messiness, but the fact that I'm a passenger in his wreckage is wholly balls.

From June to October of last year there was a hammer sitting in the middle of the living room like it was making an artistic statement. I tripped over it numerous times and might have thrice broken my left index toe. I didn't want to make a big deal about it though so, like a hero, I refused treatment.

From November to February, there was a veritable army of navy seal rodents who dodged the eighteen traps he set more successfully than I did.

And just last week, the kitchen sink backed up, choking on an entire chicken skeleton and an unopened package of soy sauce.

These are only the highlights of the low times; we have hamburger gift-wrap around every corner and Pasta Roni residue on most surfaces. I'm surprised I haven't gotten hepatitis from the dwindling sand dollar of soap in the bathroom. He is the sloppiest germaphobe on the planet.

MEANESS. He is mean, and I am not. I am the kind of person who remembers last names and birthdays and hometowns. He is the kind of person who remembers nothing. What's worse is that his mean has made me a little bit mean. So the fact that I hope a rat with Irritable Bowel Syndrome squats over his prized spatula is ultimately his fault as well. At this precise moment, I'd be willing to pay the rat in triple cream Brie.

If I had been stronger, if I had been wiser, if I hadn't allowed myself to be seduced by his poodle clause and his collection of tartan neckties, it is possible that I could have saved myself a good deal of misery. I could have found a place to live where I was more than just a forename and monthly deposit. A place where spatulas are free to serve any grilled cheese they like and where bedroom doors are firmly locked during even the quietest of coitus. But it's too late for us now. I'm moving out of the bungalow on Friday, and leaving the Phantom, his personal kitchen tools, and his cunning Craigslist advertisement to fend for themselves once again. Renter beware.

*Fourteen*

# THE MAN WHO SCARES
# THE PISS OUT OF ME

*I*f a potential suitor says, "She's really more like a kid sister to me now," it means, "She was incredibly hot before she took a highly audible horse piss in my bathroom."

Men like to imagine that the products of female digestion are small pink clouds, diamonds, baby kittens, and other members of the Lucky Charms marshmallow roster. I don't blame them. There is a reason why we're separated like nineteenth-century school children to use the commode in public buildings. There are things that we would prefer men not think about. Ever. And the image of their dainty counterparts squatting on the toilet with the *Times* is one of them.

For most of my life, I have been making clandestine trips to the powder room in order to protect what little feminine allure I have been allotted. I have ended dates early due to "work commitments." I always had something to "drop off" at the post office, and I've even set my alarm fifteen minutes early on Sundays to get time alone with the john.

When I met The Man Who Scares The Piss Out of Me approximately two months ago, "it" became impossible to conceal. The relationship developed quickly: I was given an electric toothbrush, my parents learned his middle name, and I had begun asking myself how I felt about Montessori schools for our three eventual children.

But I had yet to pee at his house.

I knew that not only our relationship, but the proliferation of the entire human race, hinged on the idea that girls pass cotton candy. I wanted my first pee to be perfect. I wanted it to be romantic, comedy-esque, grandiose, and clever. I wanted my first piss to be pithy. I pictured candlelight and a string arrangement of the "The Way You look Tonight." He would be George Clooney, and I would be a sexy aspiring mime he'd met busking by the Champs Elysees. I would hold his face close, trace his jaw line, and say with my hands, "I know we've only just met, but this white zinfandel is going right through me," before strutting to the toilets and conducting a silent, fragrance-less evacuation.

Although I was certain the fate of the first loving relationship I had ever been in would be determined by the cadence and duration of my urinary stream, on a brisk January evening, I took a leak of faith.

When Tinklebell first waved her golden wand upon my pelvis, I decided to ignore it. We were on a lumpy brown sofa, there was carefully chosen music, and I was certain that The Man Who Scares The Piss Out of Me was considering the possibility of making out in a less gentlemanly way than he had done before. "Mind over bladder," I told myself and continued to cross and re-cross my legs at thirty-second intervals.

We were trapped in a conversation about religion, a topic so personal and soul-bearing it's banned in most public schools. Even if I had wanted to pee the Victoria Falls of pees right then, I couldn't. When a date that you hope will lead to heavy petting and/or marriage is just starting to get metaphysical, you don't leave. He was explaining his place in the universe, and I was trying to figure out how I was going to explain the curious and seemingly inevitable puddle on his upholstery.

I listened as intently as I could, with an open mind and closed legs, as my date relived his Christian academy days. He was wistful and smiley and glad that I was there on his couch, at his home, three meters from his bathroom, listening to him critique institutionalism, flexing my Kegels like they were going to win a Hawaiian Tropic Pageant.

Just when I thought all the sharing would stop, a newer more exciting anecdote would succeed the last and I began to accept the fact that I might actually piss in my Levis.

Finally, after what felt like a month of theological debate, I was able to verify that God exists. The Man Who Scares The Piss Out of Me received a divine calling. His fancy telephone lit up and released the most stunning melody. It was beautiful, like celestial children playing in a meadow. He had his phone to one ear and his finger stuffed in the other. I was going to get my moment, but I had to act quickly. I allotted myself two minutes in the bathroom, the perfect time for a quick pee—too short to have dropped a log with the girth of a California Redwood, but long enough for a thorough hand-washing. If I spent three minutes, I would forever be known as "The Girl Who Whizzed like Secretariat at My House and I Never Spoke to Again."

The mission was supposed to be simple: get in there, focus, evacuate fluids, get the hell out, pat self on back for military efficiency, and resume path to romantic bliss. But right when it was all about to flow perfectly, the unthinkable happened. I had an excremental breakdown. I couldn't pee. As soon as I took my porcelain throne, I became nervous and sweaty. I went numb from the belly button down. The Man Who Scares the Piss Out of Me had stopped both my heart and my urinary tract.

I waited.

After the first thirty seconds in the loo, the air was ripe with desperation, which is actually not the worst thing bathroom air could be ripe with. But I began to wonder what my future husband must be thinking as I sat, on the can, in silence. I imagined impressive bodies of water, the rushing agua of the Rio Grande, the Danube, even the Mekong, which I have always loved because it's name sounds like an ape introducing itself, but my efforts were futile. The fear in my heart outweighed the pressure in my loins.

The Man Who Scares The Piss Out of Me was outside somewhere in the great expanse of living room-slash-kitchen-slash-foyer silently judging me. He and the dog were very quietly making jokes, wondering if I was snorting lines of cocaine with his Bic razor. Minute three rolled along, hysteria set in, and I was wound tighter than a cobra with spina bifida. As I heard him shuffling in the refrigerator for another frosty, refreshing Budweiser, I became inspired to make room for more beer and just as I was about to give up, my flood gates opened.

He was still on the telephone when the furious live stream began. He was probably picturing me like a fountain statuette, hovering above the bathtub in an arabesque position, playing a harp, and releasing a perfectly arced thoroughbred pee for all the ears in the world to rejoice in.

While my pee persisted, his talk wrapped. I could hear him throwing out, "We'll touch bases," and, "Thanks for callings." And that's when I knew: if I could hear him, he could certainly hear me. I was left with only two options: fan or faucet? Wind or water? The fan would have indicated I was creating something so toxic that when dropped from a plane, it could dissolve all vegetation in 'Nam. Running the tap would proclaim, "I pee funny, and I'm so insecure that I cling to the faucet for protection like its my mother's pant leg." Neither choice was ideal.

By minute four, I became despondent. The climate for positive decision-making was bleak. I was cold, tired, and my pants were around my ankles. So I began to do what no one should ever do in this situation: I began to whistle the saxophone part from "Careless Whisper." I suppose somewhere in my simple, simple brain, I thought it would distract him from the fact that I was peeing, but then I realized there was nothing to distract him from the fact that I was whistling George Michael while I was peeing. I could have just stopped halfway through the chorus, but I didn't. I panicked. I began to hammer out a beat on the countertop with my palms because, after all, a song that spends three weeks at the top of the charts deserves a little percussion. I was a whistling, drumming, pissing machine who sat silently hating myself against an atmospheric tinkling backdrop. It was miserable, and I became certain that bladder control was the least of my issues.

Between my intrepid fight against nature's call and my triumphant royal flush, I clocked at about 5:20. Not a horrible figure, especially considering I was paralyzed and managed to fit in a WHAM! tune. I stood up reeling from the sheer excitement. I had just passed a milestone; the first pee was over. But just as I was preparing to leave, something positively beautiful caught my eye. It glinted in the forty-watt light like the Macy's Christmas display: his medicine cabinet.

The Man Who Scares The Piss Out of Me was talking to his hound dog who, thankfully, had begun to howl incessantly. I knew it was wrong, and I knew it was risky, but so is dating someone with a colorful cocktail of drugs above his sink. I hit the cabinet like it was a hotel mini bar. I was looking for deep dark secrets, eye of newt, curative leaches, anti-depressants, a crack rock, flavored lubricant, DECEIT! LIES!—even something for chronic heartburn would have done. But there was nothing remotely exciting. There was hair wax and Q-tips. I immediately halted my morally depraved intrusion. It wasn't fair. He didn't have any drugs or anal beads, and he would be aghast to know of my suspicions.

I left everything as it was, resisting the urge to pick the stray hair off the soap and readjust the dog-eared bathmat so he would never, ever know of my presence. But as I shut the cabinet door, thinking all of my problems were flushed out, I knocked the roll of toilet paper, the ONLY roll of toilet paper, into the very wet sink. Oh, the horror! The wretched, quilted with aloe vera horror. I had no choice but to leave it there, soggy and bell-shaped from its super absorbent powers, as evidence that his bathroom had been looted. He would know exactly what I had done, and he would never trust me again with his heart or his Charmin.

I'm not sure if the toilet paper trail was ever officially traced back to me, but I do know that when I emerged from the bathroom I stopped caring. Did I take a big old piss in his bathroom? Yes. Did I try and recreate one of the most captivating woodwind solos of all time while doing so? Absolutely. Was I responsible for the sopping wet pile of paper mush on his counter? Guilty. But the moment I pushed down on that tiny silver handle, I resolved to flush all of my apprehension away because none of those things were as bad as if I had urinated on his jeans during the three positively divine hours of ungentlemanly smooching that followed.

*Fifteen*

# THE MAN WHO
# ADDS TEN POUNDS

*I*n relationships, the girl is never fat. If she spies an extra chin in a photograph, its just a "weird angle." If her jeans don't fit, the denim in question has shrunk, but she has certainly not grown. This is not a matter of opinion; this is law.

After three months of dating, I was finally treated to an expertly crafted dinner of chicken parts with my newly-minted boyfriend, The Man Who Adds Ten Pounds. And simply because I hadn't done it in a while and felt like being called pretty, I was complaining about the size of my pants. I knew I wasn't fat; sure I might have gone an Oreo or two past my daily bi-color cookie sandwich quota, but I was insecure and if I was told that my ass was the correct size and shape by somebody who loved me, I was confident that I would feel better.

I went with a rather standard anti-jeans gripe, the, "They-used-to-be-baggy-on-me-and-now-I-have-to-blackmail-the-button-to-do-up-the-fly-woe-is-me" kind of nonsense that normally elicits responses ranging from, "Are you kidding, you Goddess!" to, "If anything, I could stand to see you gain a few pounds." If luck is on your side he will also condemn the unfair pressure society places on women. He will say he can't imagine how even a beautiful specimen like you manages to cope. Eventually this longwinded tirade makes you feel like a hero. Like Joan of Arc, but with a nicer rack, and that is a lovely feeling. All men know this is the correct response to any woman accusing themselves of cellulite. But The Man Who Adds Ten Pounds did not make me feel like a sexy martyr. He was, tragically, a little behind the times. As I stared at him hopelessly, batting my eyes from across the table, just a downtrodden girl with a drumstick asking to be loved, he said, "Babe, you're just SHAPELY."

Just . . . shapely.

Immediately panic washed over me like a vat of Carolina barbeque sauce on a slab of baby back ribs. The contents of my plate magically transformed into cartoon characters dancing across the screen at a matinee movie preview. The fried chicken, mashed potatoes, and asparagus were parading across the table, singing "Big Girls Don't Cry" in perfect harmony.

The Man Who Adds Ten Pounds sat proudly in front of me, smiling and petting my left hand like it was a stray kitten. He seemed concerned that I had not yet leapt from my chair, thrown my arms around his neck, and joyfully announced to the neighborhood, "Hello world, I'm shapely!" It was as though he'd given me a surprise birthday present that he was sure I would adore but that had instead gone horribly wrong, like tickets to a high school production of *Pippin*. Recognizing the perils of his poor vocabulary choice, he attempted to diffuse the situation, adding, "Babe, shapely is a good thing."

Horseshit.

My heart began to beat a little bit faster, perhaps because my arteries were crammed full of bacon fat and other "shapely" things, or perhaps because I was almost certainly about to cry the swollen tears of a veritable hippopotamus down my shapely cheeks. The Man Who Adds Ten Pounds felt better after he said this. He thought he was a damage control aficionado and was grinning idiotically.

I was in love with this foolish man. I trusted him, so I decided to engage in a moment of reflection before beating him to death with a chicken leg. Maybe I was just like other girls cracking under the pressure of Mary-Kate Olsen and diet cola? Maybe The Man Who Adds Ten Pounds was absolutely right? Maybe shapely *is* good? I tried to convince myself that my newfound morbid obesity was an exciting thing and that I was suddenly a role model for women everywhere. My face would be on all of the progressive women's products like natural deodorants and contraceptive rings. I was going to be a trailblazer. Little girls were going to come up to me on the street and tell me that one day, when they grow up, they want to be shapely, too. I would be an embracer of all kinds of women's causes—breastfeeding, lesbianism, feminism, optional shaving, and fake sports, such as yogilates. I was going to build a shapely empire, and print business cards with the titles champion, pioneer, and crusader.

Then, I fast-forwarded twenty fantasy years to the most disturbing of Ebenezer Scroogian vignettes. We were sitting in front of a fire with our three children, his arm stretched over my mammoth, doughy shoulders, and he said, "Kids, when I first saw your mother I thought, wow, she is the most shapely woman I've ever seen."

I wanted to upchuck my chicken leg. I had tried to appreciate the sentiment, I had mulled over his oh-so-good intentions, but inevitably there was only one conclusion: The Man Who Adds Ten Pounds was an idiot. I had gone from wanting a little reassurance concerning the general state of my belly to wanting lap band surgery. Shapely never has and never will be a part of acceptable relationship vernacular. When you are a woman, shapely simply means fat.

From that moment on, if I didn't act fast, I knew my life was irrevocably changed. If I didn't make him see me in a different, thinner light, he would probably start offering me the aisle seat at the movies. So I said, "I guess I should have bought a bigger pair of jeans, but all the size fours are too baggy."

I was hoping that would make him recognize the error of his ways. He would shake his head, ask himself what he was thinking, and then we'd both collapse into a fit of laughter over how preposterous it was that he had called *me* shapely. But something horrendous happened. My philosophy cleanse failed. He contemplatively cocked his pretty, chiseled face to the side and declared with sincere disbelief, "Whoa, I can't believe it. Those pants are smaller than a four? That's *really skinny.*" He sat there for a few seconds too long, chewing and thinking, thinking and chewing, wondering how his swollen inner-tube of a girlfriend had possibly jammed herself into the Gap's latest creation. Now not only was I shapely, but it was a miracle I had fit into my clothes without WD-40.

I became utterly shocked with the outcome of my study, and when things are truly and utterly shocking, one deserves the right to engage in a melodramatic response. I began to clang, bang, and clatter. I tossed down my fork with a flourish that rattled the plasticware vociferously. Glaring, I informed him with a tone that most girls over the age of thirteen are not capable of, that he should never call a girl shapely . . . *ever.*

I swirled my potatoes angrily as though I were beating an egg, silently begging for him to explain that he had misunderstood the meaning of the word shapely and had actually meant to say I was leaner than a hummingbird. He countered with the earnestness of a star cub scout, "Hey . . . Heeeeeey, you're perfect for me. I think you're beautiful." Fantastic. *Fucking splendid*, I thought.

Now not only I am shapely, but it has been confirmed that I am attractive to exactly *one person* in our solar system. I am a fatter version of Quasimodo and will be confined to the living room, safe from prying civilian eyes, eventually going completely mad and having deep conversations about life with my Pringles before devouring them whole.

The Man Who Adds Ten Pounds could see me fiddling with the button on my jeans and sucking in my stomach like a big pale Greyhound. He knew now that I was a woman deeply troubled. In a single meal, I had gone from attractive, successful, and happy, to shapely, shapeliest, and, finally, completely disfigured. In retrospect, it might also have come to light that I was a tad vain.

And while my self-esteem felt as though it had been crushed by two giant molars, my "shapely" heart went out to him; he was one man combating the aftershocks of at least a hundred years of women's body dysmorphia. His skinny frame sat timidly in the corner probably wondering if he should be corking my utensils and mourning the probable loss of our delightfully well-rounded relationship. Our future was looking uncertain, but true love does conquer all. With enough sobbing and repeated threats of things like couples cardio-tone and ballroom dancing lessons, eventually I got what I wanted. The three simple words that are unfailingly on the hearts of women everywhere: "You're not fat."

*Sixteen*

# THE MAN FROM INDIANASSHOLIS

There's a woman standing at the door yelling my name. I've never met her before, but I imagine her name is Jean and that she was raised in some place like Bethesda, Maryland where her parents owned a dog she wasn't allowed to walk. She's got one of those very commonplace looks about her. Like the sock that goes missing in the wash. Plain and white and a little worse for use. Replaceable even. I give her bad acne as a child and three years of braces because already—probably unfairly—I don't like her. But more than her, I don't like how much she knows about me.

She taps her fingers on the clipboard and calls my name again, looking around the room to see what unfortunate soul is skulking in the corner. I get up from my chair, walk toward her, and smile meekly, peering down innocently enough at her clipboard. She's holding my chart. The one that tells all my important secrets, and she looks at me like the one we'll talk about today will blacklist me and keep me from ever getting into Harvard. Or Costco.

She pulls the clipboard up to her chest, and we go down the sterile hallway from the waiting room, past a colony of pregnant, happy women, all the way to a back room filled sparingly with expensive contraptions made to pry into inappropriate places. It's terribly cold. And white. I wouldn't be surprised if someone vacuums the walls.

Jean from Bethesda takes my weight and blood pressure, then hands me a sheet of paper that would sufficiently cover a slice of fruit. "Take off your clothes from the waist down and then drape this over you." She nods, confirming the awkwardness of it all, and exits the room so I can proceed with the undressing and draping.

I don't want to be here. Not even 3 percent. I'd rather be in Iowa, shucking corn. Or in Los Angeles traffic. Or at the bottom of a well, clawing my way out with a plastic fork. But being an adult is about being where you need to be, not where you want to be, so I obediently take off my pants.

The problem with doctors is they have it all wrong. Instead of cutting to the chase and telling you exactly what's going on, they call your home, leave a voicemail, and say something particularly vague and disconcerting. Then, quite nonchalantly, they ask you to come in. They want to talk about it. They want to play three rounds of Monopoly, letting you buy hints rather than houses.

It's no wonder after you hang up the phone that your mind starts racing. You stay up until three in the morning dissecting the tone of their voice, wondering: Were they being positive because things are positive? Or were they being positive because they know you've contracted chicken pox of the liver? You make pie charts and line graphs. Color-coded PowerPoint presentations assessing the evidence. And by the morning you're sure not only that you could pass advanced calculus, but that you're dying from a new form of plague that makes all your body parts turn purple.

"How are you doing?"

My doctor is thirty minutes late, but she gets away with it because she wears Ralph Lauren and smells like dry cleaning. She looks nothing at all like Jean from Bethesda. She has blonde, Barbie doll hair that stays in place even when the fan is moving. Her nails are manicured a bright red, and they never seem to chip, even though she's constantly sticking her hands inside strangers.

"Good," I lie, and I twiddle my thumbs while she pulls the stirrups out from the exam table and sticks my bare feet in them like I'm saddling a quarter horse.

I want her to like me. And not only because her husband looks like Humphrey Bogart, but also because, when it really matters, you take better care of the people you love.

"So, here's the deal," she says, and breaks out a clipboard where she begins drawing a chart. On one side of the chart is the word "normal" and the other side is the word "cancer." She draws some tabs in the middle and then puts a dot where I am.

I blink. I want to ask her if she drew the dot correctly. Dots can be drawn in a lot of ways. One really must be precise about such things.

"Now don't panic," she says. "This is common."

My throat goes dry. Common? My dot can't be common. It's two notches away from cancer.

I lay down on the exam table because I can't look at her or my dot. Pasted on the ceiling is a poster of a puppy playing in daisies. She explains a little more about what the dot's location means and how, if I don't have surgery, I have a 15 percent chance of getting cancer. I lie on my back and hum the "Sound of Music" in my head. This can't be real, I think. This only happens on the Hallmark Channel. I can't really have cancer's cousins inside of me.

"How many sexual partners have you had since your test last year?" she asks.

This is an easy question and I'm remotely grateful until I give my answer because it makes me think of him, and the last person I want to think about right now is him.

"One," I say. "Only one." I consider telling her how I wanted him to be the only one ever and then how he broke my heart into a thousand, million will-never-be-your-one pieces. I consider telling her how I drove four and a half hours every weekend to visit The Man from Indianassholis, and how we had named our children, and promised each other picket fences, but I stop myself before the deluge. I want her to like me, after all.

"Well, he must be a carrier then."

I sit up, all of a sudden alert.

"He did this?"

And she smiles, like she's in on a secret.

"Yes, men carry this, and while it doesn't affect them at all, it can cause cervical cancer in women. It tends to be more prevalent in men who have had multiple partners."

I immediately want to castrate him. Did he know he was carrying death around on his penis like it was an accessory? Did he deflower me knowing that one day I would be sitting here, hanging out under a piece of paper, waiting for the Grim Reaper?

More importantly, did he know I would be here alone?

When someone tells you that you have abnormal cells, you want someone to grab your hand. And not just any someone— like the postman or the manager at Dollar General—you want someone who knows what you look like at four in the morning, snoring, with spring's allergies running out your nose. You want your fingers to intertwine with that someone's fingers so you know that no matter how many abnormal cells you might acquire in your life, they still hold your hand. Even if all your abnormal cells get together and build a Burger King on top of your cervix, they'll only hold your hand tighter.

I look down at my hand. It is a very empty a hand. A lonely hand. It has so much room that it could comfortably cradle a Magic 8 Ball. Or a cheeseburger. It hasn't touched The Man from Indianassholis' hand for at least three months, and it no longer has a right to. His hand can be off doing anything it wants—giving a high five, ironing a plaid shirt, or, perhaps worst of all, hanging out with a new hand altogether.

I sit in the flying V position by myself, accompanied only by my pink sheet and 15 percent chance of cancer. I let my hands clasp the sheet and try not to vomit when she explains how much of my cervix they will cut away depending on how much cancer is hanging out in there. Hopefully it's just a few stragglers who have thrown a bad house party no one attended; worst case scenario, it could be a virus rave. She uses terms like "LEEP" and "CONE" and then says something I don't expect.

"Do you plan on having children?"

I remove my eyes from the puppy playing in the daisies to meet hers.

"I'm sorry. What did you say?"

"Children. Do you want to have children some day?"

My eyes blink at her pretty face. How could she be talking about children right now? I am husbandless and cancer-full. I am in no shape to raise a little toddler nugget and teach him how to be fluent in five languages. I am probably going to die. Alone. Parent only to an insufferable houseplant and hairless cat.

She waits.

"Of course," I say, because that, too, is the truth.

"Well, it shouldn't be a problem . . . you're just so small, we wouldn't want to cut away too much, as that can produce complications."

Complications. The word is ear vinegar. Not only has The Man from Indianassholis given me a 15 percent chance of cancer, he's given me complications. He's passed on his abnormality and potentially taken away my chance at birthing future World Cup soccer players.

"Now I just want you to relax," she says. "I'm going to take a few biopsies and once we get the results back we'll have a better handle on what we're dealing with. Just lean back and let me do the work."

I lean back onto the tissue paper covered exam table and look up again at the puppy in the daisies as I hear her jostle around the room for sharp metal objects. Jean from Bethesda comes in, the jostling stops, and they begin chatting about The Food Network while the pretty doctor extends medical tongs into my nether regions, careful not to chip her nail polish. She occasionally interrupts their conversation to say things like, "You might feel a pinch," before proceeding to erupt fireworks in my female interior. It feels like they're cleaning out a pumpkin.

And this portion—the pumpkin cleaning bit—is the worst because all I have is time to imagine what dying from 15 percent of cancer might look like. I will probably be bald and weigh thirty-seven pounds. My house will be overflowing with dust and pieces of Styrofoam that my dog has chewed up and spat out that I can no longer clean up or have the money to pay a maid to vacuum into oblivion. I will probably slur my words and look at the globe longingly, wishing I could do human things again like board a plane and eat whole pieces of asparagus. I will be despondent and reek of Vicks Vapor rub, but most of all, worst of all, my hand will be empty. I will die in a room of medicine condiments and a library of books I can no longer read and have no one to read to me. I will be alone, wilting into the abyss of people who have to hire actors to come to their funeral and cry.

I think about The Man from Indianassholis. It has been approximately three months, four days, and two hours since he last kissed me and told me he loved me. And it's been approximately three months, four days, one hour, and fifty minutes since he told me things weren't going to work out.

Right now, 85 percent of me wants to strangle him and damn him to a life of walking with a cervix tied around his wrist. But the other 15 percent of me, the portion that I don't let out in public, wants to run to him and curl up on his shoulder, letting all my pre-cancerous tears cry on to his collared shirt.

My eyes think very hard about sobbing. They lubricate slightly as the pretty doctor and Jean from Bethesda trade secrets about crab dip. But despite how much they want to rupture, I push my rivers back and breathe in deeply. Holding no hand is hard, but holding the wrong hand is harder. My body, quite literally, has rejected him. He plants tumors in my mind and in my child-making bits. If I cannot trust him with my cervix, I cannot trust him with my heart.

The pretty doctor pulls the tongs out and looks up at me, sufficiently happy with her day's work.

"All done here," she says.

And I look up at her smiling, only to confirm. "Yes, indeed. All done."

*Seventeen*

# THE CAT WHO
# GOT MY TONGUE

There is a good chance that my ex-neighbors were born before Davy Crockett was. They were old, toothless, and wore the kind of pajamas made famous in 'Twas the Night Before Christmas in public settings. But even still, living next to the Cat Who Got My Tongue and his family seemed like an ideal situation for a young married couple. We could listen to music as loud as we wanted knowing that their ancient ear canals were defunct, and we were never afraid to go on vacation because all our decrepit neighbors had to do for entertainment was stare out the window and make sure our house didn't get tagged by misguided teenagers. Plus, despite the decades, world wars, and geological eras that divided our generations, we all seemed to agree on the fundamentals: kindness, generosity, and the unsung virtues of cheap malt liquor and chain smoking.

I assumed my husband and I would live next to the ole Cat Who Got My Tongue and his wife until, well . . . you know, but after a few months it became clear that there were drawbacks that even his adorable, gummy Cheshire grin and sunny demeanor couldn't quite make up for.

## 1) Children . . . So Many Children

I imagine that in their youth, the Cat Who Got My Tongue's family, like all other mountainfolk deprived of television and formal education, engaged in the unadorned pleasures of bucolic living. They got shit-faced on moonshine and fucked until there was no moonshine left. Spending their formative years rolling in the hay (literally) proved to be mighty fruitful, and those fruits turned out to be crab apples.

The Cat Who Got My Tongue's family tree was an entire jungle—there were thousands upon thousands of children, most of whom were graduates of the esteemed Maury County Correctional Facility with degrees ranging from "How Not to Hold Up the Save-A-Lot" to "The Art of Not Shoving Your Wife Through the Drywall." When out of the clinker, these nomadic children would visit constantly, often for months at a time.

## 2) The Bartering

If you've ever shown up to find seventeen crates of stale Swiss Rolls on your doorstep and promptly been asked for a favor, then you know exactly what I'm talking about.

A few short years ago, the settlers of America maintained an amicable relationship with the natives by trading them gunpowder for, say, a beaver pelt or an indentured servant. Seeing as The Cat Who Got My Tongue was old enough to have actually participated in the great North American Fur Trade, it is not surprising that he stayed true to the values of his economic upbringing. His currency? Twinkies with manufacturing defects that he and his wife received from a family member who worked at the Little Debbie outlet. Our currency? Strong, young bones.

Mutual back scratching is fabulous, both literally and figuratively, but unfortunately there really isn't enough pound cake in the world to compensate for manual labor. One time, after we received a particularly large donation of Zebra Cakes, he asked my husband to move the largest television I'd ever seen into their squalid living room. He returned looking as though he'd had a slumber party at Guantanamo Bay.

### 3) The Cat Who Got My Tongue's Critters

I am an animal lover. I like them big, I like them small, I prefer them not to be rodents, but I'm open-minded. Our neighbor was an animal lover as well. He had a deep, unwavering affection for unvaccinated feral cats that became more steadfast by the day. The first specimen he acquired was a urine-stained Persian called White Cat. White Cat was manageable. Sure, he treated our porch like it was made of petrified Scoop Away and often sent our dogs into psychotic episodes with a simple meow, but he was The Cat Who Got My Tongue's pride and joy. He was, after all, their only dependent that wasn't on parole.

We spent months chasing him off our patio furniture and biting our tongues as our jolly ole neighbor giggled watching White Cat taking dump after mighty dump on our lawn. Sure, it grated me down to my very last nerve at times, but The Cat Who Got My Tongue liked us, and we really liked him. He was worth dodging the odd turd for.

It has been previously expressed that the once virile Cat Who Got My Tongue was not an advocate of any method of viable contraception. Neither was his cat. Things began to change.

One magical spring day, after returning from a most satisfying Sunday brunch, we noticed that there were at least three white cats glaring at us from our neighbors' porch—by Monday, there were three more. By Tuesday, there was a legitimate swarm of kittens. There must have been hundreds of them lazing on our furniture, sparring on our lawn, and hiding underneath my car, waiting to pounce on my ankles and scare the living fuck out of me. Kittens of all shapes and sizes, in so many shades and colors. They made Joseph's Technicolor Dreamcoat look like a Brooks Brothers suit.

The old man would stand out on his porch and toss cubes of stale Wonderbread at his new brood, chortling to himself as they ran out into the grass for a scrap of three day-old crust. Weeks went by and we knew something had to be done. Our life had been reduced to one giant, constant meow, sorrowfully droning and swelling morning, noon, and night. Our lawn began to look like an abandoned campsite, adorned with piles of dung and ripped up hamburger buns. The critters needed to go.

But we had a problem. The Cat Who Got My Tongue was stinking adorable. He looked like the old man in the Russell Stover commercial who takes his grandson to the fishing hole where I assume they get fat on chocolate and talk about life. He had a little belly, a hunchback, and arms that were a bit too long and skinny for his body, giving him the appearance of a wise old orangutan when he walked. These cats and his cable television were really all that he had going. His wife looked like she had been glued back together several times. I think it was safe to say he was no longer tapping that. The last thing I wanted to do was make him feel bad, but there isn't really a nice way to say, "If you don't dispose of your feral cat collection, I will burn your house to the ground with a jug of lighter fuel and barbeque torch."

The weather was starting to get warmer and the cats had become lethargic, sitting on our porch and swinging their tails back and forth like pendulums. Over the period of a few days, the cats got bolder—they slinked along our fence, sat on our front stoop, and ripped up the spinach in our vegetable garden. Their chorus of meows mutated into hellish screaming and hissing as they struggled for hierarchical power outside our front door. The tufts of white hair and cat blood become a permanent part of the landscape. We were tolerating The Cat Who Got My Tongue's felines as graciously as we could, but we were both beginning to crack.

My husband had allergies, and as the cats became more adventurous, he became afflicted with phlegm, a rattling cough, and fever. His eyes became swollen, and his sinuses tried to escape his face, pushing against his skull. It was clear that we would have to deal with this cat situation once and for all.

Then the time came when they tried to break into our house.

One quiet Saturday morning, I was awakened by the sound of an army of angry babies. I jumped out of bed in complete panic. The dogs were sweating and spinning nervously in circles. I looked outside our dusty windows to find the source of this troubled wailing, but there was nothing. I checked the TV to ensure that I hadn't left some ghastly TLC program about home births on over night, but it was silent. The sound was coming from inside the house, and it grew increasingly tortured as the seconds passed.

I raced to the kitchen and flung open the cabinets sending woks and saucers onto the floor, which made the dogs howl in despair. I shoved my head into the fireplace and stared hopefully up the chimney. Eventually, the dogs began growling at the vent so I shoved my ear to the grate and listened. It sounded like a Whiskas commercial directed by M. Night Shyamalan. There was a cat stuck in our wall.

I raced into the bedroom yelling about cats and babies trapped inside our drywall and dragged my husband out of bed. Wiping the sleep from his eyes, he told me it was just the wind. "It isn't! It isn't!" I rambled, telephone poised and ready to call animal or infant control.

The screams grew more intense, and we both started to worry. The only place I hadn't checked was the crawl space under the house. We trudged outside, peeked into the dank hollow, and perched on a slab of concrete was White Cat, one of his mistresses, and more kittens chanting like they were on the picket line. My husband began to hurl rocks, pieces of wood, and discarded coffee cups at the intruders. With a menacing hiss, White Cat and his family dashed back onto his owner's porch where the rest of clan greeted him with ambivalent stares. That was it!

Later that day, The Cat Who Got My Tongue was out with his leaf blower, making sure to clear our portion of the sidewalk, too, just as he always did. We approached him with big grins, hoping the size of our teeth and our rosy cheeks would somehow make the conversation easier.

"There sure are a whole lot of cats out there," I chirped.

"Yes ma'am, that one cat gone and had some. Then this black and white one comes on by and she goes and has some, too," he chuckles.

He was so sweet. His forehead was a little bit sweaty from his yard work and his face was glowing. I began to think about the millions of times he'd rescued our crazy escapee mutts, brought us our mail, and now the leaf blowing.

Twenty cats surveyed our conversation, skulking around like hungry hyenas.

I breathed in sharply, preparing to tell him he needed get rid of his furry children, as a tiny tabby rubbed its chin against his calf, but I couldn't do it.

I panicked and then squealed, "They are *so* cute! The little white ones look just like him," grabbing a kitten and tapping it between the ears.

"Yeah, they sure do, and would you believe we've got another litter in the back room? They ain't big enough to be outside yet, but they oughta be out here real soon." He was like a proud father, beaming and looking back at his little pride.

"Babe, we oughta be going," my husband urged, congested

and disappointed.

With a ragged exhale, he spun on his heel and walked home. I followed him, after fake congratulating our neighbor on the next generation of Fluffies and Mittenses that had been birthed in his laundry hamper.

Later that afternoon, we contacted our realtor and by week's end, our house was officially on the market: "One Bed, One Bath Bungalow. Cedar shingles. In an exciting, rapidly growing community."

After only sixteen days, we said goodbye to the Cat Who Got My Tongue and moved across town, next to dog people, where the only litter on our lawn was proper garbage.

*Eighteen*

# THE MAN WHO RUBS ME
# THE WRONG WAY

O n my twenty-fifth birthday, my boyfriend purchased me a real, professional massage. Not a thong, not a Kegerator, but something I would actually enjoy. I was ecstatic! I arrived at the spa fifteen minutes early, as instructed by the receptionist. With a Zen-like calmness, they led me inside to a room filled with silk cushions encircling a curious sandbox and sat me down.

Pan flute music drifted through the air from invisible speakers and onto the ears of robed customers slouched on the pillows beside me. I looked around at the bleary eyed women, contemplating life, drinking stinky teas, and kicking the sand with their toes. They looked so happy.

As I sat cross-legged and stiff on my cushion, a figure approached.

"Cha-No?" he asked, in a very thick accent. "Air hue Cha-No?"

I was about to correct his pronunciation, my name after all, is SHANNON, and it really isn't all that difficult to say.

But then I looked up.

BONJOURNO.

I certainly was Cha-No!

The Man Who Rubs Me the Wrong Way towered what seemed to be stories above me. His cheekbones could have cut a New York Strip, and his eyes could have cooked it, and his hair . . . well, he didn't have any, but he sure as shit didn't need it.

This was definitely the best present ever.

"Comb vith me," he crooned and dragged me to my feet.

The room was dimly lit, save for the seventy candles that sat on the ledges around the massage table. There were flower petals. What exactly had my boyfriend signed me up for? I began to worry.

"Poot yore a-tire at zee char," Zeus instructed, pointing at a stool in the corner. Then, he disappeared out the door.

Oh my. I was about to be naked with a large Italian man who should be made into a statue. He was probably going to put oil on me.

This was wrong.

I was in a relationship, a wonderful relationship that I hoped would one day be a marriage and then, a couple of years later, a family. My love had purchased me an hour with a recent immigrant who could bench press a pony. What did it all mean? Was he trying to get rid of me? I tentatively took off my clothes and got on the table, pulling the sheets up around my ears.

"Ahhh, you are reh-dee?"

He appeared in something that was decidedly not an entire shirt and flung the door open so hard I thought my sheet would be ripped off my body in a gust of wind.

I wasn't so sure I was "reh-dee."

He took a step back and stared at my body, which was covered in goose bumps. Then The Man Who Rubs Me The Wrong Way wandered over to a cabinet in his bikini top, poured some oil into his giant palms, and went to work.

I wasn't sure whether I was supposed to be enjoying this. I wasn't sure whether it was even legal in this part of the country, but his grasp of me was much, much better than his grasp of the English language. My back began to melt into a puddle of under-sunned skin. I began to relax.

About twenty minutes into our session, he began to make noises. Strange noises. At first, it was the occasional "mmm-mmmm." Then there were "oooooooohs."

"Is there something wrong?" I inquired, terrified that he was about to reach for the chocolate sauce and edible glitter.

"Yez, Yez, iz steeeef."

I wasn't sure what exactly was stiff, but I sincerely hoped it was my neck.

He dismissed my questions and continued kneading my shoulders, speaking to them, and furrowing his brow. He could tell I was uncomfortable.

"I lak to zki."

He wanted to make conversation to put me at ease. Maybe this was a good idea. That way I would stop picturing my boy-friend's disapproving face.

"Ski?" I asked.

"Yez, Zki," he replied "My Eeenglish eez…"

"Shitty?" I wanted to add.

"Lezz propor," he finished.

His English was the only thing about him that wasn't proper; the rest of him was universally proper. I felt better after our talk. He liked to ski and that was great. He was massaging my backside and talking about winter sports. He was probably gay. I hoped he was gay.

In mere seconds, he'd flipped me over and was essentially straddling the table, determined to loosen the tension in my arms. His hands drifted to my legs . . . my thighs . . . my upper thighs.

AWKWARD MOMENTS WITH MEN

I looked up at him. I had no choice. I didn't really have anything else to look at.

He was sweating. Oh God! There was a large Italian on top of me, and he was perspiring.

"I'm in love!" I wanted to scream. I wanted to tell him that it would never work out, that I should probably leave and never come back again. I pretended to close my eyes.

But just then, a faint buzzing broke the stream of ethereal music. Saved by the egg timer.

The Man Who Rubs Me the Wrong Way leapt away from me and grabbed a towel to wipe the lavender oil off of his paws.

"Dare, you are feenish."

I thanked him and returned the sheet to its place around my ears.

Just as he was leaving, I asked him where he was from.

"Genova. Es bootiful."

"Genoa?" I repeated.

I was definitely going to vacation there.

# Nineteen

# THE BEE WHO STINGS
# LIKE A BUTTERFLY

*I*f you learn one thing from this collection of embarrassments, let it be this: Don't let just anybody weed your spiritual garden. Yoga has never appealed to me. Yoga is for people who claim they "used to be dancers," and patronizing new-ageists who refuse to take Tylenol and swear by a combination Ginkgo Biloba and aromatherapy. It will transform you into none of the following: Telekinetic healer, street ninja, coordinated human being, or master of stress management. Yoga is just stretching while watching other people stretch, just another opportunity for spandex, and another reason to shave your legs.

The Bee Who Stings Like a Butterfly looked like Chuck Norris. I first noticed him meditating on a brown couch in the hallway of the YMCA; sometimes during the winter months I wondered if he were actually hibernating. I went to the Y exactly three times a week to stave off obesity; I trotted on the treadmill for twelve minutes and pumped three pounds of baby iron for eight. It was a routine that I never deviated from until locker room reconnaissance revealed that The Bee Who Stings Like a Butterfly was a yoga instructor at this very faith-based community center. Naturally,

I assumed this "teaching" business was merely a cover: a way to unwind when he wasn't Jiu-Jitsuing Asian warlords or reading the Dalai Lama's mind. I was intrigued. Regardless of my utter abhorrence for ethereal music, bohemians, and physical activity, I knew if I wanted to be "The Prodigy Who Will One Day Sting Like a Bee," I had to let him educate me. So I bought a forty-dollar rubber mat, a new pair of stretchy pants, and I enlisted.

What I came to find out is that The Bee Who Stings Like a Butterfly didn't actually speak in class. Instead he brought an instructional cassette tape . . . of himself. After a brief musical introduction, the prerecorded guru spoke. It was just as intoxicating as I hoped it would be. It was as though somebody had French braided the vocal chords of Laurence Fishburne and God. I had entered a new world where *Tadasana* meant "stand" and *Upavistha Konasana* meant "sit," and these things were considered exercise. He told me to feel myself connecting with the ground (very difficult to not do, unless you happen to be a goldfish) and to allow myself to breathe (something very difficult to not do, unless you're a dead goldfish). I have never concentrated so deeply on things of such absurdity.

He floated around the room in his tunic, mashing our limbs into improbable geometrically advanced shapes, slowly molding us into fleshy vessels of mystical healing. Then he said he wanted to "weed our spiritual gardens." The unenlightened version of me would have pepper sprayed a person for saying something like that, but the new free-thinking woman I had been crushed into wanted him to do it. I wanted him to landscape my spiritual garden.

I really wanted to ask him what he was packing his hookah with and what squalid alley one had to coincidently wander into to acquire some.

I had been upside down for approximately thirty-six minutes when I was shoved from the summit of my spiritual development and sent tumbling back down to earth with the other hollow drones. The Bee Who Stings Like a Butterfly glided over to me and opened his mouth.

"Are those tattoos birds or airplanes?" he lisped.

Impossible. He speaks! Like Sally Field in *Steel Magnolias*.

"Ooooweeee! That must have hurt like the Dickens."

He continued pointing at the miniscule spot of ink on my foot as he gingerly placed one hand on his brow, and swooned. The melodrama would have reduced Chuck Norris to tears.

He then pulled me off my mat, ruining what was a perfectly sculpted downward dog, and rolled up his sleeve. Perched daintily on his deadly bicep sat a fluttering pink butterfly, a double rainbow, and a tiny hibiscus flower.

Goodbye, Crouching Tiger. Hello Kitty.

I began to wonder where on his lower back "My Little Pony" was hiding.

Delivering the fatal blow, he divulged with all sorts of pride that he designed it all by himself and it took him forty whole years to get it just right.

I wanted to kick Baby Bear out of my spiritual garden in which he had likely erected pink flamingos and tiki torches. I could picture him laughing diabolically, wine spritzer in his hand, decimating my sacred flora and fauna with his army of rainbows and butterflies.

With a final pre-recorded ding of the gong, he rolled down his sleeve, and floated away leaving me, mouth agape on my giant rubber square. He curled himself into a perfect lotus position at the front of the room.

"*Namaste*," bellowed the tape.

"*Namaste, girlfriend,*" I replied in my head, still a little shocked. As it turns out, I had been right. He definitely knew how to take a man out, but probably just for frozen yogurt, not with his roundhouse kick.

# Twenty

# THE MAN WHO HAD
# TOO MANY

*I* had wanted to do the right thing. I had wanted to talk figures with The Man Who Had Too Many a thousand times during the early phases of our relationship, but I didn't. Not because the opportunity never presented itself, but because I was certain I had slept with at least twice as many people as he had and, frankly, I didn't want him to think I was a tramp and leave me for somebody with longer legs and better morals.

I had made mistakes in my youth. I had sometimes been irresponsible, other times, naïve, and at least one time jacked up on Mike's Hard Lemonade. He was not the sort of man who made mistakes. He was old fashioned and had been raised among churchy folk. He valued marriage, children, and general good behavior—things that, prior to our romance, I found rather silly and not all that much fun. But we fell in love and, before I knew it, we were engaged, then married, and I had let the conversation elude us.

Until our honeymoon.

We had decided to vacation in Mexico. It was cheap, had a seemingly endless supply of nacho cheese, and it was romantic—

that is until the one fateful evening over complimentary cocktails in the lobby when I decided to ask my new husband exactly how many there were before me. Our heads were pressed together over the table, we were drinking things we'd never heard of, and I decided the time was right. He deserved to know the truth about me, for better or worse.

I leaned back, grabbed his hand, prayed silently that he wouldn't think I was a harlot by the end of the night, and I asked very matter of factly: "How many people have you had sex with?"

He paused for a moment, eyes darting from Hawaiian shirt to Hawaiian shirt in the bustling atrium, and he cleared his throat.

"Twenty-ish," he guessed.

I felt like I had been punched in the throat. Impossible. Not HIM. I was supposed to be the libertine.

Twenty-ish.

Ish.

What was ish?

Should I be angry about ish?

The number of women he'd shagged was not supposed to be a guessing game. It was supposed to be an exact calculation.

He looked across the table into my eyes, which in their entire ocular history had never been so large, and asked timidly, "What about you?"

I had been preparing for this conversation before we'd met. I could justify every sexual encounter I'd ever had, even the more embarrassing ones that could only be explained by an empty box of wine. I knew all of them, their full names, ages, eye colors, and at least one interesting bit of potpourri.

Zachary Bryzowski: Caucasian. Black hair. Brown eyes. 2004. Futon. Former spelling bee champion. One testicle.

Robert Welch: Thirty-two. Guitar player. Cat person . . . And so on.

I'd been storing all of this information in a very cramped corner of my brain. All for nothing.

"Seven," I replied. "Just seven."

Alongside his wholesome upbringing, the Christian school, the table manners, and the slightly patriarchal southern charm, the number seven had seemed like an astronomical figure, or so I had thought. Seven had made me feel like a fast woman, a hussy, a floozy, and a complete degenerate!

He lit up a cigarette and kicked the terracotta tiles on the ground.

I was certain he had slept with a maximum of three people, maybe three and a half. I had never once even dreamed that a man of such sterling character would be capable of promiscuity.

I needed to think about this.

I leaned back, taking in a big gulp of recycled lobby air, and I stared at him, all freckly, dewy eyed, and pink from the sun.

"Twenty-ish," I repeated to him just to be sure.

He nodded.

My life was over.

I felt blindsided and manipulated and . . . liberated?

Yes!

Liberated!

I wasn't the slut.

Oh. Snap.

This was excellent news.

I wanted to leap out of my seat and do cartwheels; I wanted to introduce myself as Shannon Lee Miller, upstanding citizen. If we hadn't been in Mexico, I would have called my parents just to tell them what a fabulous job they did. The results were in: "Shannon-1, The Power of Jesus in your Life-0."

I was a pillar of moral fortitude in a decadent, vice-ridden world. I had absolutely nothing to feel guilty about. I sat back in my hibiscus covered wicker chair sipping my Singapore Sling, feeling like I was exceptional at doing the right thing. I was going to run for office when we got home.

The Man Who Had Too Many was swirling his index finger idly in a bowl of cocktail peanuts looking like he might begin to whimper. *Why was he so upset?* I wondered. His wife hadn't spent her bachelorette-hood prowling the streets like some fiery strumpet. This was good news for everybody.

Or was it?

I paused for a moment. Something was awry. The thrill of being a sensible young woman had jarred my perspective. This wasn't cause for acrobatic celebration at all. It was a mother frickin' disaster. A monkey hawking jungle tours cackled wickedly from across the lobby, and it all became clear.

If I wasn't the slut, then who was?

Oh no.

My husband was . . . easy.

And all of a sudden, just like that, I had hurt feelings.

There had to be some sort of mistake. He couldn't have slept with that many people; he was a Republican. Were Republicans even allowed to have that much sex?

Apparently so.

I wanted to vomit into the pounding steel drum to my left, mid-*La Bamba*.

Twenty-ISH people.

I was The Woman Who Had Too Few.

I felt betrayed, outfoxed, and strangely uncool. I wasn't a pillar of moral anything; I was just a sad old prude, and nobody likes a prude. He sat across from me rolling his Modelo across his nervous brow. He was picturing me, picturing him with other women. My mind was overwhelmed with profound questions. Should I have done it with more people? Did I have any bed cred left at all? Did he have a secret slutty baby somewhere out in this great expanse of universe who would one day show up at our door on Christmas?

"Babe, are you okay?" he offered, clasping my hand.

I was not prepared for this. I was supposed to be the tramp with the shady past who'd turned her life around; not him! I was outraged.

"I love you so much. None of those girls meant anything," he offered.

At this point I could have been an adult, but the endless supply of dark liquor and emotions I was experiencing made it impossible. I wanted to know why, and who, and how my sweet rose-purchasing, door opening, God-fearing husband ended up with more bedfellows than Keith Richards.

"So sex doesn't mean anything to you? It's just some way to pass the time? We have feelings you know . . . girls have feelings," I squawked at him.

He began to explain, to count each of his conquests on each of his fingers until he had run out of digits. He'd had more sexual partners than he did appendages and that was troubling.

He strained to remember details and dates, but there were just so many of them. In some instances, he couldn't even recall first names; instead they were tagged "this girl" or "that girl" or just plain "her." He certainly didn't have any interesting trivia about them.

The samba band began to play a grossly mispronounced version of an AC/DC "Let Me Put My Love Into You." He had probably had sex to that song before; he'd probably had sex to every song on *Back in Black*. This was the worst honeymoon ever. There wasn't enough free rum in the world to fix this.

The Man Who Had Too Many pulled his chair closer to mine and decided to get into the psychology of it all. He connected the lurid exploits of his past to his low self-esteem, earnestly expressing that these one-night stands were a product of feeling lonely and unloved.

Touching.

But not to a newly married wife.

*Great*, I thought. *If he watches* Shawshank Redemption *on a rainy day, I'm going to find him going at it on the kitchen counter with a hooker named Fawn.*

With each shake of the maracas, our future was looking grimmer. For a moment, I considered staying in Mexico and roaming the vast nation until vultures in the Sonora desert ate me, but I couldn't. I was married. To a gigolo.

He could tell I was upset, but we were both upset. This was our honeymoon, we were in Mexico, there was a dude playing the classical guitar, and a domesticated monkey promoting eco-tourism. We should have been feeding each other chimichangas and naming our future children, not our ex-lovers.

"Why didn't you tell me?" I demanded between loud, medicinal slurps of piña colada.

"Because I didn't want to know about you. I didn't want to think about you with other guys," he countered.

This was a lie. This was a lie of Nixon-esque proportions.

But I probably would have lied, too. I knew exactly why he didn't tell me, and it was the very reason I didn't tell him: because he didn't want me to think he was a dirty, dirty scoundrel. With a creak, The Man Who Had Too Many rose from his chair and began rubbing my back.

"I'm so sorry," he pleaded. "I never meant to disappoint you."

Ugh.

I hated that he'd slept with enough people to fill up a school bus, and I hated that he didn't tell me, but he was a nervous wreck.

I began to ponder.

Maybe if more than seven people had wanted to have sex with me, I would have done it too. Probably not unless there were Rohypnols and White Russians involved, but I would never really know.

We both leaned back in our wickers and stared. We were married. We had a lot to learn about each other. We would probably have to go through something like this again.

The band was playing "Lady In Red." There were couples all around us twirling and dipping and getting positively hammered. They were all so happy, stumbling along to the Casio in their docksiders. At some point, they had all been forced to reveal the scandals of their premarital existence, and they still survived. They managed to make screaming children, and buy plane tickets, and come to Mexico, and dance to a Latino Chris de Burgh who sounded partially deaf. It was certainly worth finding out if we could make it, too. Later on that evening, after a bottle of sparkling wine, we went back to our room where he offered me a very compelling apology (twice). I decided we would be just fine.

*Twenty-one*

# THE "QUEEN" OF
# MY CASTLE

t was Tuesday, and I needed a new apartment. I was an
adult living with my parents, and it had come to my
attention this was unacceptable. I needed my own place.
Even if I didn't feel like an adult, I certainly needed to keep
up appearances. I needed to be able to make ice cubes without
supervision. And this required investing in my very own set
of keys, doors, and electrical wiring issues. I wrote down the
necessities in no particular order, then headed to a coffee shop
with my computer and strict policies of renterhood: hardwood
floors; enough space to play Twister; no more than $600 a
month; and a location that would be unsuitable as a crime scene
for a Quentin Tarantino film.

I was excited. Thrilled even. Since I had never had a bat
mitzvah, I considered this equally monumental. I waited in line,
peering at my fellow coffee drinkers. The man in the blazer. The
woman in the silk blouse. I bet they all had their own apartments.
I bet they paid for their own utilities and knew how to use a
plunger. I imagined them all getting together on Friday nights at
Applebees, exchanging horror stories about gas bills over pints. It

was so romantic. I beamed as I walked back to my table. I couldn't wait to forget to water my plants.

The ad was sitting there discretely, squeezed right between a studio the size of a matchbox and a landlord who mandated a wake-up call every morning at 5:30.

"Craftsman artist loft," it promised. "Newly restored with hardwood floors, marble bathroom, and granite counter tops. Princess balcony. 2 bedroom. 2 bath. Move in immediately. First and last month's rent due on signing."

I thumbed over the pictures, mouth agape. I couldn't believe it. The place couldn't possibly be real. It was like Pinterest on crack. The toilet could practically wipe your ass for you. I wanted to tap my MCAT-studying, coffee neighbor on the shoulder and show him the closet space. Did he want to live there? I certainly did.

I scrolled down the ad and came to the price tag. Wince. Not quite as pleasant as the pictures, so I scrolled back up. The Craftsman Artist's Loft was well over my budget. And it was in an area of town that had seen more guns than Gettysburg. But what was an extra zero—or two—when you could bathe in a shower built by Romans?

Some people are born with the thrifty bone. They order waters when they go to restaurants. And not because they want their pee to be clear, but because they want to save $2.50. These people participate in an act called saving—an occupation where individuals set money aside and simply let it stay there. Untouched. Like brussel sprouts in front of a five year old. The difference between these people and me is that they expect life to go poorly. They know radiators are prone to break. (Moreover, they know what radiators are.) These people understand the lifespan of a refrigerator and the durability of rubber band. They pledge allegiance to the rainy day. I, on the other hand, can't imagine the needs of my yet-to-be-born children. My heating unit is working just fine, and no Brooks Brothers wearing accountant can convince me that driving through Starbucks every once in a while will cause me to become homeless and smell like a wet yak. *It doesn't hurt to just look. You can say no*, I told myself. But even I knew I was lying.

The house was on the west side of town, on the dividing line between the old neighborhood—complete with ghetto and gunshots—and the new neighborhood—complete with freshly restored bungalows and slightly uppity white women who had miniature J.Crew stores in their walk-in closets. The house looked plucked from the antebellum south. A wraparound porch and large glass doors beckoned, "Come inside and drink tea!" I promptly knocked on them, brushing back my hair and flattening the creases out of my shirt so I would look like I could win consecutive roommate of the year awards. The man who came to the door, whose name was Burton, was in his mid-forties and slightly balding. He wore horn-rimmed glasses and the expression of a toddler who just drank cough syrup. Everything he did was quick and gnat-like. I figured him for a closet gay, and smiled at the prospect. I didn't have any gay friends and my out-of-touch reasoning told me that if I moved into a craftsman artist loft above a gay landlord, my status in society would bolster. I would almost be cool enough to sit at the table with kids who were bringing back leg warmers. I could picture us at Christmas getting terribly excited about yams and stringing together Fruit Loops on a piece of yarn.

"It's so nice to meet you," I said, and I extended my hand as a gesture to prove just how friendly and southern I was. I waited for him to do something, like flail his voice or his hands, but instead he merely propped his glasses onto the top of his nose and said,

"Don't come inside; follow me."

I should have known from that moment to walk away. Curt, closet gays aren't the type of people you should rent from, live near, or acknowledge in public. They're the kind who initial their eggs and log your water usage. You feel guilty when you do a load of whites and a load of colors because you know they're standing below you counting how many times your washer rotates.

Even still, if the curtness hadn't been enough, the sweep around the house and the introduction to his six "security" cameras should have lit a spasm in my brain that he was at best anal retentive and at worst featured on *America's Most Wanted*. The only person who needs that many angles of a fence is an inmate trying to escape Folsom. Besides, if there were that many outside, how many were there *inside*? Would he tape me walking around in my underwear making scrambled eggs? More importantly, would he find out that I didn't even know how to make scrambled eggs?

I swallowed my concerns and tried to remember why I was there. *After all,* I reminded myself, *people don't get to live in restored bungalows and penthouses just by being nice. If I have to give up my ability to change in private, so be it.*

We walked around the edge of the lawn and the curt, gay landlord lectured me on the rules of the house. "Under no circumstances should you use the front door. Do you understand? And no banging after 9:00 p.m."

I nodded my head. Entries and exits I could manage. Banging I could define. What confused me is what I found when we turned the corner. There are a number of things you expect to see in the back of a house. For instance, a car. Or a lawnmower. Even a sandbox would be reasonable. But when you come across a hole the size of Savannah, Georgia, you take pause. And that's exactly what I did. While my potential future landlord stopped his huffing and puffing about what areas of the house were "forbidden," I stopped to assess the situation. Where there should have been grass and enough space to play Frisbee golf, there was a large expanse of dirt that fell magnificently downward, the edges full of bricks roosting on their decaying red perches. One could easily trip and become body one in a mass grave of trespassers and tenants who were overly zealous with their laundry.

I suspiciously eyed the evaporated Lake Eerie in the backyard, and my potential future landlord waved it off, as though the abyss were as common as a belly on an alcoholic. Bothersome perhaps. But nothing to trifle over.

"Oh that?" he said, scratching his chin in the exact spot where he wished he could grow a goatee. "I'm building a driveway out of bricks. It's hard work you know. Very careful work. Not everyone can do it."

Clearly.

"When will it be done?" I asked.

"Oh within the month. Just need to tidy up some loose ends. Until then you can park out front," and then he continued trekking up the steps, as though 'loose ends' wasn't code for the twenty-three people he was going to murder and then bury in his clearly marked grave.

My potential future landlord didn't seem to care about his overt parallels to Charles Manson. And when he unlocked the door to the loft and we walked inside, I have to confess I didn't either. I had never seen such pristine hardwood floors and shiny marble bathrooms. I could easily floss my teeth with silk from the lace curtains. I had heard people talk about stainless steel appliances and granite countertops, but I had never before been so overwhelmed by their proximity. Apparently places like this didn't only exist in *Better Homes & Gardens*; they existed in real life.

Before my fingers even knew what was happening, I was

sitting at the kitchen counter writing a deposit check to move in, in one week. I was practically squealing, and the curt, gay landlord was, too. Apparently he wasn't such an egg labeler once he realized how much I appreciated his newly buffered windows. We spent the afternoon in the master bathroom, watching the imported Japanese toilet lid open and close on its own. It's hard to find people who really appreciate the finer things in life. Most of my friends eat at combination Pizza Hut/Taco Bells and live in sublet basements. And with the luck of Craigslist and a slight lack of financial prudence, I'd finally found a kindred spirit. One with a mass grave, perhaps, but a kindred spirit no less.

As it turns out, The "Queen" of My Castle did not become my best friend. He became a hot dog salesman. He bought an old metal motor home and steamed buns in our backyard before driving downtown and selling foot longs to men who believe flinging ties over their shoulder can avoid mustard stains. He spent his weekends driving to Kentucky trying to discover the "best burger," and he blogged about it to an audience of three. In his spare time, he built two sheds in the backyard that served no discernible purpose except to make the neighbors believe that he might, in fact, be the next Unabomber.

About a week after moving in, I came to find out that my next door neighbor, who I'd been told was an aging grandfather, wasn't as geriatric as I had assumed, but instead an electric wheelchair driving drug dealer who hadn't taken a shower since the 1982 Olympics. I found out about "Gary" at three in the morning on a Saturday when I was fast asleep and heard blaring sirens fly down the street. They stopped directly in front of the house and flashed their lights. I got out of bed, expecting, I suppose, to see someone pulled over, but instead I found three police officers barricading themselves behind their car, guns drawn, pointed at my neighbor's house. They were yelling intensely. "Get the fuck down! Get the fuck down!"

I did not appreciate their language or their arrival time.

I tried to peer at my neighbor's house and see who needed to get the fuck down, but the window blocked my view. Immediately I broke into a sheer panic. What if the person who needed to get the fuck down escaped behind the house and decided to climb my stairs and seek refuge in my apartment? What if I was going to become a hostage, forever known as the girl who got between the police and the drugs? I knew I had to do something. I had to stop the electric wheelchair driving drug dealer from breaking in. My move? I pushed my one hundred-year-old cherry dresser in front of my door and barricaded myself in the bedroom.

The police rushed the house guns drawn and five minutes later came out, quite nonchalantly got in their cars, and drove off as though they were headed to a picnic to eat pimento cheese sandwiches.

I was confused. Amazed. And entirely frightened.

Had anyone gotten the fuck down? Where was Gary? Had he outrun them in his wheelchair?

The next morning I saw my curt, gay landlord sitting out on his porch, contemplating our giant crater in the backyard. "Did you see all that last night, Burton?" I asked. "What in the world was going on?"

"Oh, that was probably just Gary," he mused as he sipped his orange soda. "He deals coke sometimes. You know, on the side."

On the side? On the side of what?

As the months progressed, I began to realize that the moment The "Queen" of the Castle and I shared with the Japanese toilet would be an isolated event. While we both strongly believed everyone should own a set of china and know how to drink tea with pinkie finger extended, we had an entire English Channel of differences to muck through. This become remarkably clear when the house alarm went off on a Thursday afternoon. My curt, gay landlord was in Mississippi trying out a jalapeno-flavored burger for his blog, when the entire Victorian house erupted in what sounded like a jailbreak.

I called him immediately, yelling in the phone, "Burton, Burton, how do I turn this thing off?"

He was calm and collected, slurping ketchup off his fingers.

"Go downstairs. The alarm is right by the back door, next to the bathroom," he said. "The code is 9847#."

Simple enough, I thought, and opened the door that led down to his portion of the house and walked straight into a place I'd never been: his hallway. The alarm was louder down there, but I hardly recognized it due to what I saw. Resting against the walls in multiples were large, framed pictures of nude women. They were clustered together, each taking up space the size of a refrigerator. On the left-hand side, resting by a disheveled bookcase, was a picture of our neighbor, Miss Johnson. She was holding an apple in her hand and extending it toward me. I was horribly confused. What was this? *Biblical Playboy?* I hurried to the back of the house to shut off the alarm, catching a glimpse of the head of our Neighborhood Watch, then quickly returned to my upstairs haven where I wouldn't have to see Miss Johnson shoving fresh fruit in my face from her earthly "basket."

After the naked people, it was all downhill. I began to see far more of my curt, gay landlord than I ever would have liked. He let himself into my loft with disturbing frequency. I'd get home from work to find him "fixing a light fixture" or "repairing the sink" when indeed my lights had been appropriately bright that morning and the sink had done its job just fine. Sometimes I thought about hiring a naked midget to hang out in my apartment all day waiting for him. I wondered if he would try to fix that as well. Or perhaps merely charge me more rent. Moreover, despite all promises of parking on bricks born in the same century as Humphrey Bogart, the great expanse daily looked more and more like a landfill and less and less like a home for my vehicle.

In September, and nearly five months into the driveway project, there was light at the end of the tunnel. Bricks were actually being placed on the ground in a driveway like fashion, giving me hope that I would be able to stop parking on the street in the front the wheelchair drug dealer's house.

Spotting my landlord below, I walked down the steps to get an update. But before I could say, "Hello," or, "How are you doing?" or anything remotely resembling a normal exchange between two human beings, he simply came out with it: "My mother died."

It was short and simple and monotone, like how you would expect someone to talk about going to the grocery store to pick up cucumbers. Only this wasn't produce at all, but rather the woman who had given birth to his curt, gay self. His eyes started to well up and he sniffled. I'd had no idea his mother was sick. Or that he had a mother at all. Some part of me just assumed he was born in swaddling clothes and left outside a Mitchell & Gold.

I looked at him and for the first time in months I didn't want to slip weed killer in his coffee. He was annoying and spoiled and very bad at cooking hot dogs, but the picture of him sitting there so sullen in his mound of bricks broke my heart.

"I'm so sorry," I said. "How are you doing?"

I expected him to thank me for my concern, say, "It was her time," and continue paving his yellow brick road, but instead he said, "I'm burying her hair in the driveway. Right here. And I'm going to cover it over with this large white stone so I can always know where she is."

For the first time that afternoon, I noticed the dexterity with which he was working. There was so much intentionality in his action that had been missing before.

"How lovely," I said, when what I really wanted to say was, "Are you really sure that's what her hair wants?"

I have never been the kind of person to understand urns. Housing a person's remains in a porcelain cat on the mantle bothers me. No part of me wants to remember the person I loved encased in an object smaller than an easy-bake oven. And certainly not under a white stone in the backyard where I can drive over them every day to my heart's content. I stifled my disapproval and told him I was upstairs if he needed anything. But as it turns out, the one thing he "needed," I couldn't supply.

The Tuesday after his mother died, I peered over my balcony to see The "Queen" of My Castle beaming. I had truthfully never seen him so happy. Perhaps she isn't really dead, I thought. Perhaps it was a coma and everyone was mistaken.

"Burton," I called down. "What's going on?"

He looked up at me with the large beady eyes of a puppy and told me to stay where I was and close my eyes. I did as I was told, with a slight fear in my heart, and heard him rustling through the shed, pulling something out that was certainly more bulky and less flexible than a living, breathing mother. Had he made a cement mold of her? Or had her inducted into the wax museum?

"Alright," he called a few minutes later, "You can look." And I opened my eyes to see something I never would have expected: A Vespa. A shiny blue Vespa. I didn't say anything. What could I say? That's a lovely replacement for your mother? I'm sure it's quicker than she was?

The "Queen" of My Castle looked up at me, proud, waiting for my response, but when nothing audible was able to escape my mouth, he spoke for me: "It's my reward for taking care of my mother for so long."

I couldn't believe it. I was more shocked by this than John Edwards' infidelity. And as he sat there beaming, literally parked on top of his mother, I finally realized the only thing we had in common was our appreciation for craftsman architecture and crown molding. I had to move out. Immediately. My penny pinching friends might not realize the grandeur of a Japanese toilet, but at least they recognize what's actually important in life, and it's not hardwood flooring.

*Twenty-two*

# THE MAN WITH
# THE GOLDEN GROIN

*Y*ou should never get too close to a man in spandex; it reveals only the worst in him. I am reminded of this on a daily basis as I spend a minimum of thirty-three seconds every evening watching an insecure seventy-year-old cyclist display his penis like it's a new Corvette being unveiled on a rotating stage.

Every evening, at approximately 5:30 p.m., I find The Man with the Golden Groin standing, glutes flexed, water bottle holstered, in the middle of the apartment building elevator looking like a bike courier for the Fantastic Four. Accompanying him is his unit, which I can quite surely assume, based on his appreciation for Nike dri-fit products, is nicknamed Magic Johnson.

The effect of this penis on my general state of health and happiness has been catastrophic. Not only has it thwarted my every effort at striking up a neighborly conversation, but it has caused me to develop a great distaste for somebody I hardly know based solely on the contents of his shorts. I resent him, Monday through Saturday, for thrusting this age old, paradoxical question upon me: "Why can't I stop staring at the nasty junk of this very old man?"

There is much I admire in this aged cyclist. He takes his health seriously, he subscribes to *The New Yorker*, and his whistle-friendly repertoire of sad Irish laments is limitless. In another outfit, in another elevator, in another life, we could have been the dearest of friends. Unfortunately, there has always been and will always be a great distance of insurmountable inches that stand between us. I have resigned myself to the following humiliating routine, which I expect will continue until the end of time, or until he gets even older and moves to South Florida.

At first, I resolve to treat the penis like it's a screaming toddler. I walk onto the elevator, stare straight ahead, and ignore its desperate cries for attention. I tell myself, most matter of factly, that the penis is not there. I do my best to deny, deny, deny, but the unblinking one-eyed monster stares at me through its neon mustard hued enclosure. We have been engaged in this juvenile debate for the better part of a year and frankly, I've grown rather tired.

I wait for the doors to close, I check imaginary messages on my telephone, I tap my foot, and I read the flyer from Rollo Fine Foods as though it's the *Da Vinci Code*. Despite the fact that I study Black Forest Hams that I will never buy with remarkable intensity, the penis refuses to surrender. It taunts me, chanting, "Chicken Wangs: $8.95, Peckerino Romano: $10.65/lb, Oscar Meyer Weiners $2.99, Pixie Sticks .75 cents," under its breath.

At this point, I become furious. I know exactly what the little prick is doing, trying to make *me* seem like the pervy one so that if and when the cat lady walks onto the elevator, I'll get caught staring at the wedding tackle of a friendly senior who probably drinks sleepytime tea and has flocks of mallard ducks sitting on his side tables. I fix my gaze and picture unsexual things like slices of toast and pumice stones and spectator shoes. This strategy proves effective until The Man With the Golden Groin starts stretching.

It's entirely unfair to talk to a stranger when you've dressed up your member like an Academy Award. My cyclist neighbor is always sprained or twisted or torn, and he uses the thirty-three seconds of travel from the lobby to the thirteenth floor to detail his injuries to his fellow passengers as though we are the committee doctors for the Tour de France. Curiously, all of his ailments appear to stem from his crotch. As he settles into a set of deep lunges, grunting like a suspicious Rottweiler, he begins filling the air with semi-rhetorical questions and statements: *"Could my quads ever use some Eucalyptus Oil?" "Did that bike ever do a number on my pelvis." "These abductors, they don't work like they used to, do they?"* He is daring me to examine the state of his pelvic region. I say nothing, but inside I scream, "NO, NO, NO! No to Eucalyptus! And to bicycles! And to styling your penis like a Formula One racecar! But before I can even finish my string of melodramatic thoughts, I realize that I have been staring directly at his package for at least ten and a half seconds. He has snared me with his acrobatics, his popping joints, and his mind control. The world has faded away, and its just me versus one complicated man and his Shaft.

As we near the third floor, I attempt to evaluate the condition of my ass in the mirrored walls, which is what all normal women do when they are confronted with an appropriate amount of reflective surface. But The Man With the Golden Groin has stepped in front of me and foiled my plan. All of the sudden, the one golden groin has multiplied into thousands. There is a kaleidoscopic line of infinite penises hurtling toward me. I am watching Phallus in Wonderland.

After numerous elevator rides with The Man With the Golden Groin, I know that this type of limb multiplying reflection pleases him. Sometimes, he even lifts up his many arms and waves hello at himself and his mystical Octopenis. At this point,

I want to punch him directly in the jaw, but unfortunately his freakish height and clasped helmet prevent me. How convenient.

By the seventh floor, I'm a goner. I feel like a mirrorball should be dropping from the ceiling and I should be stuffing my leftover cab fare down his bicycle shorts. He is an exotic dancer named Lance Armshlong, and I am a fat forty-five-year-old administrative assistant named Cathy escaping from my unhappy marriage. He is pumping his pelvis to the strains of "Eye of the Tiger" and screaming. Begging for me to "Just Do It!" There are strobe lights and whiskey sours and cigarettes long enough to conduct the Berlin Philharmonic. I am smiling and flapping my chubby arms in the air pleading for an encore.

"Almost time to get off," smiles The Man with the Golden Groin as he finishes his stretches and prepares to strut his Olympic medal off the elevator's dance floor. The dry ice curls back and the strobe lights stop flashing and slowly it becomes clear that I'm in my apartment building and not "Ladies Drink Free Night" at the Swinging Banana. The doors open, and he's gone.

Later in the evening, I step onto the crowded elevator in my own bicycle shorts and nobody seems to notice. There are no beads of sweat forming upon the brows of the businessmen surrounding me, and the elderly woman in the pink beret seems utterly transfixed by her Pomeranian's tangled coat. I stretch and shuffle my feet, but not a single person seems as though they're fighting to ignore the throbbing house music in their head. As we reach the ground floor, my neighbors exit, their pulses at a safe, resting rate. I look in the waist-high mirror and examine my condition for the second time that day, grey shorts clinging to my lady parts half-heartedly. Images of that dazzling gilded penis begin to pop up in my mind, and I must admit, I am a bit envious.

*Twenty-three*

# THE MAN WHO STOLE
# MY EGO

*I*t is incredibly difficult to be famous when you aren't particularly attractive or good at anything, but I never let those obstacles get in my way. As soon as I was old enough to threaten to run away, I made my mother plaster my bedroom with *90210* wallpaper and purchase every CD at HMV with a spurned looking woman on the front. Tiny Me would spend hours, sunk deep into folds of a giant blue beanbag thinking about exactly how breathtakingly famous Giant Me was going to be one day. I also thought a lot about the kid from *Home Improvement* from this exact location, as well. If I was going to go on to be some form of sensation, I wanted to be at least famous enough to own a Maserati and a mid-major sports team.

Moreover, a true famous person is far too materially successful to experience the following unholy emotions: grief, sadness, heartache, or, of course, utter humiliation. And avoiding said feelings is kind of the whole point of being famous in the first place. Even as a seven year old, I didn't want to wake up one day in a Studio City apartment, all old and spooning an empty bottle of Johnny Walker with nothing but an acoustic guitar or a demo reel filled with failed pilots and small time commercials; I was having enough trouble making friends in the school yard as it was. Nobody wants to be kind of famous. Being kind of famous means that you don't have sports cars and a stable of professional athletes to protect your pride when life decides to punch you in the tit.

Despite my best efforts at becoming an instant celebrity, I learned the earth shattering pains of moderate success the hard way.

Once upon a time, I was kind of famous. Or at least kind of, kind of famous. I learned that being kind of famous and being T-Pain are very different. No matter how many clippings of yourself you snip out of magazines and stash in your secret "I Love Me" shoebox that lives under the bed, unless you are T–Pain famous, you can still experience enough utter embarrassment to "I Hate" yourself all over again. All it takes is an ex-boyfriend and a powder fresh douche. Allow me to explain.

One day, years ago, in a land far, far-ish away, I decided to be a country music sensation. I had sizable hair, sizable breasts, and harbored a deep, dark desire to make sure that every kid who even thought about teasing me in high school was truly ashamed. I eventually wiggled my way into a recording studio, onto the radio, and then, television.

I was filming my first big television commercial. Sure, it was going to be a badly lit, thirty-second blip on a division of Country Music Television. But it was a nationally aired ad starring me. To the best of my knowledge, Natalie Hale, who used to tie me up by my windbreaker to the tetherball pole in front of the entire fifth grade, did not have a blip and that was all that mattered.

I woke up the morning of the shoot feeling like Faith fucking Hill. I'd spent the week dousing my face in salicylic acid until it shone like waxed linoleum, and I'd ingested nothing but aspartame for five straight days. I stared at myself in the mirror, and in a slightly naïve moment of pure vanity, felt wholly superior. I began to envision myself in the winners' circle at the Preakness with one of the racehorses I planned to buy after I hit it big. I was wearing a large, expensive hat flanked by large expensive men. That was, until I looked closer. I snapped out of my National Velvet fantasy and glared at my reflection. I was not wearing a large expensive hat. In fact, I looked quite cheap. There were roots. About an inch of mousy brown un-famous hair was destroying the shade of Jessica Simpson that had catapulted me into the spotlight. For a moment, I mourned the molehill that had popped up in my glorious meadow of perfect day, but luckily I had a solution.

When I was younger, the folks at *Seventeen Magazine* had told me to put baby powder in my hair, and I listened. Up until that point, it was the best life advice I had ever received. It made me look blonder, it made me smell better, and it meant that I didn't have to wash my hair every single day. Sometimes, it also made me look like I had acute psoriasis, but I figured looking like a blonde with psoriasis was better that not being blonde at all. So off to the convenience store I went to save my television debut, unaware that I was about to make a transaction that would dismantle all the accolades of my self-important career.

The Sudsy Express was located a mere three meters from my house. It was a Laundromat/Internet café/florist/hardware store, run by an Asian man that looked like Kim Jong-il. They carried everything from cigarettes to jigsaw puzzles so I was certain that somewhere between the deli meats and power tools, I would find the rather pedestrian toiletry I so desperately desired. If not, they had a collection of sensible wigs displayed between the mini-cactuses and the rain sticks.

The jingle bell above the door announced my arrival as I breezed inside and looked around to see if anybody had recognized me. This was a habit I developed from being asked for an autograph in a food court . . . once. There was a shady looking fellow in girl jeans on a computer who glanced up briefly and a middle-aged woman folding her briefs who smelled of cat urine. I allowed myself to believe that they wanted to snap pictures of me on their camera phones but had chosen to respect my privacy. I pretended like I didn't want to be recognized as I strutted down the aisles, even though I probably would have given out free hand jobs to anybody who said I looked remotely familiar.

I began sorting through the merchandise under the watchful eye of Kim Jong-il, who seemed very concerned that I might steal a package of sponges and make a run for it, but I quickly spotted a cardboard box that read talcum powder and stuffed it under my arm along with some Pizza Combos and a peppermint patty. Then *it* happened.

I had been fantasizing about this moment my entire life, since before I was even kind of famous. I was about to experience true vindication. There under the fluorescent lights of the Sudsy Express, buying Listerine and frozen waffles, was the first boy to ever break my heart, The Man Who Stole My Ego. I could not believe my luck.

"Shannon?" he asked quizzically.

Fucking liar. Like he didn't own my record and listen to it in bed after a long, hard day of mowing lawns.

I began cackling in my head.

Of course, in true celebrity fashion, I ran over and gave him a warm and slightly desperate embrace that allowed me to adjust my breasts to the appropriate level of bustiness. I hugged him hard, the box of baby powder creaking between us.

"He is going to need a hug," I thought. I was about to be in a television commercial; he was still living with his parents. I was also probably going to gloat and suggest that I made more money than I actually did. HA.

He looked good, but I looked better. I was wearing fake eyelashes that could have cut plate glass, and I had grown a few crucial cup sizes since I was sixteen, which I noticed he had noticed . . . and I loved it.

We briefly commiserated over his family and then he began telling me about hearing my song on the radio and his cousin buying a ticket to my concert. It was like poetry. I handled it like how Beyoncé circa early Destiny's Child would have handled it, but he was terribly awkward. His gaze was shifting. He cleared his throat at least six phlegm-rattling times, and he began to perspire. I was intimidating him and enjoying every second of it. I told him how overwhelming my new flawless life was, even though it wasn't, and then transitioned effortlessly into recounting how very burnt out I was on talking about my illustrious career. I might have even mentioned how much I missed the simplicity of the old days. He was sweating through his polo shirt, he was blushing, and his junk had to be shrinking exponentially. This was the best day of my life.

I felt important. I had told a colorful assortment of half-truths convincingly and looked good doing it. If egos were battleships, I had already sunk his destroyer. Then, he made the mistake of asking where I was off to, and I began to feel a twinge of guilt. He would never recover from this.

"Oh, I'm just off to shoot a commercial."

NAIL.

IN.

COFFIN.

His eyes grew wide, and he began to act a bit shifty. He couldn't even look me in the eye.

Poor thing, maybe it was wrong to so blatantly flaunt my success over his head, but I couldn't stop. I liked that I had gotten somewhere, and he was living in a moldy, suburban basement.

Still something just didn't seem right, something that kept me from enjoying the sweet, sweet nectar of revenge as much as I would have liked to. He seemed troubled; I didn't want him to feel defeated by life, only defeated by me.

Just as I about to get into the part of my speech about how blessed I was and maybe give him a little hopeful but also condescending advice about following his dreams, I dropped the bundle of goods I'd been clutching and looked down.

Combos. Peppermint Patty. TALCUM POWDER SCENTED DOUCHE.

No.

No.

NO, NO, NO, NO, NO!

There before us lay the pink box plastered with the image of a middle-aged man in a white linen suit, clutching his wife whose vagina probably smelled like a new car.

He began to wiggle his knee uncomfortably as my heart visibly jumped into my esophagus. I had never even seen a douche before. I didn't even know anybody who had seen a douche before. I wanted talcum powder. He had to have known it was a mistake. He just had to!

I stared down at the italicized script on the box, then I stared at him, then I stared at the Asian. This cycle was repeated at least a dozen times; each time the silence grew more silent.

"I should probably let you get going. Congratulations on everything," he insisted.

With a half-hearted hug and a jingle of the doorbell, he was gone and I was left standing in the Sudsy Express with my candy. And my douche. He probably thought I had an STD, and he was probably going to tell all of our old friends about it.

That bastard.

My career was over.

My life was over.

And my one true moment of triumph and vindication lay dead, albeit smelling fabulous, on the floor of a Laundromat. Despite the fact that I had almost purchased an antiquated feminine hygiene product, I would never feel like a fresh new talent again.

*Twenty-four*

# THE FATHER WHO
# WORKED OVERTIME

*T*he first looked like an inkblot.

The second looked like an addition mistake that had been half erased on a math exam.

The third was definitely a plus sign.

Holy Fuck. I was pregnant.

I unwrapped a copy of the Yellow Pages previously employed as a giant coaster and dialed the OB with the fancy, full color ad.

I parallel parked seamlessly, an incredible feat for somebody who just lost a fetus, and I sat, half listening to a sports radio program. I had just returned from the doctor's office where a gynecologist who appeared no older than fifteen had told me with a customer service-y grin that I had a miscarriage. I was pregnant for the span of a summer camp semester and now it was over.

The car was mercifully hovering just above empty outside of our house, where I sat for nearly an hour watching the mailman trot up and down the street and the neighborhood vagrants gulp their morning swill. Normally, watching the hobos spar with their imaginary friends brought me an unsuitable amount of pleasure, but not that day. I was going to have to tell my husband about this, and I knew that eventually we would probably have to tell our parents, and then our friends. Ugh. They would probably want to bring us lovingly prepared casseroles that would never get eaten. They would only sit on the counter top and remind us that something bad had happened.

Crying felt like the politically correct thing to do, but I couldn't. All I could do was listen to the voices of angry sports fans on the radio, chew gum, and wonder if I was feeling the right things. The broadcast went to a commercial. I was afraid to take my seat belt off, so I just sat, poking my tummy, wondering if maybe they'd made a mistake this time. Maybe they'd mixed up the cups of pee or vials of blood. Maybe she was still in there. That's right, at no more than six weeks along, I had already arbitrarily decided it was a girl.

I looked out the window at our tiny house, the porch three sizes too big. My husband was in there asleep, dreaming of something nice like a craft beer and a billiards festival. I wasn't about to ruin it for him. I was going to be practical. I was going to stay in the car . . . forever.

I was just about to begin planning what would be a custard-filled eternity of emotional eating when my phone rang. It was early enough in the morning that I knew it could only be one person: The Father Who Worked Overtime.

Let it be known that my father and I are a living, breathing public service announcement. Before I was married, we'd go to baseball games, watch *American Idol*, and talk about life on the back deck in matching Adirondack chairs. Though he has always had a general understanding of my peptic ulcer-inducing personal life, it is the small talk at which we really excel, the mundane dinner conversations that float across the lasagna and remind you that you are part of a family and you will never be alone . . . ever . . . even when you want to be.

Despite the fact that I got married and moved to a shiny new country with a new kitchen table and terrible lasagna, and had a new fellow to gab with, our relationship never changed. Every night, one of us got bored in our respective living rooms, hundreds of miles apart, picked up the phone, and all of a sudden were not bored, not alone, and were probably laughing. It wasn't commiserating over pork chops and instant mashed potatoes, but it was a simple, perfect comfort for two people who loved each other and lived entirely too far away.

The phone was growling angrily from my cup holder, a picture of my snaggle-toothed dog blinking on the screen like a marquee sign.

I wasn't going to pick up.

I stared at Bob the Dog and Bob the Dog stared back at me as if for once I was the one disobeying simple commands.

The screen went blank and I settled back into my seat, reclining and closing my eyes. But of course, The Father Who Worked Overtime called again, like he always did.

"Dad, what's crackin'?"

I'm not sure why I greeted him as though I were a member

of the Wu Tang Clan.

The Father Who Worked Overtime was always delightful in the morning and today was no exception. He was jovial and had seen enough of the six o'clock news to make sure we had plenty of things to talk about. He had even read enough of my local newspaper to fill me in on restaurant openings and the ten-day forecast. He began talking about a carnivore-chic hamburger joint that opened in town. It had designer mustard.

I could picture his steely blue eyes, the same as mine, flickering as his morning coffee. The baby would have had those eyes, I was certain.

The buoyancy of his voice was helping me to breathe easier. I was comfortable debating the virtues of Dijon vs. yellow mustard. I tried to forget the last two hours of my life. It's not like he needed to know I had moved into my SUV and that he would probably never have a grandchild. I was twenty-six years old; I could deal with it later and leave him out of it.

"How was your doctor's appointment?" he crowed.

The back of my throat began to burn so badly I thought I had swallowed a curling iron. I had told my parents the week before that I thought I might be pregnant, but it was nothing new to them. I'd been imaginary pregnant at least seventeen times and have pissed on more sticks than a major-league hitter. I was a card-carrying babychondriac. Every twenty-eight days, there were embryos lurking around dark corners, poised and ready to rob me of my youth and destroy my vagina.

"Hello?" he barked into the phone. "I think you're fading out." I felt like I was fading out, but I was certain the reception was just fine. He liked to pretend he was going through a dead zone when I took too long to answer questions, thus prompting me to give him my full attention.

"Oh it was fine, but they made me wait for three bloody hours and all they had to read was *Road and Track*! Honestly, what kind of gynecologist subscribes to *Road and Track*?!"

Of course, they didn't have *Road and Track* but in my mind it was a funny little scenario that would make him laugh.

It did.

I smiled a little as I heard him chuckling on the other line. I began to giggle.

Giggling is always a mistake for a girl in tears. I kind of yelped a bit, like a dog whose tail had gotten underfoot.

"Are you okay?" he inquired, probably wondering why I sounded like a wounded terrier.

I looked up, attempting to contain the pools of saltwater that peeked over the edge of my eyelids. I wished we were at the kitchen table making fun of Alex Trebek's cocky French accent, eating chicken à la something, and snickering at the Magnavox.

"No, I'm fine, I'm just a bit hung over . . . and my allergies . . . and I just don't think I'm going to go back to that doctor ever again."

He wanted to know why.

"She looked like fucking Pippi Longstocking!" I spat into the phone, shaking.

It had become clear to him that something other than my doctor's pigtails was distressing me.

"Shannon," he said in a voice I hadn't heard since I was about eleven—a serious voice.

"I'm not pregnant . . . anymore."

It just popped out.

I'm not pregnant anymore.

I don't live in Boston anymore.

I can't eat dairy anymore.

It was mechanical, computer generated.

I'm not pregnant anymore. Just like that.

Now it was his turn to be silent. I could hear the cars whooshing past him, and the ticking of his turn signal. He was breathing heavily, the way hockey players sound during the post-game wrap up. He took a loud a sip of coffee, the pieces of the puzzle slowing merging together.

She was pregnant. Now she isn't pregnant.

Baby. No baby.

Miscarriage.

He had really called at the wrong time. This was a mom conversation, a husband conversation, or even a shrink conversation. There wasn't even any lasagna on the table to talk across. He had been thrust into the crosshairs of No Dad's Land. He wasn't supposed to be on the line; he was supposed to be off the hook, playing spider solitaire, listening to Aerosmith, and doing regular dad things. Not counseling his daughter through one of the most devastating pitfalls of womanhood.

He exhaled, "Oh."

He had no idea whether this was good news or bad news.

I began to whimper.

I was married. So by all accounts, I was allowed to have sex. Heck, I was eligible for a legitimate baby. I was of hearty northern stock and had a post-secondary education. I might have even been a tad overqualified! I wasn't, however, qualified to deal with THIS.

"It's probably for the best," I conceded, trying to pull my shit together. "Babies are expensive."

Unfortunately, that's as good as I could do. That was my primo line. Losing the baby was God's way of being frugal. As far I was concerned, all that my dad needed to know was that I had everything under control.

He asked, "Are you guys okay?"

And that was when the whimpers turned into full-on crying.

I told him that I hadn't said anything to my husband yet because I was stuck in the car like a complete lunatic. I started to feel embarrassed. My Dad knew I had sex and he knew I was effective enough at sex to make a baby. This was a disaster. I was a grown up! These were my issues, not his. We were supposed to be talking about reality TV.

"You know, it's supposed to be emotionally devastating for a woman. You're supposed to be upset," he offered.

The Father Who Worked Overtime was talking like an experienced pediatrician, calmly assuring me that I was perfectly normal, despite the fact that there were tears and snot all over the dashboard.

My shallow breathing began to even up. I was afraid nothing would be the same again: my marriage would be strained, and we'd probably start sleeping in separate beds. My father would stop being my friend and resume just being my father—no more joking and idle chatter, just worrying.

I could hear the hum of his engine and the bustle of my old hometown in the background.

"You need to go inside," he reasoned. "It might take a while to feel better but just so you know, you will get through this . . . both of you together. Mom and I are here for you. I love you. Oh, and make sure you blow your snotty, old nose."

It was just what I needed.

Eventually the foggy world outside the car came into focus, the sidewalk didn't seem as though it were a million miles away, and the low drone in my ears gave way to an ensemble of regular neighborhood sounds. I still felt like shit, but a nicer version of shit. I told him that I loved him too and said goodbye. He was a good friend and a rather amazing father.

I walked lazily up to our house, still tentative but unashamed. I removed my large key ring from my handbag and opened the door. I remembered back to my wedding day when The Father Who Worked Overtime placed my hand in my husband's and walked to his seat. He gave me away, but that didn't mean I had to go away. Even though I was somebody's wife and would eventually be somebody's mother, I would always be his daughter.

# *The Credits*

After writing, editing, re-writing, and reading this book, we are most grateful that we have managed to survive the stories within it. It is nothing short of miraculous that we aren't eating, praying, or loving in Nepal. Or for that matter mopping the floors at a convent. We aren't even all that screwed up. We are starting to realize the fact that we elected to write a book instead of drowning in our respective pools of romantic discontent might have something to do with the truly fantastic people in our lives. Thank you to our friends, families, and all other delightful scamps associated with the publication of this book and the preservation of our sanity.

## I. KICKSTARTERS

We would still be here without you (barring any incarcerations, deportations, or unfortunate accidents), but this book would not be. Thank you for intrepidly reaching down the side of the cushions for couch change, for saying "no" to that sale at Sharper Image and "yes" to *Awkward Moments*. Thank you for daring to see us as more than a couple of angry broads with MacBook Pros, a box of wine, and too much time on their hands. We are so very grateful for you from the bottom of our cruel, shriveled, little raisin hearts:

*Art and Debbie Briggs, Gary Belsky, Alice and Emmett Byrd, Ryan Sisson, Tyler Cain, Ashley Simpson, Ian Crozier, Brandy Blanton, Bryan Monzon, Kim Baldwin, John Preston, Carlee Brossard, Brian Waidelich, Jamie Holmes, Melissa Dinwoodie, Bill Fletcher, Alice Sullivan, Shelby Miller, Jeremy Reppy, Erin Briggs, Arthur Briggs, James Pearson, James Tipton, Sam Harrison, Erik Jahner, Marc Weingarten, Maggie Young, Michael Lavelle, Bethany Kirby, Renee Herrell, Katie Thompson, Jacklyn Johnston, Melissa Roth, Mark Thorrington, Mark Karis, ImportGenius.com, Liva Smith, Molly Kempf, Noah Mintz, John O'Neill, Merrill Farnsworth, Beverly Walsh, Lisa Reilly, Emil Fiorantis, Matthew Brown, Jaclyn Johnson, Meredith Edwards, Dana Gelin, Tyler Lafreniere, Kevin and Lauren Christopher, Erin Briggs, Jaime Derensis, Katie Landers, Jennifer Luckett, Casey Summar, Jason Russell, Julia Millard, Siggi Smarason, Kelsey Burr, Alexander Teitz, Josh Roberts, John Baldwin, Ashley Guy, James Turnbull, Warda Shazadi, Scott Fort, Alex Hodgson, Stan Golden, Brooke Carbo, Carolyn Fabrici, Sarah Ivany, Jeffrey Walsh, Molly Smith, Sarah Waitkus, Ashley Earnhardt, Reid Shippen, Lee Bridges, Mary Miller, Mariana Blanco, Tiffany Keesey, Dave Taylor, Christine Fisher and Elizabeth Murphy, Whitney Griffin, Kyle Andrews, Claudia Levy, Jas Mogwood, Taylor Nyquist, Caroline Mitchell, Kristen Trettevik, Stuart Bradley, Rene Inman, Leo Lui, Megan S., J. Curtis, Jude Coombe, Charley Dingboom, Nathan Abhigan, Wendy Chow, Dean Rossetti, Dimitar Kolev, Mark Gedak*

## 2. MARK KARIS

Sometimes you just meet people in life who are better than you. Mark is one of those people. Not only is he better looking and more talented, but he also fathered the most absurdly adorable daughter on the planet. This generous, successful bloke typeset our manuscript and designed our cover for the price of a high five. We are grateful. And indebted. And vow to some day pay him in something more valuable than war bonds. Mark you are really, really good at life; never forget it.

## 3. ALICE SULLIVAN

Normally, we do everything in our power to avoid criticism. Criticism makes us sad. But in this case, we quite enjoyed it. Thank you for navigating the terrifying collection of words we presented you with and fishing out all the decent ones. We love you. You made us look like we write pretty good.

## 4. PATRICK WEBER

You have programs on your desktop that we've never even heard of. You might even have an entirely new futuristic computing machine for tech savvy design people who are "ahead of the curve." Thank you for spending more time on our facial hair than your own.

## 5. ARIEL RENAE

Most days we don't shower before noon. We can't remember the last time we voluntarily plucked an eyebrow or did a calf raise. Yet somehow you were able to make us look like we don't belong in an Occupy Wall Street camp. Thank you and your lucky lens for keeping us presentable and downright purty.

## 6. BRYAN MONZON

If it weren't for you, we would still believe cookies were just the glorious products of Nabisco. Thank you for prying open our technology-deprived eyes and harnessing the power of the Internet for reasons more precious than online dating. You created such a stunning virtual home for us all the way from your dreadfully overcast weather in San Diego. You make us look like we know what we're doing. A feat of Olympic proportions. Thank you.

## 7. OUR PARENTS

While we were birthed in two different countries with two different colors of hair, we are remarkably similar in one respect: we have incredible and immensely supportive parents. Art, Debbie, Rick, and Carol—we might hope you didn't read the actual contents of this book, but we certainly hope you read this: we love you.

## 8. BUCKLEY MILLER

Buckley is Shannon's husband. Unlike the majority of fellows in this tome, he is pretty recognizable throughout the entire thing and will have to live with that for the rest of eternity. Thank you for allowing us to convey the unremitting, endearing awkwardness that is marriage. Shannon loves you very, very much. Megan loves you too, but in a different way.

## 9. MEGAN'S FUTURE HUSBAND

Thank you for not appearing yet. We'll need material for the sequel.

# Book Club Questions

What can we say? We've put this page in here on the ill-advised hopes that not only has more than one person read this book, but that at least two people who live in the same state have read it and are trekking two hours to an Interstate rest stop to discuss the fascinating inner workings of our awkward experiences and thoughts.

We are floored. And honored. And hope someone remembered the wine.

1) We're all horribly awkward human beings from the very day we are born, each and every darling one of us. Do you think there is a dominantly awkward sex? Why?

2) You have to date one of the awkward men in this book . . . Who's the lucky guy?

3) Obviously this book is going to be picked up by some star spangled Hollywood studio. Cast a few of your favorite characters, and explain your selections.

4) Do relationships with the opposite sex get more or less awkward over time?

5) What is the worst "meet the parents" story you have in your arsenal?

6) Which story in this book wins gold in the "Most Painfully Uncomfortable Situation" category at the next Olympic games?

7) Eating is almost always awkward, especially when you're trying to seduce the person across the table. What is the most awkward date food and why?

8) If the Blonde and the Brunette were to brighten the world with another tome in their awkward series, what would you like to read next? *Awkward Moments with* (fill in the blank).

9) Do you think it's important to talk about awkward moments or just ignore them and hope they disappear?

10) Don't pretend you didn't know this was coming! We've all had our fair share of awkward moments . . . Which one of yours takes the cake?

# Don't Make Me Think, Revisited
A COMMON SENSE APPROACH TO WEB USABILITY

STEVE KRUG

**Don't Make Me Think, Revisited**
**A Common Sense Approach to Web Usability**

New Riders
www.newriders.com
To report errors, please send a note to errata@peachpit.com
New Riders is an imprint of Peachpit, a division of Pearson Education.

Editor: Elisabeth Bayle
Project Editor: Nancy Davis
Production Editor: Lisa Brazieal
Copy Editor: Barbara Flanagan
Interior Design and Composition: Romney Lange
Illustrations by Mark Matcho and Mimi Heft
Farnham fonts provided by The Font Bureau, Inc. (www.fontbureau.com)

ISBN-13: 978-0-321-96551-6
ISBN-10:    0-321-96551-5

28 2020

Printed and bound in the United States of America

First Edition

*To my father, who always wanted me to write a book,*

*My mother, who always made me feel like I could,*

*Melanie, who married me—the greatest
stroke of good fortune of my life,*

*and my son, Harry, who will surely write books
much better than this one whenever he wants to.*


Second Edition

*To my big brother, Phil, who was a mensch his whole life.*

Third Edition

*To all the people—from all parts of the world—who have
been so nice about this book for fourteen years.
Your kind words—in person, in email, and in your
blogs—have been one of the great joys of my life.*

*Especially the woman who said it made her laugh so hard
that milk came out of her nose.*

# MAKING SURE YOU GOT THEM RIGHT

# LARGER CONCERNS AND OUTSIDE INFLUENCES

# About this edition

*People come and go so quickly here!*

—DOROTHY GALE (JUDY GARLAND)
IN *THE WIZARD OF OZ* (1939)

I wrote the first edition of *Don't Make Me Think* back in 2000.

By 2002, I began to get a few emails a year from readers asking (very politely) if I'd thought about updating it. Not complaining; just trying to be helpful. "A lot of the examples are out of date" was the usual comment.

My standard response was to point out that since I wrote it right around the time the Internet bubble burst, many of the sites I used as examples had already disappeared by the time it was published. But I didn't think that made the examples any less clear.

Finally, in 2006 I had a strong personal incentive to update it.[1] But as I reread it to see what I should change, I just kept thinking "This is all still true." I really couldn't find much of anything that I thought should be changed.

If it was a new edition, though, *something* had to be different. So I added three chapters that I didn't have time to finish back in 2000, hit the snooze button, and happily pulled the covers back over my head for another seven years.

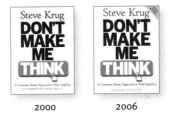

2000          2006

(Writing is really hard for me, and I'm always happy to have a reason not to do it. Give me a good old root canal over writing any day.)

So why now, finally, a new edition? Two reasons.

---

[1]   *Half of the royalties for the book were going to a company that no longer existed, and doing a new edition meant a new contract—and twice the royalties—for me.*

# #1. Let's face it: It's old

There's no doubt about it at this point: It feels dated. After all, it's thirteen years old, which is like a hundred years in Internet time. (See? Nobody even says things like "in Internet time" anymore.)

Most of the Web pages I used for examples, like Senator Orrin Hatch's campaign site for the 2000 election, look really old-fashioned now.

Sites these days tend to look a lot more sophisticated, as you might expect.

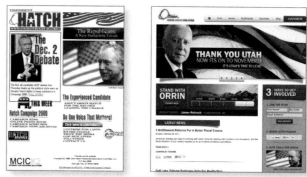

www.orrinhatch.com 1999          www.orrinhatch.com 2012

Recently I've been starting to worry that the book would finally reach a point where it felt *so* dated that it would stop being effective. I know it hasn't happened yet because

- It's still selling steadily (thank heavens), without any sign of slowing down. It's even become required reading in a lot of courses, something I never expected.

- New readers from all over the world continue to tweet about things they've learned from it.

- I still keep hearing this story: "I gave it to my boss, hoping he'd finally understand

what I'm talking about. He actually read it, and then he bought it for our whole team/department/company!" (I love that story.)

- People keep telling me that they got their job thanks in part to reading it or that it influenced their choice of a career. [2]

But I know that eventually the aging effect is going to keep people from reading it, for the same reason that it was so hard to get my son to watch black and white movies when he was young, no matter how good they were.

Clearly, it's time for new examples.

# #2. The world has changed

To say that computers and the Internet and the way we use them have changed a lot lately is putting it mildly. Very mildly.

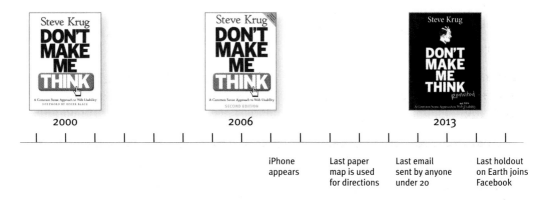

| 2000 | 2006 | 2013 |

iPhone
appears

Last paper
map is used
for directions

Last email
sent by anyone
under 20

Last holdout
on Earth joins
Facebook

The landscape has changed in three ways:

- **Technology got its hands on some steroids.** In 2000, we were using the Web on relatively large screens, with a mouse or touchpad and a keyboard. And we were sitting down, often at a desk, when we did.

  Now we use tiny computers that we carry around with us all the time, with still and video cameras, magical maps that know exactly where we are, and

---

[2] *I'm enormously pleased and flattered, but I have to admit there's always a part of me that's thinking "Yikes! I hope she wasn't meant to be a brain surgeon. What have I done?"*

our entire libraries of books and music built in. And are always connected to the Internet. Oh, and they're phones, too.

Heck, I can use my "phone" to

...book a restaurant reservation in seconds

...adjust the heat in my house from anywhere

...or deposit a check without going to an ATM

It's no flying car (which, come to think of it, we were promised we'd have by now), but it's pretty impressive.

- **The Web itself kept improving.** Even when I'm using my desktop computer to do all the things I've always done on the Web (buying stuff, making travel plans, connecting with friends, reading the news, and settling bar bets), the sites I use tend to be much more powerful and useful than their predecessors.

We've come to expect things like autosuggest and autocorrect, and we're annoyed when we *can't* pay a parking ticket or renew a driver's license online.

- **Usability went mainstream.** In 2000, not that many people understood the importance of usability.

Now, thanks in large part to Steve Jobs (and Jonathan Ive), almost everyone understands that it's important, even if they're still not entirely sure what it is. Except now they usually call it User Experience Design (UXD or just UX), an umbrella term for any activity or profession that contributes to a better experience for the user.

It's great that there's now so much more emphasis on designing for the user, but all the new job descriptions, subspecialties, and tools that have come along with this evolution have left a lot of people confused about what they should actually *do* about it.

I'll be talking about all three of these changes throughout the book.

# Don't get me wrong...

This edition has new examples, some new principles, and a few things I've learned along the way, but it's still the same book, with the same purpose: It's still a book about designing great, usable Web sites.

And it's also still a book about designing anything that people need to interact with, whether it's a microwave oven, a mobile app, or an ATM.

The basic principles are the same even if the landscape has changed, because usability is about people and how they understand and use things, not about technology. And while technology often changes quickly, people change very slowly.[3]

Or as Jakob Nielsen so aptly put it:

> The human brain's capacity doesn't change from one year to the next, so the insights from studying human behavior have a very long shelf life. What was difficult for users twenty years ago continues to be difficult today.

I hope you enjoy the new edition. And don't forget to wave in a few years when you pass me in your flying car.

STEVE KRUG
NOVEMBER 2013

---

[3] *There's a wonderful Norwegian video (with subtitles) about this that shows a monk getting help as he struggles to use the newfangled "book." (Search for "medieval helpdesk" on YouTube.)*

# Read me first

## THROAT CLEARING AND DISCLAIMERS

*I can't tell you anything you don't already know.*
*But I'd like to clarify a few things.*

—JOE FERRARA, A HIGH SCHOOL FRIEND OF MINE

I have a great job. I'm a usability consultant. Here's what I do:

- People ("clients") send me something they're working on.

  It could be designs for a new Web site they're building, or the URL of a site that they're redesigning, or a prototype of an app.

Web site design by Interval (ThinkInterval.com)

- I try using what they send me, doing the things that their users would need or want to do with it. I note the places where people are likely to get stuck and the things that I think will confuse them (an "expert usability review").

  Sometimes I get other people to try using it while I watch to see where *they* get stuck and confused ("usability testing").

[ 3 ]

- I have a meeting with the client's team to describe the problems I found that are likely to cause users grief ("usability issues") and help them decide which ones are most important to fix and how best to fix them.

Sometimes we work by the phone...

...and sometimes in person

I used to write what I called the "big honking report" detailing my findings, but I finally realized that it wasn't worth the time and effort. A live presentation allows people to ask me questions and voice their concerns—something a written report doesn't do. And for teams doing Agile or Lean development, there's no time for written reports anyway.

- They pay me.

Being a consultant, I get to work on interesting projects with a lot of nice, smart people. I get to work at home most of the time and I don't have to sit in mind-numbing meetings every day or deal with office politics. I get to say what I think, and people usually appreciate it. And I get paid well.

On top of all that, I get a lot of job satisfaction, because when we're finished, the things they're building are almost always much better than when we started.[1]

---

[1] Almost *always. Even when people know about usability problems, they can't always fix them completely, as I'll explain in Chapter 9.*

# The bad news: You probably don't have a usability professional

Almost every development team could use somebody like me to help them build usability into their products. Unfortunately, the vast majority of them can't afford to hire a usability professional.

And even if they could, there aren't enough to go around. At last count there were umpteen billion Web sites (and umpteen billion apps for the iPhone alone[2]) and only about 10,000 usability consultants worldwide. You do the math.

And even if you do have a professional on your team, that person can't possibly look at everything the team produces.

In the last few years, making things more usable has become almost everybody's responsibility. Visual designers and developers now often find themselves doing things like interaction design (deciding what happens next when the user clicks, taps, or swipes) and information architecture (figuring out how everything should be organized).

I wrote this book mainly for people who can't afford to hire (or rent) someone like me.

Knowing some usability principles will help you see the problems yourself—and help keep you from creating them in the first place.

No question: If you can afford to, hire someone like me. But if you can't, I hope this book will enable you to do it yourself (in your copious spare time).

---

[2]  *I'm not quite sure why Apple brags about this. Having thousands of good apps for a platform is a really good thing. Having millions of mediocre apps just means it's really hard to find the good ones.*

# The good news: It's not rocket surgery™

Fortunately, much of what I do is just common sense, and anyone with some interest can learn to do it.

Like a lot of common sense, though, it's not necessarily obvious until *after* someone's pointed it out to you.[3]

I spend a lot of my time telling people things they already know, so don't be surprised if you find yourself thinking "I knew *that*" a lot in the pages ahead.

# It's a thin book

More good news: I've worked hard to keep this book short—hopefully short enough so you can read it on a long plane ride. I did this for two reasons:

- **If it's short, it's more likely to actually be used.**[4] I'm writing for the people who are in the trenches—the designers, the developers, the site producers, the project managers, the marketing people, and the people who sign the checks—and for the one-man-bands who are doing it all themselves.

Usability isn't your life's work, and you don't have time for a long book.

---

3 *...which is one reason why my consulting business is called Advanced Common Sense. "It's not rocket surgery" is my corporate motto.*

4 *There's a good usability principle right there: If something requires a large investment of time—or looks like it will—it's less likely to be used.*

- **You don't need to know everything.** As with any field, there's a lot you *could* learn about usability. But unless you're a usability professional, there's a limit to how much is *useful* for you to learn.[5]

I find that the most valuable contributions I make to each project always come from keeping just a few key usability principles in mind. I think there's a lot more leverage for most people in understanding these principles than in another laundry list of specific do's and don'ts. I've tried to boil down the few things I think everybody involved in design should know about usability.

# Not present at time of photo

Just so you don't waste your time looking for them, here are a few things you won't find in this book:

- **Hard and fast usability rules.** I've been at this for a long time, long enough to know that there is no one "right" answer to most usability questions. Design is a complicated process and the real answer to most of the questions people ask me is "It depends." But I do think that there are a few useful guiding principles it always helps to have in mind, and those are what I'm trying to convey.

- **Predictions about the future of technology and the Web.** Honestly, your guess is as good as mine. The only thing I'm sure of is that (a) most of the predictions I hear are almost certainly wrong, and (b) the things that will turn out to be important will come as a surprise, even though in hindsight they'll seem perfectly obvious.

---

[5] *I've always liked the passage in* A Study in Scarlet *where Dr. Watson is shocked to learn that Sherlock Holmes doesn't know that the earth travels around the sun. Given the finite capacity of the human brain, Holmes explains, he can't afford to have useless facts elbowing out the useful ones:*

> *"What the deuce is it to me? You say that we go round the sun. If we went round the moon it would not make a pennyworth of difference to me or to my work."*

- **Bad-mouthing of poorly designed sites and apps.** If you enjoy people poking fun at things with obvious flaws, you're reading the wrong book. Designing, building, and maintaining a great Web site or app isn't easy. It's like golf: a handful of ways to get the ball in the hole, a million ways not to. Anyone who gets it even half right has my admiration.

As a result, you'll find that the examples I use tend to be from excellent products with minor flaws. I think you can learn more from looking at good designs than bad ones.

# Now with Mobile!

One of the dilemmas I faced when updating this book was that it's always been a book about designing usable Web sites. Even though the principles apply to the design of anything people have to interact with (including things like election ballots and voting booths, and even PowerPoint presentations), its focus was clearly on Web design, and all the examples were from Web sites. Until recently, that's what most people were working on.

But now there are a lot of people designing mobile apps, and even the people working on Web sites have to create versions of them that work well on mobile devices. I know they're very interested in how all of this applies to them.

So I did three things:

- Included mobile examples wherever it made sense

- Added a new chapter about some mobile-specific usability issues

- And the most important one: Added "and Mobile" to the subtitle on the cover

And as you'll see, in some places where it made things clearer, instead of "Web site" I've written "Web site or mobile app." In most cases, though, I used the Web-centric wording to keep things from getting cumbersome and distracting.

# One last thing, before we begin

One crucial thing, really: My definition of usability.

You'll find a lot of different definitions of usability, often breaking it down into attributes like

- **Useful:** Does it do something people need done?

- **Learnable:** Can people figure out how to use it?

- **Memorable:** Do they have to relearn it each time they use it?

- **Effective:** Does it get the job done?

- **Efficient:** Does it do it with a reasonable amount of time and effort?

- **Desirable:** Do people want it?

and recently even

- **Delightful:** Is using it enjoyable, or even fun?

I'll talk about these later. But to me, the important part of the definition is pretty simple. If something is usable—whether it's a Web site, a remote control, or a revolving door—it means that

> A person of average (or even below average) ability and experience can figure out how to use the thing to accomplish something without it being more trouble than it's worth.

Take my word for it: It's really that simple.

I hope this book will help you build better products and—if it lets you skip a few of the endless arguments about design—maybe even get home in time for dinner once in a while.

# Don't make me think!

## KRUG'S FIRST LAW OF USABILITY

*Michael, why are the drapes open?*

—KAY CORLEONE IN *THE GODFATHER, PART II*

P eople often ask me:

> "What's the most important thing I should do if I want to make sure
> my site or app is easy to use?"

The answer is simple. It's not "Nothing important should ever be more than two
clicks away" or "Speak the user's language" or "Be consistent."

It's...

## "Don't make me think!"

For as long I can remember, I've been telling people that this is my first law of
usability.

It's the overriding principle—the ultimate tie breaker when deciding whether a
design works or it doesn't. If you have room in your head for only one usability
rule, make this the one.

For instance, it means that as far as is humanly possible, when I look at a Web
page it should be self-evident. Obvious. Self-explanatory.

I should be able to "get it"—what it is and how to use it—without expending any
effort thinking about it.

Just how self-evident are we talking about?

Well, self-evident enough, for instance, that your next door neighbor, who has
no interest in the subject of your site and who barely knows how to use the Back
button, could look at your Home page and say, "Oh, it's a ___." (With any luck,
she'll say, "Oh, it's a ___. Great!" But that's another subject.)

Think of it this way:

When I'm looking at a page that doesn't make me think, all the thought balloons over my head say things like "OK, there's the___. And that's a ___. And there's the thing that I want."

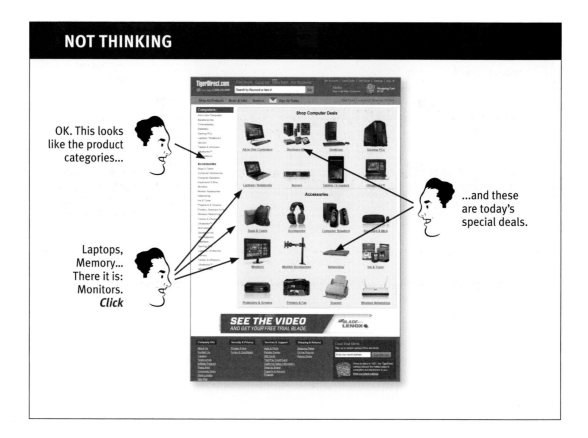

But when I'm looking at a page that makes me think, all the thought balloons over my head have question marks in them.

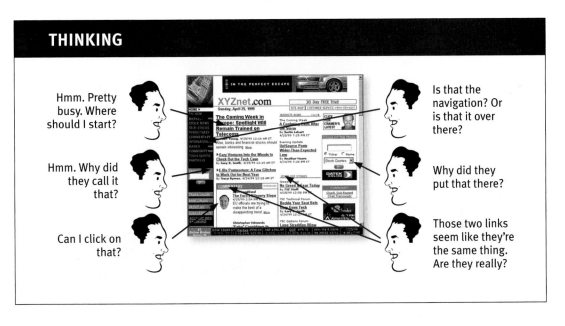

**THINKING**

Hmm. Pretty busy. Where should I start?

Hmm. Why did they call it that?

Can I click on that?

Is that the navigation? Or is that it over there?

Why did they put that there?

Those two links seem like they're the same thing. Are they really?

When you're creating a site, your job is to get rid of the question marks.

# Things that make us think

All kinds of things on a Web page can make us stop and think unnecessarily. Take names, for example. Typical culprits are cute or clever names, marketing-induced names, company-specific names, and unfamiliar technical names.

For instance, suppose a friend tells me that XYZ Corp is looking to hire someone with my exact qualifications, so I head off to their Web site. As I scan the page for something to click, the name they've chosen for their job listings section makes a difference.

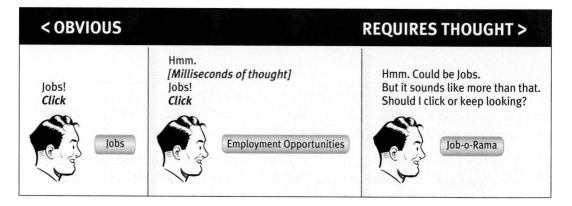

Note that these things are always on a continuum somewhere between "Obvious to everybody" and "Truly obscure," and there are always tradeoffs involved.

For instance, "Jobs" may sound too undignified for XYZ Corp, or they may be locked into "Job-o-Rama" because of some complicated internal politics or because that's what it's always been called in their company newsletter.[1] My main point is that the tradeoffs should usually be skewed further in the direction of "Obvious" than we think.

---

[1] *There's almost always a plausible rationale—and a good, if misguided, intention—behind every usability flaw.*

Another needless source of question marks over people's heads is links and buttons that aren't obviously clickable. As a user, I should never have to devote a millisecond of thought to whether things are clickable—or not.

You may be thinking, "Well, it really doesn't matter that much. If you click or tap it and nothing happens, what's the big deal?"

The point is that every question mark adds to our cognitive workload, distracting our attention from the task at hand. The distractions may be slight but they add up, especially if it's something we do all the time like deciding what to click on.

And as a rule, people don't *like* to puzzle over how to do things. They enjoy puzzles in their place—when they want to be entertained or diverted or challenged—but not when they're trying to find out what time their dry cleaner closes. The fact that the people who built the site didn't care enough to make things obvious—and easy—can erode our confidence in the site and the organization behind it.

#### CHAPTER 1

Another example from a common task: booking a flight.

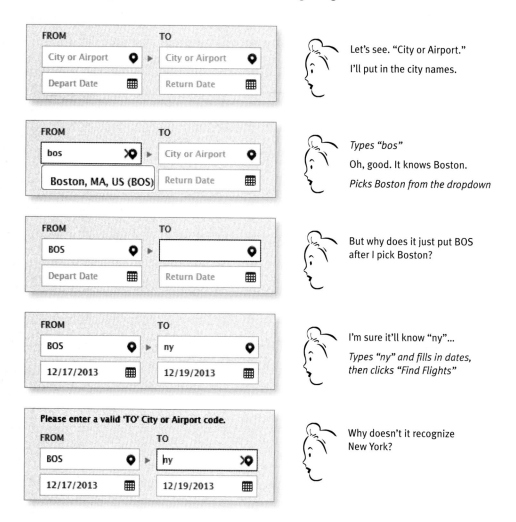

Granted, most of this "mental chatter" takes place in a fraction of a second, but you can see that it's a pretty noisy process, with a lot of question marks. And then there's a puzzling error at the end.

Another site just takes what I type and gives me choices that make sense, so it's hard to go wrong.

*Starts typing "bos" and gets a list of choices*

*Starts typing "ny" and gets a list of choices*

Good.

No question marks. No mental chatter. And no errors.

I could list dozens of things that users shouldn't spend their time thinking about, like

- Where am I?
- Where should I begin?
- Where did they put ___?
- What are the most important things on this page?
- Why did they call it that?
- Is that an ad or part of the site?

But the last thing you need is another checklist to add to your stack of design checklists. The most important thing you can do is to understand the basic principle of eliminating question marks. When you do, you'll begin to notice all the things that make *you* think in the sites and apps *you* use. And eventually you'll learn to recognize and avoid them in the things you're building.

# You can't make everything self-evident

Your goal should be for each page or screen to be self-evident, so that just by looking at it the average user[2] will know what it is and how to use it. In other words, they'll "get it" without having to think about it.

Sometimes, though, particularly if you're doing something original or groundbreaking or something that's inherently complicated, you have to settle for *self-explanatory*. On a self-explanatory page, it takes a *little* thought to "get it"— but only a little. The appearance of things (like size, color, and layout), their well-chosen names, and the *small* amounts of carefully crafted text should all work together to create a sense of nearly effortless understanding.

Here's the rule: If you can't make something self-evident, you at least need to make it self-explanatory.

# Why is all of this so important?

Oddly enough, not for the reason people usually cite:

On the Internet, the competition is always just one click away, so if you frustrate users they'll head somewhere else.

It's true that there's a lot of competition out there. Especially in things like mobile apps, where there are often many readily available (and equally attractive) alternatives, and the cost of changing horses is usually negligible (99 cents or even "Free").

---

[2] *The actual Average User is kept in a hermetically sealed vault at the International Bureau of Standards in Geneva. We'll get around to talking about the best way to think about the "average user" eventually.*

But it's not *always* true that people are fickle. For instance:

- They may have no choice but to stick with it, if it's their only option (e.g., a company intranet, or their bank's mobile app, or the only site that sells the rattan they're looking for).

- You'd be surprised at how long some people will tough it out on sites that frustrate them, often blaming themselves and not the site. There's also the "I've waited ten minutes for this bus already, so I may as well hang in a little longer" phenomenon.

- Besides, who's to say that the competition will be any less frustrating?

## So why, then?

Making every page or screen self-evident is like having good lighting in a store: it just makes everything seem better. Using a site that doesn't make us think about unimportant things feels effortless, whereas puzzling over things that don't matter to us tends to sap our energy and enthusiasm—and time.

But as you'll see in the next chapter when we examine how we really use the Web, the main reason why it's important not to make me think is that most people are going to spend far less time looking at the pages we design than we'd like to imagine.

As a result, if Web pages are going to be effective, they have to work most of their magic at a glance. And the best way to do this is to create pages that are self-evident, or at least self-explanatory.

# 2

# How we *really* use the Web

SCANNING, SATISFICING, AND MUDDLING THROUGH

*Why are things always in the last place you look for them?*
*Because you stop looking when you find them!*

—CHILDREN'S RIDDLE

In all the time I've spent watching people use the Web, the thing that has struck me most is the difference between how we think people use Web sites and how they actually use them.

When we're creating sites, we act as though people are going to pore over each page, reading all of our carefully crafted text, figuring out how we've organized things, and weighing their options before deciding which link to click.

What they actually do most of the time (if we're lucky) is *glance* at each new page, scan *some* of the text, and click on the first link that catches their interest or vaguely resembles the thing they're looking for. There are almost always large parts of the page that they don't even look at.

We're thinking "great literature" (or at least "product brochure"), while the user's reality is much closer to "billboard going by at 60 miles an hour."

## WHAT WE DESIGN FOR...   THE REALITY...

Read

Read

Read

Read

[Pause for reflection]

Finally. click on carefully chosen link

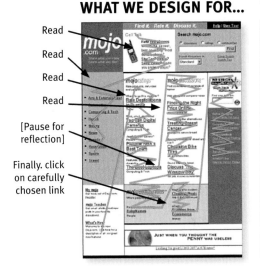

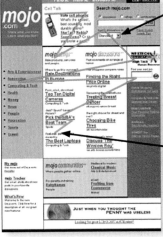

Look around feverishly for anything that

a) is interesting, or vaguely resembles what you're looking for, and

b) is clickable.

As soon as you find a halfway-decent match, click.

If it doesn't pan out, click the Back button and try again.

As you might imagine, it's a little more complicated than this, and it depends on the kind of page, what the user is trying to do, how much of a hurry she's in, and so on. But this simplistic view is much closer to reality than most of us imagine.

It makes sense that we picture a more rational, attentive user when we're designing pages. It's only natural to assume that everyone uses the Web the same way we do, and—like everyone else—we tend to think that our own behavior is much more orderly and sensible than it really is.

If you want to design effective Web pages, though, you have to learn to live with three facts about real-world Web use.

## FACT OF LIFE #1:
# We don't read pages. We scan them.

One of the very few well-documented facts about Web use is that people tend to spend very little time *reading* most Web pages. Instead, we scan (or skim) them, looking for words or phrases that catch our eye.

The exception, of course, is pages that contain documents like news stories, reports, or product descriptions, where people will revert to reading—but even then, they're often alternating between reading and scanning.

Why do we scan?

- **We're usually on a mission.** Most Web use involves trying to get something done, and usually done quickly. As a result, Web users tend to act like sharks: They have to keep moving, or they'll die. We just don't have the time to read any more than necessary.

- **We know we don't *need* to read everything.** On most pages, we're really only interested in a fraction of what's on the page. We're just looking for the bits that match our interests or the task at hand, and the rest of it is irrelevant. Scanning is how we find the relevant bits.

- **We're good at it.** It's a basic skill: When you learn to read, you also learn to scan. We've been scanning newspapers, magazines, and books—or if you're under 25, probably reddit, Tumblr, or Facebook—all our lives to find the parts we're interested in, and we know that it works.

The net effect is a lot like Gary Larson's classic Far Side cartoon about the difference between what we say to dogs and what they hear. In the cartoon, the dog (named Ginger) appears to be listening intently as her owner gives her a serious talking-to about staying out of the garbage. But from the dog's point of view, all he's saying is "blah blah GINGER blah blah blah blah GINGER blah blah blah."

What we see when we look at a page depends on what we have in mind, and it's usually just a fraction of what's there.

Like Ginger, we tend to focus on words and phrases that seem to match (a) the task at hand or (b) our current or ongoing personal interests. And of course, (c) the trigger words that are hardwired into our nervous systems, like "Free," "Sale," and "Sex," and our own name.

FACT OF LIFE #**2**:

# We don't make optimal choices.
# We satisfice.

When we're designing pages, we tend to assume that users will scan the page, consider all of the available options, and choose the best one.

In reality, though, most of the time we *don't* choose the best option—we choose the *first reasonable option*, a strategy known as satisficing.[1] As soon as we find a link that seems like it might lead to what we're looking for, there's a very good chance that we'll click it.

I'd observed this behavior for years, but its significance wasn't really clear to me until I read Gary Klein's book *Sources of Power: How People Make Decisions*.

Klein spent many years studying naturalistic decision making: how people like firefighters, pilots, chessmasters, and nuclear power plant operators make high-stakes decisions in real situations with time pressure, vague goals, limited information, and changing conditions.

Klein's team of observers went into their first study (of field commanders at fire scenes) with the generally accepted model of rational decision making: Faced with a problem, a person gathers information, identifies the possible solutions, and chooses the best one. They started with the hypothesis that because of the high stakes and extreme time pressure, fire captains would be able to compare only two options, an assumption they thought was conservative.

As it turned out, the fire commanders didn't compare *any* options. They took the first reasonable plan that came to mind and did a quick mental test for possible problems. If they didn't find any, they had their plan of action.

---

[1]  *Economist Herbert Simon coined the term (a cross between satisfying and sufficing) in* Models of Man: Social and Rational *(Wiley, 1957).*

So why don't Web users look for the best choice?

- **We're usually in a hurry.** And as Klein points out, "Optimizing is hard, and it takes a long time. Satisficing is more efficient."

- **There's not much of a penalty for guessing wrong.** Unlike firefighting, the penalty for guessing wrong on a Web site is usually only a click or two of the Back button, making satisficing an effective strategy. (Back is the most-used button in Web browsers.)

- **Weighing options may not improve our chances.** On poorly designed sites, putting effort into making the best choice doesn't really help. You're usually just as well off going with your first guess and using the Back button if it doesn't work out.

- **Guessing is more fun.** It's less work than weighing options, and if you guess right, it's faster. And it introduces an element of chance—the pleasant possibility of running into something surprising and good.

Of course, this is not to say that users never weigh options before they click. It depends on things like their frame of mind, how pressed they are for time, and how much confidence they have in the site.

**FACT OF LIFE #3:**

# We don't figure out how things work. We muddle through.

One of the things that becomes obvious as soon as you do any usability testing—whether you're testing Web sites, software, or household appliances—is the extent to which people use things all the time without understanding how they work, or with completely wrong-headed ideas about how they work.

Faced with any sort of technology, very few people take the time to read instructions. Instead, we forge ahead and muddle through, making up our own vaguely plausible stories about what we're doing and why it works.

It often reminds me of the scene at the end of *The Prince and the Pauper* where the real prince discovers that the look-alike pauper has been using the Great Seal of England as a nutcracker in his absence. (It makes perfect sense—to him, the seal is just this great big, heavy chunk of metal.)

*The Prince and the Pauper (Classics Illustrated)*

And the fact is, we get things done that way. I've seen lots of people use software, Web sites, and consumer products effectively in ways that are nothing like what the designers intended.

Take the Web browser, for instance—a crucial part of Internet use. To people who build Web sites, it's an application that you use to view Web pages. But if you ask users what a browser is, a surprisingly large percentage will say something like "It's what I use to search...to find things" or "It's the search engine." Try it yourself: ask some family members what a Web browser is. You may be surprised.

Many people use the Web extensively without knowing that they're using a browser. What they know is you type something in a box and stuff appears.[2] But it doesn't matter to them: They're muddling through and using the thing successfully.

And muddling through is not limited to beginners. Even technically savvy users often have surprising gaps in their understanding of how things work. (I wouldn't be surprised if even Mark Zuckerberg and Sergey Brin have some bits of technology in their lives that they use by muddling through.)

Why does this happen? *you don't have to know how a clock works to get the time*

- **It's not important to us.** For most of us, it doesn't matter to us whether we understand how things work, as long as we can use them. It's not for lack of intelligence, but for lack of caring. It's just not important to us.[3]

- **If we find something that works, we stick to it.** Once we find something that works—no matter how badly—we tend not to look for a better way. We'll use a better way if we stumble across one, but we seldom look for one.

---

[2] *Usually a box with the word "Google" next to it. A lot of people think Google is the Internet.*

[3] *Web developers often have a particularly hard time understanding—or even believing—that people might feel this way, since they themselves are usually keenly interested in how things work.*

It's always interesting to watch designers and developers observe their first usability test. The first time they see a user click on something completely inappropriate, they're surprised. (For instance, when the user ignores a nice big fat "Software" button in the navigation bar, saying something like, "Well, I'm looking for software, so I guess I'd click here on 'Cheap Stuff' because cheap is always good.") The user may even find what he's looking for eventually, but by then the people watching don't know whether to be happy or not.

The second time it happens, they're yelling "Just click on 'Software'!" The third time, you can see them thinking: "Why are we even bothering?"

And it's a good question: If people manage to muddle through so much, does it really matter whether they "get it"? The answer is that it matters a great deal because while muddling through may work sometimes, it tends to be inefficient and error-prone.

On the other hand, if users "get it":

- There's a much better chance that they'll find what they're looking for, which is good for them and for you.

- There's a better chance that they'll understand the full range of what your site has to offer—not just the parts that they stumble across.

- You have a better chance of steering them to the parts of your site that you want them to see.

- They'll feel smarter and more in control when they're using your site, which will bring them back. You can get away with a site that people muddle through only until someone builds one down the street that makes them feel smart.

# If life gives you lemons...

By now you may be thinking (given this less than rosy picture of your audience and how they use the Web), "Why don't I just get a job at the local 7-Eleven? At least there my efforts *might* be appreciated."

So, what's a girl to do?

I think the answer is simple: If your audience is going to act like you're designing billboards, then design great billboards.

# 3

# Billboard
# Design 101

## DESIGNING FOR SCANNING, NOT READING

Faced with the fact that your users are whizzing by, there are some important things you can do to make sure they see and understand as much of what they need to know—and of what you *want* them to know—as possible:

- Take advantage of conventions

- Create effective visual hierarchies

- Break pages up into clearly defined areas

- Make it obvious what's clickable

- Eliminate distractions

- Format content to support scanning

## Conventions are your friends

One of the best ways to make almost anything easier to grasp in a hurry is to follow the existing conventions—the widely used or standardized design patterns. For example:

- **Stop signs.** Given how crucial it is that drivers see and recognize them at a glance, at a distance, in all kinds of weather and lighting conditions, it's a really good thing that all stop signs look the same. (Some of the specifics may vary from country to country, but overall they're remarkably consistent around the world.)

  The convention includes a distinctive shape, the word for "Stop," a highly visible color that contrasts with most natural surroundings, and standardized size, height, and location.

- **Controls in cars.** Imagine trying to drive a rental car if the gas pedal wasn't always to the right of the brake pedal, or the horn wasn't always on the steering wheel.

In the past twenty years, many conventions for Web pages have evolved. As users, we've come to have a lot of expectations about

- **Where things will be located on a page.** For example, users expect the logo identifying the site to be in the top-left corner (at least in countries where reading is left-to-right) and the primary navigation to be across the top or down the left side.

- **How things work.** For example, almost all sites that sell products use the metaphor of a shopping cart and a very similar series of forms for specifying things like your method of payment, your shipping address, and so on.

- **How things look.** Many elements have a standardized appearance, like the icon that tells you it's a link to a video, the search icon, and the social networking sharing options.

Conventions have also evolved for different *kinds* of sites—commerce, colleges, blogs, restaurants, movies, and many more—since all the sites in each category have to solve the same set of problems.

SomeSlightlyIrregular.com

cityislandmovie.com

These conventions didn't just come out of thin air: They all started life as somebody's bright idea. If an idea works well enough, other sites imitate it and eventually enough people have seen it in enough places that it needs no explanation.

Want proof that conventions help? See how much you know about this page—even if you can't understand a word of it—just because it follows some conventions.

When applied well, Web conventions make life easier for users because they don't have to constantly figure out what things are and how they're supposed to work as they go from site to site.

One problem with conventions, though: Designers are often reluctant to take advantage of them.

Faced with the prospect of following a convention, there's a great temptation for designers to try reinventing the wheel instead, largely because they feel (not incorrectly) that they've been hired to do something new and different, not the same old thing. Not to mention the fact that praise from peers, awards, and high-profile job offers are rarely based on criteria like "best use of conventions."

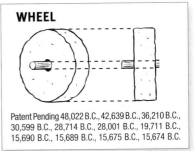

**WHEEL**

Patent Pending 48,022 B.C., 42,639 B.C., 36,210 B.C., 30,599 B.C., 28,714 B.C., 28,001 B.C., 19,711 B.C., 15,690 B.C., 15,689 B.C., 15,675 B.C., 15,674 B.C.

Occasionally, time spent reinventing the wheel results in a revolutionary new rolling device. But usually it just amounts to time spent reinventing the wheel.

If you're going to innovate, you have to understand the value of what you're replacing (or as Dylan put it, "To live outside the law, you must be honest"), and it's easy to underestimate just how much value conventions provide. The classic example is custom scrollbars. Whenever a designer decides to create scrollbars from scratch—usually to make them prettier—the results almost always make it obvious that the designer never thought about how many hundreds or thousands of hours of fine tuning went into the evolution of the standard operating system scrollbars.

If you're not going to use an existing Web convention, you need to be sure that what you're replacing it with either (a) is so clear and self-explanatory that there's no learning curve—so it's as good as the convention, or (b) adds so much value that it's worth a small learning curve.

My recommendation: Innovate when you *know* you have a better idea, but take advantage of conventions when you don't. ⟳

Don't get me wrong: I'm not in any way trying to discourage creativity. I love innovative and original Web design.

One of my favorite examples is Harlem.org. The whole site is built around Art Kane's famous photo of 57 jazz musicians, taken on the steps of a brownstone in Harlem in August 1957. Instead of text links or menus, you use the photo to navigate the site.

Clicking on any area of the photo...    identifies the people there and...    lets you click on them to see their bios.

Not only is it innovative and fun, but it's easy to understand and use. And the creators were smart enough to understand that the fun might wear off after a while so they also included a more conventional category-based navigation.

You can also browse the musicians by name, instrument, or jazz style.

The rule of thumb is that you can—and *should*—be as creative and innovative as you want, and add as much aesthetic appeal as you can, *as long as you make sure it's still usable*.

And finally, a word about consistency.

You often hear consistency cited as an absolute good. People win a lot of design arguments just by saying "We can't do that. It wouldn't be consistent."

Consistency *is* always a good thing to strive for within your site or app. If your navigation is always in the same place, for instance, I don't have to think about it or waste time looking for it. But there will be cases where things will be clearer if you make them *slightly* inconsistent.

Here's the rule to keep in mind:

CLARITY TRUMPS CONSISTENCY

If you can make something *significantly* clearer by making it *slightly* inconsistent, choose in favor of clarity.

# Create effective visual hierarchies

Another important way to make pages easy to grasp in a hurry is to make sure that the appearance of the things on the page—all of the visual cues—accurately portray the relationships between the things on the page: which things are most important, which things are similar, and which things are part of other things. In other words, each page should have a clear visual hierarchy.

Pages with a clear visual hierarchy have three traits:

- **The more important something is, the more prominent it is.** The most important elements are either larger, bolder, in a distinctive color, set off by more white space, or nearer the top of the page—or some combination of the above.

- **Things that are related logically are related visually.** For instance, you can show that things are similar by grouping them together under a heading, displaying them in the same visual style, or putting them all in a clearly defined area.

- **Things are "nested" visually to show what's part of what.** For instance, a site section name ("Computer Books") would appear above the titles of the individual books, reflecting the fact that the books are part of the section. And each book title in turn would span all the elements that make up the description of that book.

There's nothing new about visual hierarchies. Every newspaper page, for instance, uses prominence, grouping, and nesting to give us useful information about the contents of the page before we read a word. *This* picture goes with *this* story because they're both spanned by this headline. *This* story is the most important because it has the biggest headline and a prominent position on the page.

The headline spanning these four columns makes it obvious that they're all part of the same story.

The size of this headline makes it clear at a glance that this is the most important story.

We all parse visual hierarchies every day, but it happens so quickly that the only time we're even vaguely aware that we're doing it is when we *can't* do it—when the visual cues (or absence of them) force us to think.

A good visual hierarchy saves us work by preprocessing the page for us, organizing and prioritizing its contents in a way that we can grasp almost instantly.

But when a page doesn't have a clear visual hierarchy—if everything looks equally important, for instance—we're reduced to the much slower process of scanning the page for revealing words and phrases and then trying to form our own sense of what's important and how things are organized. It's a lot more work.

Parsing a page with a visual hierarchy that's even slightly flawed—where a heading spans things that aren't part of it, for instance—is like reading a carelessly constructed sentence ("Bill put the cat on the table for a minute because it was a little wobbly").

This flawed visual hierarchy suggests that all the major sections of the site are part of the Computer Books subsection.

Putting the heading where it belongs makes the relationship clearer.

Even though we can usually figure out what the sentence is supposed to mean, it still throws us momentarily and forces us to think when we shouldn't have to.

# Break up pages into clearly defined areas

Ideally, on any well-designed Web page users can play a variation of the old TV game show *$25,000 Pyramid*.[1] Glancing around, they should be able to point at the different areas of the page and say, "Things I can do on this site!" "Links to today's top stories!" "Products this company sells!" "Things they're eager to sell me!" "Navigation to get to the rest of the site!"

Dividing the page into clearly defined areas is important because it allows users to decide quickly which areas of the page to focus on and which areas they can safely ignore. Eye-tracking studies of Web page scanning suggest that users decide very quickly in their initial glances which parts of the page are likely to have useful information and then rarely look at the other parts—almost as though they weren't there. (Banner blindness—the ability of users to completely ignore areas they think will contain ads—is just the extreme case.)

---

[1] Contestants had to get their partners to guess a category like "Things a plumber uses" by giving them examples ("a wrench, a pipe cutter, pants that won't stay up...").

# Make it obvious what's clickable

Since a large part of what people are doing on the Web is looking for the next thing to click, it's important to make it easy to tell what's clickable.

As we scan a page, we're looking for a variety of visual cues that identify things as clickable (or "tappable" on touch screens)—things like shape (buttons, tabs, etc.), location (in a menu bar, for instance), and formatting (color and underlining).[2]

This process of looking for clues in the appearance of things that tell us how to use them isn't limited to Web pages. As Don Norman explains so enjoyably in his recently updated usability classic *The Design of Everyday Things*, we're constantly parsing our environment (like the handles on doors) for these clues (to decide whether to pull or push). Read it. You'll never look at doors the same way again.

Easily identifying what's clickable on a page has waxed and waned as a problem since the beginning of the Web.

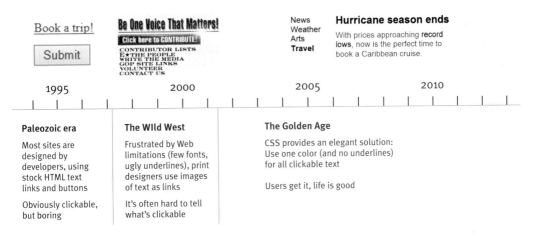

| Paleozoic era | The Wild West | The Golden Age |
|---|---|---|
| Most sites are designed by developers, using stock HTML text links and buttons | Frustrated by Web limitations (few fonts, ugly underlines), print designers use images of text as links | CSS provides an elegant solution: Use one color (and no underlines) for all clickable text |
| Obviously clickable, but boring | It's often hard to tell what's clickable | Users get it, life is good |

---

2 *People also rely on the fact that the cursor in a Web browser changes from an arrow to a hand when you point it at a link, but this requires deliberately moving the cursor around, a relatively slow process. Also, it doesn't work on touch screens because they don't have a cursor.*

It's currently resurfacing as an issue in mobile design, though, as you'll see in Chapter 10.

In general, you'll be fine if you just stick to one color for all text links or make sure that their shape and location identify them as clickable. Just don't make silly mistakes like using the same color for links and nonclickable headings.

# Keep the noise down to a dull roar

One of the great enemies of easy-to-grasp pages is visual noise.

Users have varying tolerances for complexity and distractions; some people have no problem with noisy pages, but many find them downright annoying. Users have even been known to put Post-its on their screen to cover up animation that's distracting them while they're trying to read.

There are really three different kinds of noise:

- **Shouting.** When everything on the page is clamoring for your attention, the effect can be overwhelming: Lots of invitations to buy! Lots of exclamation points, different typefaces, and bright colors! Automated slideshows, animation, pop-ups, and the never-ending array of new attention-grabbing ad formats!

  The truth is, *everything* can't be important. Shouting is usually the result of a failure to make tough decisions about which elements are really the most important and then create a visual hierarchy that guides users to them first.

- **Disorganization.** Some pages look like a room that's been ransacked, with things strewn everywhere. This is a sure sign that the designer doesn't understand the importance of using grids to align the elements on a page.

- **Clutter.** We've all seen pages—especially Home pages—that just have too much *stuff.* The net effect is the same as when your email inbox is flooded with things like newsletters from sites that have decided that your one contact with them has made you lifelong friends: It's hard to find and focus on the messages you actually care about. You end up with what engineers call a low signal-to-noise ratio: Lots of noise, not much information, and the noise obscures the useful stuff.

When you're editing your Web pages, it's probably a good idea to start with the assumption that *everything* is visual noise (the "presumed guilty until proven innocent" approach) and get rid of anything that's not making a real contribution. In the face of limited time and attention, everything that's not part of the solution must go.

# Format text to support scanning

Much of the time—perhaps most of the time—that users spend on your Web pages is spent scanning the text in search of something.

The way your text is formatted can do a lot to make it easier for them.

Here are the most important things you can do to make your pages scan-friendly:

Which one would you rather scan?

- **Use plenty of headings.** Well-written, thoughtful headings interspersed in the text act as an informal outline or table of contents for a page. They tell you what each section is about or, if they're less literal, they intrigue you. Either way they help you decide which parts to read, scan, or skip.

In general, you'll want to use more headings than you'd think and put more time into writing them.

[ 39 ]

Also, be sure to format headings correctly. Two very important things about the styling of headings that people often overlook:

If you're using more than one level of heading, make sure there's an obvious, impossible-to-miss visual distinction between them. You can do this by making each higher level larger or by leaving more space above it.

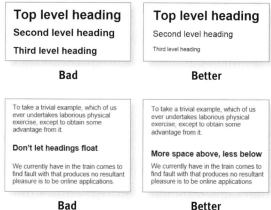

Even more important: Don't let your headings float. Make sure they're closer to the section they introduce than to the section they follow. This makes a huge difference.

- **Keep paragraphs short.** Long paragraphs confront the reader with what Caroline Jarrett and Ginny Redish call a "wall of words." They're daunting, they make it harder for readers to keep their place, and they're harder to scan than a series of shorter paragraphs.

  You may have been taught that each paragraph has to have a topic sentence, detail sentences, and a conclusion, but reading online is different. Even single-sentence paragraphs are fine.

  If you examine a long paragraph, you'll almost always find that there's a reasonable place to break it in two. Get in the habit of doing it.

- **Use bulleted lists.** Think of it this way: Almost anything that *can* be a bulleted list probably *should* be. Just look at your paragraphs for any series of items separated by commas or semicolons and you'll find likely candidates.

  And for optimal readability, there should be a small amount of additional space between the items in the list.

- **Highlight key terms.** Much page scanning consists of looking for key words and phrases. Formatting the most important ones in bold where they first appear in the text makes them easier to find. (If they're already text links, you obviously don't have to.) Don't highlight too many things, though, or the technique will lose its effectiveness.

If you really want to learn about making content scannable (or about anything related to writing for screens in general), run, do not walk, to an Internet-connected device and order Ginny Redish's book *Letting Go of the Words*.

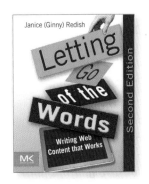

And while you're at it, order a copy for anyone you know who writes, edits, or has anything to do with creating digital content. They'll end up eternally indebted to you.

# 4

# Animal, Vegetable, or Mineral?

## WHY USERS LIKE MINDLESS CHOICES

*It doesn't matter how many times I have to click, as long*
*as each click is a mindless, unambiguous choice.*

—KRUG'S SECOND LAW OF USABILITY

Web designers and usability professionals have spent a lot of time over the years debating how many times you can expect users to click (or tap) to get what they want without getting too frustrated. Some sites even have design rules stating that it should never take more than a specified number of clicks (usually three, four, or five) to get to any page in the site.

On the face of it, "number of clicks to get anywhere" seems like a useful metric. But over time I've come to think that what really counts is not the number of clicks it takes me to get to what I want (although there are limits), but rather how *hard* each click is—the amount of thought required and the amount of uncertainty about whether I'm making the right choice.

In general, I think it's safe to say that users don't mind a lot of clicks *as long as each click is painless and they have continued confidence that they're on the right track*—following what's often called the "scent of information."[1] Links that clearly and unambiguously identify their target give off a strong scent that assures users that clicking them will bring them nearer to their "prey." Ambiguous or poorly worded links do not.

I think the rule of thumb might be something like "three mindless, unambiguous clicks equal one click that requires thought."[2]

---

[1]  *This term comes from Peter Pirolli and Stuart Card's "information foraging" research at Xerox PARC in which they drew parallels between people seeking information ("informavores") and animals following the scent of their prey.*

[2]  *Of course, there are exceptions. For instance, if I'm going to have to drill down through the same path in a site repeatedly, or if the pages are going to take a long time to load, then the value of fewer clicks increases.*

The classic first question in the word game Twenty Questions—"Animal, vegetable, or mineral?"—is a wonderful example of a mindless choice. As long as you accept the premise that anything that's not a plant or an animal—including things as diverse as pianos, limericks, and cheesecake, for instance—falls under "mineral," it requires almost no thought to answer the question correctly.[3]

Unfortunately, many choices on the Web aren't as clear.

For example, as recently as a few years ago when I was trying to buy a product or service to use in my home office (like a printer, for instance), most of the manufacturers' sites asked me to make a top-level choice like this:

Which one was me? I had to think about it, and even when I made my choice I wasn't very confident it was the right one. In fact, what I had to look forward to when the target page finally loaded was even *more* thinking to figure out whether I was in the right place.

It was the feeling I get when I'm standing in front of two mailboxes labeled Stamped Mail and Metered Mail with a business reply card in my hand. What do *they* think it is—stamped or metered? And what happens if I drop it in the wrong box?

---

[3] *In case you've forgotten the game, there's an excellent version that you can play against at www.20q.net. Created by Robin Burgener, it uses a neural net algorithm and plays a mean game.*

Here's another example:

I'm trying to read an article online. The page I arrive at gives me all these options:

| Already a Magazine Subscriber But Not an Online Member? | Already an Online Member? | Not a Member or Subscriber Yet? |
|---|---|---|
| **Create/Access Your Account Now** (You only need to do this once) | **Log in using your email address and password** | **Get FREE Access Online Instantly!** |
| Enter 6-digit Account Number: [____] | Enter Email Address: [____] | • Subscribe to the print magazine (Quirk's Marketing Research Review) |
| Enter Last Name: [____] | Enter Password: [____] | • Gain access to all the articles in our online database |
| *Continue* » | ☐ Keep me logged in. | • Post and reply to research discussion groups |
| Where can I find my account number? | *Log In* » | • Create and post job openings |
| | Did you forget your password? | • Send RFP's |
| | | *Continue* » |

Now I've got to scan all this text and work out whether I'm a subscriber but not a member, or a member, or neither one. And then I'll have to dig up the account number or the password that I used or decide whether it's worth joining.

At this point, the question I'm asking myself is probably changing from "How do I answer this question?" to "Just how interested am I in this article?"

*The New York Times* makes the same kind of choice seem much easier by not confronting you with all the details at once. Making an initial selection (to log in or to see your options for subscribing) takes you to another screen where you see only the relevant questions or information for that selection.

This problem of giving the user difficult choices and questions that are hard to answer happens all the time in forms. Caroline Jarrett has an entire chapter about it ("Making Questions Easy to Answer") in her book *Forms that Work: Designing Web Forms for Usability.*

As with Ginny Redish's book about writing for the Web, anyone who works on forms should have a well-worn copy sitting on their desk.

# Some assistance may be required

Life is complicated, though, and some choices really aren't simple.

When you can't avoid giving me a difficult choice, you need to go out of your way to give me as much guidance as I need—but no more.

This guidance works best when it's

- **Brief:** The smallest amount of information that will help me

- **Timely:** Placed so I encounter it exactly when I need it

- **Unavoidable:** Formatted in a way that ensures that I'll notice it

Examples are tips adjacent to form fields, "What's this?" links, and even tool tips.

My favorite example of this kind of just-in-time guidance is found on street corners throughout London.

It's brief ("LOOK RIGHT" and an arrow pointing right), timely (you see it at the instant you need to be reminded), and unavoidable (you almost always glance down when you're stepping off a curb).

I have to think it's saved the lives of a lot of tourists who expect traffic to be coming from the other direction. (I know it saved mine once.)

Whether you need to offer some help or not, the point is that we face choices all the time on the Web and making those choices mindless is one of the most important things you can do to make a site easy to use.

# 5

# Omit ~~needless~~ words

## THE ART OF NOT WRITING FOR THE WEB

O f the five or six things that I learned in college, the one that has stuck with me the longest—and benefited me the most—is E. B. White's seventeenth rule in *The Elements of Style:*

### 17. Omit needless words.

> Vigorous writing is concise. A sentence should contain no unnecessary words, a paragraph no unnecessary sentences, for the same reason that a drawing should have no unnecessary lines and a machine no unnecessary parts.[1]

When I look at most Web pages, I'm struck by the fact that most of the words I see are just taking up space, because no one is ever going to read them. And just by being there, all the extra words suggest that you may actually *need* to read them to understand what's going on, which often makes pages seem more daunting than they actually are.

My Third Law probably sounds excessive, because it's meant to. Removing half of the words is actually a realistic goal; I find I have no trouble getting rid of half the words on most Web pages without losing anything of value. But the idea of removing half of what's left is just my way of trying to encourage people to be ruthless about it.

Getting rid of all those words that no one is going to read has several beneficial effects:

- It reduces the noise level of the page.

- It makes the useful content more prominent.

- It makes the pages shorter, allowing users to see more of each page at a glance without scrolling.

---

[1] *William Strunk, Jr., and E. B. White,* The Elements of Style *(Allyn and Bacon, 1979).*

I'm not suggesting that the articles at WebMD.com or the stories on NYTimes.com should be shorter than they are. But certain kinds of writing tend to be particularly prone to excess.

# Happy talk must die

We all know happy talk when we see it: It's the introductory text that's supposed to welcome us to the site and tell us how great it is or to tell us what we're about to see in the section we've just entered.

If you're not sure whether something is happy talk, there's one sure-fire test: If you listen very closely while you're reading it, you can actually hear a tiny voice in the back of your head saying, "Blah blah blah blah blah...."

A lot of happy talk is the kind of self-congratulatory promotional writing that you find in badly written brochures. Unlike good promotional copy, it conveys no useful information, and it focuses on saying how great we are, as opposed to explaining what makes us great.

Although happy talk is sometimes found on Home pages—usually in paragraphs that start with the words "Welcome to..."—its favored habitat is the front pages of the sections of a site ("section fronts"). Since these pages are often just a list of links to the pages in the section with no real content of their own, there's a temptation to fill them with happy talk. Unfortunately, the effect is as if a book publisher felt obligated to add a paragraph to the table of contents page saying, "This book contains many interesting chapters about ___, ___, and ___. We hope you enjoy them."

Happy talk is like small talk—content-free, basically just a way to be sociable. But most Web users don't have time for small talk; they want to get right to the point. You can—and should—eliminate as much happy talk as possible.

# Instructions must die

Another major source of needless words is instructions. The main thing you need to know about instructions is that no one is going to read them—at least not until after repeated attempts at "muddling through" have failed. And even then, if the instructions are wordy, the odds of users finding the information they need are pretty low.

Your objective should always be to eliminate instructions entirely by making everything self-explanatory, or as close to it as possible. When instructions are absolutely necessary, cut them back to the bare minimum.

*Similar to comments in code*

For example, here are the instructions I found at the beginning of a site survey:

> The following questionnaire is designed to provide us with information that will help us improve the site and make it more relevant to your needs. Please select your answers from the drop-down menus and radio buttons below. The questionnaire should only take you 2–3 minutes to complete.
>
> At the bottom of this form you can choose to leave your name, address, and telephone number. If you leave your name and number, you may be contacted in the future to participate in a survey to help us improve this site.
>
> If you have comments or concerns that require a response please contact Customer Service.
>
> **1. How many times have you visited this site?**
>
> This is my first visit ∨

I think some aggressive pruning makes them much more useful:

## BEFORE: 103 WORDS

The following questionnaire is designed to provide us with information that will help us improve the site and make it more relevant to your needs.

The first sentence is just introductory happy talk. I know what a survey is for; all I need is the words "help us" to show me that they understand that I'm doing them a favor by filling it out.

Please select your answers from the drop-down menus and radio buttons below.

Most users don't need to be told how to fill in a Web form, and the ones who do won't know what a "drop-down menu" and a "radio button" are anyway.

The questionnaire should only take you 2-3 minutes to complete.

At this point, I'm still trying to decide whether to bother with this questionnaire, so knowing that it's short is useful information.

At the bottom of this form you can choose to leave your name, address, and telephone number. If you leave your name and number, you may be contacted in the future to participate in a survey to help us improve this site.

This instruction is of no use to me at this point. It belongs at the end of the questionnaire where I can act on it. As it is, its only effect is to make the instructions look daunting.

If you have comments or concerns that require a response please contact Customer Service.

The fact that I shouldn't use this form if I want an answer is useful and important information. Unfortunately, though, they don't bother telling me how I contact Customer Service—or, better still, giving me a link so I can do it from right here.

## AFTER: 34 WORDS

Please help us improve the site by taking 2-3 minutes to complete this survey.

NOTE: If you have comments or concerns that require a response, don't use this form. Instead, please contact Customer Service.

# And now for something completely different

In these first few chapters, I've been trying to convey some guiding principles that I think are good to have in mind when you're building a Web site.

Now we're heading into two chapters that look at how these principles apply to two of the biggest and most important challenges in Web design: navigation and the Home page.

You might want to pack a lunch. They're very long chapters.

# 6

# Street signs and Breadcrumbs

## DESIGNING NAVIGATION

*And you may find yourself | in a beautiful house | with a beautiful wife*
*And you may ask yourself | Well... | How did I get here?!*

—TALKING HEADS, "ONCE IN A LIFETIME"

I t's a fact:

*People won't use your Web site if they can't find their way around it.*

You know this from your own experience as a Web user. If you go to a site and can't find what you're looking for or figure out how the site is organized, you're not likely to stay long—or come back. So how do you create the proverbial "clear, simple, and consistent" navigation?

# Scene from a mall

Picture this: It's Saturday afternoon and you're headed for the mall to buy a chainsaw.

As you walk through the door at Sears, you're thinking, "Hmmm. Where do they keep chainsaws?" As soon as you're inside, you start looking at the department names, high up on the walls. (They're big enough that you can read them from all the way across the store.)

"Hmmm," you think, "Tools? Or Lawn and Garden?" It could be either one, but you've got to start somewhere so you head in the direction of Tools.

When you reach the Tools department, you start looking at the signs at the end of each aisle.

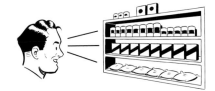

When you think you've got the right aisle, you start looking at the individual products.

If it turns out you've guessed wrong, you try another aisle, or you may back up and start over again in the Lawn and Garden department. By the time you're done, the process looks something like this:

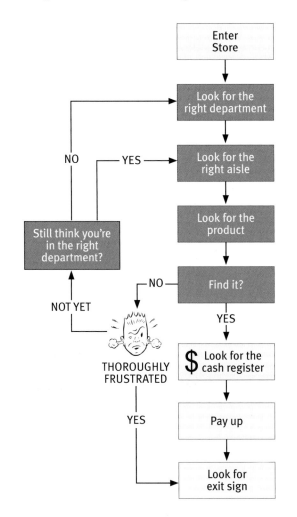

Basically, you use the store's navigation systems (the signs and the organizing hierarchy that the signs embody) and your ability to scan shelves full of products to find what you're looking for.

Of course, the actual process is a little more complex. For one thing, as you walk in the door you usually devote a few microseconds to a crucial decision: Are you going to start by looking for chainsaws on your own or are you going to ask someone where they are?

It's a decision based on a number of variables—how familiar you are with the store, how much you trust their ability to organize things sensibly, how much of a hurry you're in, and even how sociable you are.

When we factor this decision in, the process looks something like this:

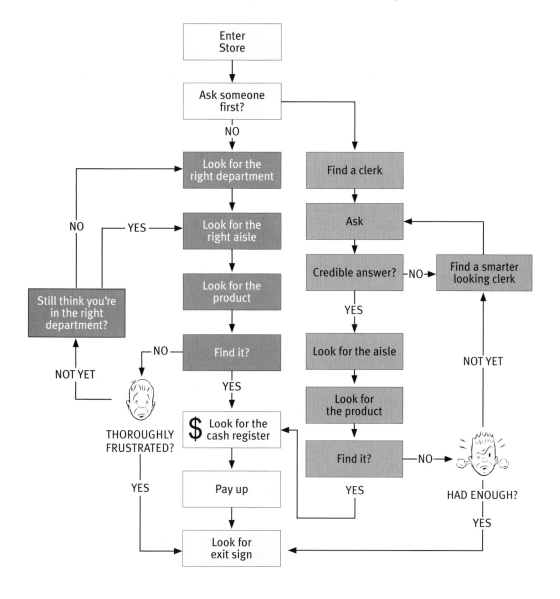

Note that even if you start looking on your own, if things don't pan out there's a good chance that eventually you'll end up asking someone for directions anyway.

# Web Navigation 101

In many ways, you go through the same process when you enter a Web site.

- **You're usually trying to find something.** In the "real" world it might be the emergency room or a family-size bottle of ketchup. On the Web, it might be a pair of headphones or the name of the actor in Casablanca who played the headwaiter at Rick's.[1]

- **You decide whether to ask first or browse first.** The difference is that on a Web site there's no one standing around who can tell you where things are. The Web equivalent of asking directions is searching—typing a description of what you're looking for in a search box and getting back a list of links to places where it *might* be.

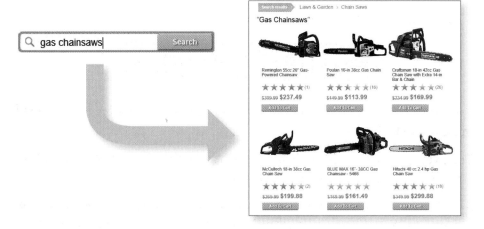

Some people (Jakob Nielsen calls them "search-dominant" users) will almost always look for a search box as soon as they enter a site. (These may be the same people who look for the nearest clerk as soon as they enter a store.)

---

[1]  *S. Z. "Cuddles" Sakall, born Eugene Sakall in Budapest in 1884. Ironically, most of the character actors who played the Nazi-hating denizens of Rick's Café were actually famous European stage and screen actors who landed in Hollywood after fleeing the Nazis.*

Other people (Nielsen's "link-dominant" users) will almost always browse first, searching only when they've run out of likely links to click or when they have gotten sufficiently frustrated by the site.

For everyone else, the decision whether to start by browsing or searching depends on their current frame of mind, how much of a hurry they're in, and whether the site appears to have decent browsable navigation.

- **If you choose to browse, you make your way through a hierarchy, using signs to guide you.** Typically, you'll look around on the Home page for a list of the site's main sections (like the store's department signs) and click on the one that seems right.

Then you'll choose from the list of subsections.

With any luck, after another click or two you'll end up with a list of the kind of thing you're looking for.

Then you can click on the individual links to examine them in detail, the same way you'd take products off the shelf and read the labels.

- **Eventually, if you can't find what you're looking for, you'll leave.** This is as true on a Web site as it is at Sears. You'll leave when you're convinced they haven't got it or when you're just too frustrated to keep looking.

Here's what the process looks like:

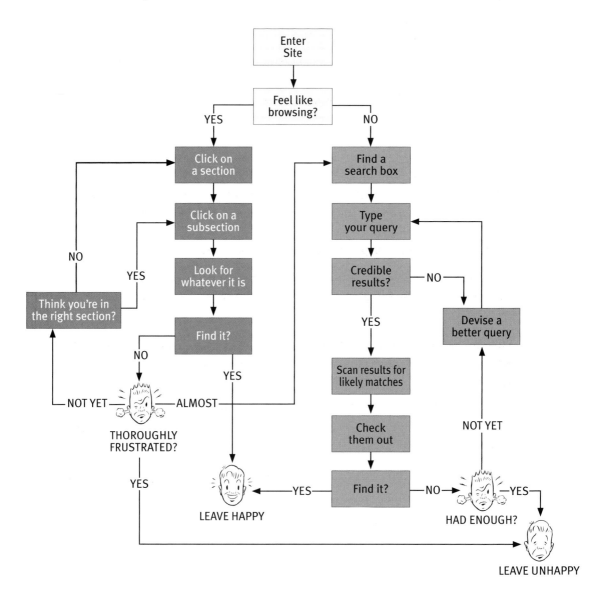

# The unbearable lightness of browsing

Looking for things on a Web site and looking for them in the "real" world have a lot of similarities. When we're exploring the Web, in some ways it even *feels* like we're moving around in a physical space. Think of the words we use to describe the experience—like "cruising," "browsing," and "surfing." And clicking a link doesn't "load" or "display" another page—it "takes you to" a page.

But the Web experience is missing many of the cues we've relied on all our lives to negotiate spaces. Consider these oddities of Web space:

- **No sense of scale.** Even after we've used a Web site extensively, unless it's a very small site we tend to have very little sense of how big it is (50 pages? 1,000? 17,000?).[2] For all we know, there could be huge corners we've never explored. Compare this to a magazine, a museum, or a department store, where you always have at least a rough sense of the seen/unseen ratio.

  The practical result is that it's very hard to know whether you've seen everything of interest to you in a site, which means it's hard to know when to stop looking.[3]

- **No sense of direction.** In a Web site, there's no left and right, no up and down. We may talk about moving up and down, but we mean up and down in the hierarchy—to a more general or more specific level.

- **No sense of location.** In physical spaces, as we move around we accumulate knowledge about the space. We develop a sense of where things are and can take shortcuts to get to them.

  We may get to the chainsaws the first time by following the signs, but the next time we're just as likely to think,

  > "Chainsaws? Oh, yeah, I remember where they were: right rear corner, near the refrigerators."

---

[2] *Even the people who manage Web sites often have very little idea how big their sites really are.*

[3] *This is one reason why it's useful for links that we've already clicked on to display in a different color. It gives us some small sense of how much ground we've covered.*

And then head straight to them.

**FIRST TIME**  **SUBSEQUENT VISITS**

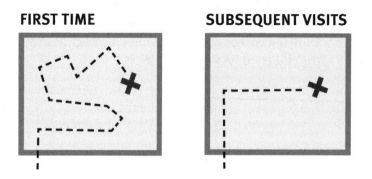

But on the Web, your feet never touch the ground; instead, you make your way around by clicking on links. Click on "Power Tools" and you're suddenly teleported to the Power Tools aisle with no traversal of space, no glancing at things along the way.

When we want to return to something on a Web site, instead of relying on a *physical* sense of where it is we have to remember where it is in the conceptual hierarchy and retrace our steps.

This is one reason why bookmarks—stored personal shortcuts—are so important, and why the Back button is the most used button in Web browsers.

It also explains why the concept of Home pages is so important. Home pages are—comparatively—fixed places. When you're in a site, the Home page is like the North Star. Being able to click Home gives you a fresh start.

This lack of physicality is both good and bad. On the plus side, the sense of weightlessness can be exhilarating and partly explains why it's so easy to lose track of time on the Web—the same as when we're "lost" in a good book.

On the negative side, I think it explains why we use the term "Web navigation" even though we never talk about "department store navigation" or "library navigation." If you look up navigation in a dictionary, it's about doing two things: getting from one place to another, and figuring out where you are.

I think we talk about Web navigation because "figuring out where you are" is a much more pervasive problem on the Web than in physical spaces. We're inherently lost when we're on the Web, and we can't peek over the aisles to see where we are. Web navigation compensates for this missing sense of place by embodying the site's hierarchy, creating a sense of "there."

Navigation isn't just a *feature* of a Web site; it is the Web site, in the same way that the building, the shelves, and the cash registers are Sears. Without it, there's no there there.

The moral? Web navigation had better be good.

# The overlooked purposes of navigation

Two of the purposes of navigation are fairly obvious: to help us find whatever it is we're looking for and to tell us where we are.

But navigation has some other equally important—and easily overlooked—functions:

- **It tells us what's here.** By making the hierarchy visible, navigation tells us what the site contains. Navigation reveals content! And revealing the site may be even more important than guiding or situating us.

- **It tells us how to use the site.** If the navigation is doing its job, it tells you *implicitly* where to begin and what your options are. Done correctly, it should be all the instructions you need. (Which is good, since most users will ignore any other instructions anyway.)

- **It gives us confidence in the people who built it.** Every moment we're in a Web site, we're keeping a mental running tally: "Do these guys know what they're doing?" It's one of the main factors we use in deciding whether to bail out and deciding whether to ever come back. Clear, well-thought-out navigation is one of the best opportunities a site has to create a good impression.

# Web navigation conventions

Physical spaces like cities and buildings (and even information spaces like books and magazines) have their own navigation systems, with conventions that have evolved over time like street signs, page numbers, and chapter titles. The conventions specify (loosely) the appearance and location of the navigation elements so we know what to look for and where to look when we need them.

Putting them in a standard place lets us locate them quickly, with a minimum of effort; standardizing their appearance makes it easy to distinguish them from everything else.

*not in MA*

For instance, we expect to find street signs at street corners, we expect to find them by looking up (not down), and we expect them to look like street signs (horizontal, not vertical).

We also take it for granted that the name of a building will be above or next to its front door. In a grocery store, we expect to find signs near the ends of each aisle. In a magazine, we know there will be a table of contents somewhere in the first few pages and page numbers somewhere in the margin of each page—and that they'll look like a table of contents and page numbers.

Think of how frustrating it is when one of these conventions is broken (when magazines don't put page numbers on advertising pages, for instance).

Although their appearance can vary significantly, these are the basic navigation conventions for the Web:

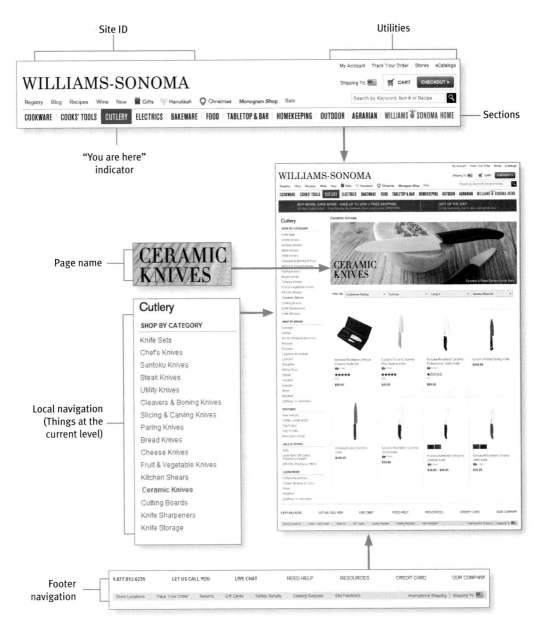

Site ID

Utilities

Sections

"You are here" indicator

Page name

Local navigation (Things at the current level)

Footer navigation

# Don't look now, but I think it's following us

Web designers use the term *persistent navigation* (or *global navigation*) to describe the set of navigation elements that appear on every page of a site.

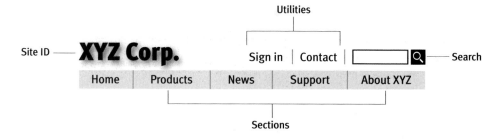

Done right, persistent navigation should say—preferably in a calm, comforting voice:

> *"The navigation is over here. Some parts will change a little depending on where you are, but it will always be here, and it will always work the same way."*

Just having the navigation appear in the same place on every page with a consistent look gives you instant confirmation that you're still in the same site—which is more important than you might think. And keeping it the same throughout the site means that (hopefully) you only have to figure out how it works once.

Persistent navigation should include the four elements you most need to have on hand at all times:

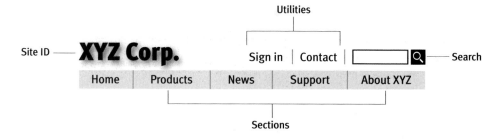

We'll look at each of them in a minute. But first...

# Did I say every page?

I lied. There is one exception to the "follow me everywhere" rule: forms.

On pages where a form needs to be filled in, the persistent navigation can sometimes be an unnecessary distraction. For instance, when I'm paying for my purchases on an e-commerce site, you don't really want me to do anything but finish filling in the forms. The same is true when I'm registering, subscribing, giving feedback, or checking off personalization preferences.

For these pages, it's useful to have a minimal version of the persistent navigation with just the Site ID, a link to Home, and any Utilities that might help me fill out the form.

# Now I know we're not in Kansas

The Site ID or logo is like the building name for a Web site. At Sears, I really only need to see the name on my way in; once I'm inside, I know I'm still in Sears until I leave. But on the Web—where my primary mode of travel is teleportation—I need to see it on every page.

OK. Now I'm in South Park

OK. I'm still in South Park

And now I'm on Facebook

In the same way that we expect to see the name of a building over the front entrance, we expect to see the Site ID at the top of the page—usually in (or at least near) the upper left corner.[4]

Why? Because the Site ID represents the whole site, which means it's the highest thing in the logical hierarchy of the site.

> This site
> Sections of this site
> Subsections
> Sub-subsections, etc.
> This page
> Areas of this page
> Items on this page

And there are two ways to get this primacy across in the visual hierarchy of the page: either make it the most prominent thing on the page, or make it frame everything else.

Since you don't want the ID to be the most prominent element on the page (except, perhaps, on the Home page), the best place for it—the place that is least likely to make me think—is at the top, where it frames the entire page.

| Site ID |
| --- |
| Everything else |

And in addition to being where we would expect it to be, the Site ID also needs to *look* like a Site ID. This means it should have the attributes we would expect to see in a brand logo or the sign outside a store: a distinctive typeface and a graphic that's recognizable at any size from a button to a billboard.

---

[4]   *... on Web pages written for left-to-right reading languages.*

# The Sections

The Sections—sometimes called the *primary navigation*—are the links to the main sections of the site: the top level of the site's hierarchy.

In some designs the persistent navigation will also include space to display the *secondary* navigation: the list of subsections in the current section.

In others, pointing at a section name or clicking on it reveals a dropdown menu. And in others, clicking takes you to the front page of the section, where you'll find the secondary navigation.

# The Utilities

Utilities are the links to important elements of the site that aren't really part of the content hierarchy.

These are things that either can help me use the site (like Sign in/Register, Help, a Site Map, or a Shopping Cart) or provide information about its publisher (like About Us and Contact Us).

Like the signs for the facilities in a store, the Utilities list should be slightly less prominent than the Sections.

**Men's Shoes**

Restrooms ▶
◀ Telephones
◀ Customer Service
Gift Wrapping ▶

Utilities will vary for different types of sites. For a corporate or e-commerce site, for example, they might include any of the following:

| | | | |
|---|---|---|---|
| About Us | Downloads | How to Shop | Register |
| Archives | Directory | Jobs | Search |
| Checkout | Forums | My _____ | Shopping Cart |
| Company Info | FAQs | News | Sign in |
| Contact Us | Help | Order Tracking | Site Map |
| Customer Service | Home | Press Releases | Store Locator |
| Discussion Boards | Investor Relations | Privacy Policy | Your Account |

As a rule, the persistent navigation can accommodate only four or five Utilities— the ones users are likely to need most often. If you try to squeeze in more than that, they tend to get lost in the crowd. The less frequently used leftovers belong in the footer: the small text links at the bottom of each page.

# Just click your heels three times and say, "There's no place like home"

One of the most crucial items in the persistent navigation is a button or link that takes me to the site's Home page.

Having a Home button in sight at all times offers reassurance that no matter how lost I may get, I can always start over, like pressing a Reset button or using a "Get out of Jail Free" card.

Almost all Web users expect the Site ID to be a button that can take you to the Home page. I think it's also a good idea to include Home with the main sections of the site.

# A way to search

Given the power of searching and the number of people who prefer searching to browsing, unless a site is very small and very well organized, every page should have either a search box or a link to a search page. And unless there's very little reason to search your site, it should be a search box.

Keep in mind that for a large percentage of users their first official act when they reach a new site will be to scan the page for something that matches one of these three patterns:

It's a simple formula: a box, a button, and either the word "Search" or the universally recognized magnifying glass icon. Don't make it hard for them—stick to the formula. In particular, avoid

- **Fancy wording.** They'll be looking for the word "Search," so use the word Search, not Find, Quick Find, Quick Search, or Keyword Search. (If you use "Search" as the label for the box, use the word "Go" as the button name.)

- **Instructions.** If you stick to the formula, anyone who has used the Web for more than a few days will know what to do. Adding "Type a keyword" is like saying, "Leave a message at the beep" on your voice mail message: There was a time when it was necessary, but now it just makes you sound clueless.

- **Options.** If there is any possibility of confusion about the *scope* of the search (what's being searched: the site, part of the site, or the whole Web), by all means spell it out.

But think very carefully before giving me options to limit the scope (to search just the current section of the site, for instance). And also be wary of providing options for how I specify what I'm searching for (search by title or by author, for instance, or search by part number or by product name).

I seldom see a case where the potential payoff for adding options to the persistent search box is worth the cost of making me figure out what the options are and whether I need to use them (i.e., making me think).

If you want to give me the option to scope the search, give it to me when it's useful—when I get to the search results page and discover that searching everything turned up far too many hits, so I *need* to limit the scope.

# Secondary, tertiary, and whatever comes after tertiary

It's happened so often I've come to expect it: When designers I haven't worked with before send me preliminary page designs so I can check for usability issues, I almost inevitably get a flowchart that shows a site four levels deep...

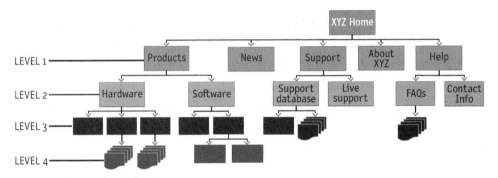

...and sample pages for the Home page and the top *two* levels.

Home | Second-level page | Subsection page

I keep flipping the pages looking for more, or at least for the place where they've scrawled "Some magic happens here," but I never find even that. I think this is one of the most common problems in Web design (especially in larger sites): failing to give the lower-level navigation the same attention as the top. In so many sites, as soon as you get past the second level, the navigation breaks down and becomes *ad hoc*. The problem is so common that it's actually hard to find good examples of third-level navigation.

Why does this happen?

Partly, I think, because good multi-level navigation is just plain hard to design— given the limited amount of space on the page and the number of elements that have to be squeezed in.

Partly because designers usually don't even have enough time to figure out the first two levels.

Partly because it just doesn't seem that important. (After all, how important can it be? It's not primary. It's not even secondary.) And there's a tendency to think that by the time people get that far into the site, they'll understand how it works.

And then there's the problem of getting sample content and hierarchy examples for lower-level pages. Even if designers ask, they probably won't get them, because the people responsible for the content usually haven't thought things through that far, either.

But the reality is that users usually end up spending as much time on lower-level pages as they do at the top. And unless you've worked out top-to-bottom navigation from the beginning, it's very hard to graft it on later and come up with something consistent.

The moral? It's vital to have sample pages that show the navigation for all the potential levels of the site before you start arguing about the color scheme.

# Page names, or Why I love to drive in L.A.

If you've ever spent time in Los Angeles, you understand that it's not just a song lyric—L.A. really *is* a great big freeway. And because people in L.A. take driving seriously, they have the best street signs I've ever seen. In L.A.,

- **Street signs are big.** When you're stopped at an intersection, you can read the sign for the next cross street.

- **They're in the right place**—hanging over the street you're driving on, so all you have to do is glance up.

Now, I'll admit I'm a sucker for this kind of treatment because I come from Boston, where you consider yourself lucky if you can manage to read the street sign while there's still time to make the turn.

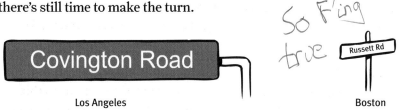

So F'ing true

Los Angeles                                      Boston

The result? When I'm driving in L.A., I devote less energy and attention to dealing with where I am and more to traffic, conversation, and listening to *All Things Considered*. I love driving in L.A.

Page names are the street signs of the Web. Just as with street signs, when things are going well I may not notice page names at all. But as soon as I start to sense that I may not be headed in the right direction, I need to be able to spot the page name effortlessly so I can get my bearings.

There are four things you need to know about page names:

- **Every page needs a name.** Just as every corner should have a street sign, every page should have a name.

Designers sometimes think, "Well, we've highlighted the page name in the navigation. That's good enough." It's a tempting idea because it can save space, and it's one less element to work into the page layout, but it's not enough. You need a page name, too.

- **The name needs to be in the right place.** In the visual hierarchy of the page, the page name should appear to be framing the content that is unique to this page. (After all, that's what it's naming—not the navigation or the ads, which are just the infrastructure.)

- **The name needs to be prominent.** You want the combination of position, size, color, and typeface to make the name say "This is the heading for the entire page." In most cases, it will be the largest text on the page.

- **The name needs to match what I clicked.** Even though nobody ever mentions it, every site makes an implicit social contract with its visitors:

  *The name of the page will match the words I clicked to get there.*

In other words, if I click on a link or button that says "Hot mashed potatoes," the site will take me to a page named "Hot mashed potatoes."

It may seem trivial, but it's actually a crucial agreement. Each time a site violates it, I'm forced to think, even if only for milliseconds, "Why are those two things different?" And if there's a major discrepancy between the link name and the page name or a lot of minor discrepancies, my trust in the site—and the competence of the people who publish it—will be diminished.

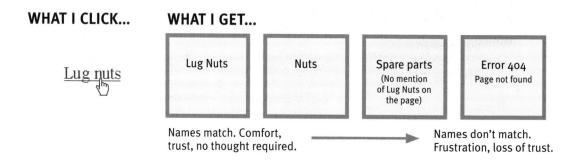

**WHAT I CLICK...**

Lug nuts

**WHAT I GET...**

| Lug Nuts | Nuts | Spare parts (No mention of Lug Nuts on the page) | Error 404 Page not found |

Names match. Comfort, trust, no thought required. ——→ Names don't match. Frustration, loss of trust.

Of course, sometimes you have to compromise, usually because of space limitations. If the words I click on and the page name don't match exactly, the important thing is that (a) they match as closely as possible, and (b) the reason for the difference is obvious. For instance, if I click buttons labeled "Gifts for Him" and "Gifts for Her" and get pages titled "Gifts for Men" and "Gifts for Women," even though the wording isn't identical they feel so equivalent that I'm not going to think about the difference.

# "You are here"

One of the ways navigation can counteract the Web's inherent "lost in space" feeling is by showing me where I am in the scheme of things, the same way that a "You are here" indicator does on the map in a shopping mall—or a National Park.

On the Web, this is accomplished by highlighting my current location in whatever navigation bars, lists, or menus appear on the page.

| Living room | Bedroom | Kitchen & Appliances | Children's IKEA |
| --- | --- | --- | --- |
| Mattresses | Beds | Bedroom storage | Lighting | Textiles & rugs |

Looks like I'm in bedroom lighting

In this example, the current section (Bedroom) and subsection (Lighting) have both been "marked."

There are a number of ways to make the current location stand out:

| Put a pointer next to it | Change the text color | Use bold text | Reverse the button | Change the button color |
|---|---|---|---|---|
| **Sports** | **Sports** | Sports | **Sports** | Sports |
| **Business** | **Business** | Business | **Business** | Business |
| ▸ **Entertainment** | Entertainment | **Entertainment** | **Entertainment** | **Entertainment** |
| **Politics** | **Politics** | Politics | **Politics** | Politics |

The most common failing of "You are here" indicators is that they're too subtle. They need to stand out; if they don't, they lose their value as visual cues and end up just adding more noise to the page. One way to ensure that they stand out is to apply more than one visual distinction—for instance, a different color *and* bold text.

Too-subtle visual cues are actually a very common problem. Designers love subtle cues, because subtlety is one of the traits of sophisticated design. But Web users are generally in such a hurry that they routinely miss subtle cues.

In general, if you're a designer and you think a visual cue is sticking out like a sore thumb, it probably means you need to make it twice as prominent.

# Breadcrumbs

Like "You are here" indicators, Breadcrumbs show you where you are.

They're called Breadcrumbs because they're reminiscent of the trail of crumbs Hansel dropped in the woods so he and Gretel could find their way back home.[5]

Breadcrumbs show you the path from the Home page to where you are and make it easy to move back up to higher levels in the hierarchy of a site.

For a long time, Breadcrumbs were an oddity, found only in sites that were really just enormous databases with very deep hierarchies. But these days they show up in more and more sites, sometimes in lieu of well-thought-out navigation.

---

[5] *In the original story, H & G's stepmother persuades their father to lose them in the forest during lean times so the whole family won't have to starve. The suspicious and resourceful H spoils the plot by dropping pebbles on the way in and following them home. But the next time (!) H is forced to use breadcrumbs instead, which prove to be a less-than-suitable substitute since birds eat them before H & G can retrace their steps. Eventually the tale devolves into attempted cannibalism, grand larceny, and immolation, but basically it's a story about how unpleasant it is to be lost.*

Done right, Breadcrumbs are self-explanatory, they don't take up much room, and they provide a convenient, consistent way to do two of the things you need to do most often: back up a level or go Home. They're most useful in a large site with a deep hierarchy.

Here are a few best practices for implementing them:

- **Put them at the top.** Breadcrumbs seem to work best if they're at the top of the page. I think this is probably because it literally marginalizes them—making them seem like an accessory, like page numbers in a book or magazine.

- **Use > between levels.** Trial and error seems to have shown that the best separator between levels is the "greater than" character (>), probably because it visually suggests forward motion down through the levels.

- **Boldface the last item.** The last item in the list should be the name of the current page, and making it bold gives it the prominence it deserves. And because it's the page that you're on, naturally it's not a link.

# Three reasons why I *still* love tabs

I haven't been able to prove it (yet), but I strongly suspect that Leonardo da Vinci invented tab dividers sometime in the late 15th century. As interface devices go, they're clearly a product of genius.

Tabs are one of the very few cases where using a physical metaphor in a user interface actually works. Like the tab dividers in a three-ring binder or tabs on folders in a file drawer, they divide whatever they're sticking out of into sections. And they make it easy to open a section by reaching for its tab (or, in the case of the Web, clicking on it).

I think they're an excellent and underused navigation choice. Here's why I like them:

- **They're self-evident.** I've never seen anyone—no matter how "computer illiterate"—look at a tabbed interface and say, "Hmmm. I wonder what *those* do?"

- **They're hard to miss.** When I do usability tests, I'm surprised at how often people can overlook horizontal navigation bars at the top of a Web page. But tabs are so visually distinctive that they're hard to overlook. And because they're hard to mistake for anything *but* navigation, they create the kind of obvious-at-a-glance division you want between navigation and content.

- **They're slick.** Web designers are always struggling to make pages more visually interesting. If done correctly, tabs can add polish and serve a useful purpose.

If you're going to use tabs, though, you have to do them right.

For tabs to work to full effect, the graphics have to create the visual illusion that the active tab is in front of the other tabs. This is the main thing that makes them feel like tabs—even more than the distinctive tab shape.

To create this illusion, the active tab needs to be a different color or contrasting shade, and it has to physically connect with the space below it. This is what makes the active tab "pop" to the front.

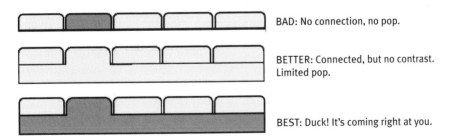

BAD: No connection, no pop.

BETTER: Connected, but no contrast. Limited pop.

BEST: Duck! It's coming right at you.

# Try the trunk test

Now that you have a feeling for all of the moving parts, you're ready to try my acid test for good Web navigation. Here's how it goes:

Imagine that you've been blindfolded and locked in the trunk of a car, then driven around for a while and dumped on a page somewhere deep in the bowels of a Web site. If the page is well designed, when your vision clears you should be able to answer these questions without hesitation:

- What site is this? (Site ID)

- What page am I on? (Page name)

- What are the major sections of this site? (Sections)

- What are my options at this level? (Local navigation)

- Where am I in the scheme of things? ("You are here" indicators)

- How can I search?

Why the *Goodfellas* motif? Because it's so easy to forget that the Web experience is often more like being abducted than following a garden path. When you're designing pages, it's tempting to think that people will reach them by starting at the Home page and following the nice, neat paths you've laid out. But the reality is that we're often dropped down in the middle of a site with no idea where we are because we've followed a link from a search engine, a social networking site, or email from a friend, and we've never seen this site's navigation scheme before.

And the blindfold? You want your vision to be slightly blurry, because the true test isn't whether you can figure it out given enough time and close scrutiny. The standard needs to be that these elements pop off the page so clearly that it doesn't matter whether you're looking closely or not. You want to be relying solely on the overall appearance of things, not the details.

Here's how you perform the trunk test:

**Step 1:** Choose a page anywhere in the site at random, and print it.

**Step 2:** Hold it at arm's length or squint so you can't really study it closely.

**Step 3:** As quickly as possible, try to find and circle each of these items:

- Site ID
- Page name
- Sections (Primary navigation)
- Local navigation
- "You are here" indicator(s)
- Search

Try it on your own site and see how well it works. Then ask some friends to try it, too. You may be surprised by the results.

# 7

# The Big Bang Theory of Web Design

## THE IMPORTANCE OF GETTING PEOPLE OFF ON THE RIGHT FOOT

Designing a Home page often reminds me of the classic TV game show *Beat the Clock*.

Each contestant would listen patiently while emcee Bud Collyer explained the "stunt" she had to perform. For instance, "You have 45 seconds to toss five of these water balloons into the colander strapped to your head."

The stunt always looked tricky, but doable with a little luck.

But then just as the contestant was ready to begin, Bud would always add, "Oh, there's just one more thing: you have to do it...blindfolded." Or "...under water." Or "...in the fifth dimension."

Bud Collyer offers words of encouragement to a plucky contestant

It's that way with the Home page. Just when you think you've covered all the bases, there's always just *one...more...thing*.

Think about all the things the Home page has to accommodate:

- **Site identity and mission.** Right off the bat, the Home page has to tell me what site this is and what it's for—and if possible, why I should be here and not at some other site.

- **Site hierarchy.** The Home page has to give an overview of what the site has to offer—both content ("What can I find here?") and features ("What can I do here?")—and how it's all organized. This is usually handled by the persistent navigation.

- **Search.** Most sites need to have a prominently displayed search box on the Home page.

- **Teases.** Like the cover of a magazine, the Home page needs to entice me with hints of the "good stuff" inside.

- **Content promos** spotlight the newest, best, or most popular pieces of content, like top stories and hot deals.

- **Feature promos** invite me to explore additional sections of the site or try out features.

- **Timely content.** If the site's success depends on my coming back often, the Home page probably needs to have some content that gets updated frequently. And even a site that doesn't need regular visitors needs some signs of life—even if only a link to a recent press release—to signal to me that it's not abandoned or hopelessly outdated.

- **Deals.** Home page space needs to be allocated for whatever advertising, cross-promotion, and co-branding deals have been made.

- **Shortcuts.** The most frequently requested pieces of content (software updates, for instance) may deserve their own links on the Home page so that people don't have to hunt for them.

- **Registration.** If the site uses registration, the Home page needs links or text boxes for new users to register and old users to sign in and a way to let me know that I'm signed in ("Welcome back, Steve Krug").

In addition to these concrete needs, the Home page also has to meet a few abstract objectives:

- **Show me what I'm looking for.** The Home page needs to make it obvious how to get to whatever I want—assuming it's somewhere on the site.

- **...and what I'm *not* looking for.** At the same time, the Home page needs to expose me to some of the wonderful things the site has to offer that I might be interested in—even though I'm not actively looking for them.

- **Show me where to start.** There's nothing worse than encountering a new Home page and having no idea where to begin.

- **Establish credibility and trust.** For some visitors, the Home page will be the only chance your site gets to create a good impression.

# And you have to do it...blindfolded

As if that wasn't daunting enough, it all has to be done under adverse conditions. Some of the usual constraints:

- **Everybody wants a piece of it.** Since it's likely to be the page seen by more visitors than any other—and the only page some visitors will see—things that are prominently promoted on the Home page tend to get significantly greater traffic.

  As a result, the Home page is the waterfront property of the Web: It's the most desirable real estate, and there's a very limited supply. Everybody who has a stake in the site wants a promo or a link to their section on the Home page, and the turf battles for Home page visibility can be fierce. Sometimes when I look at a Home page, I feel like the boy in *The Sixth Sense*: "I see stakeholders."

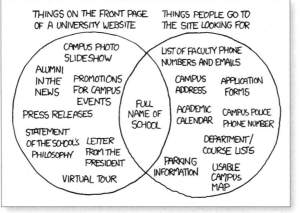

THINGS ON THE FRONT PAGE OF A UNIVERSITY WEBSITE

THINGS PEOPLE GO TO THE SITE LOOKING FOR

CAMPUS PHOTO SLIDESHOW

ALUMNI IN THE NEWS PROMOTIONS FOR CAMPUS EVENTS

PRESS RELEASES

STATEMENT OF THE SCHOOL'S PHILOSOPHY LETTER FROM THE PRESIDENT

VIRTUAL TOUR

FULL NAME OF SCHOOL

LIST OF FACULTY PHONE NUMBERS AND EMAILS

CAMPUS ADDRESS APPLICATION FORMS

ACADEMIC CALENDAR CAMPUS POLICE PHONE NUMBER

DEPARTMENT/ COURSE LISTS

PARKING INFORMATION USABLE CAMPUS MAP

The result of design by stakeholders.

The Venn diagram isn't entirely accurate: Some university sites don't have the full name of the school on the Home page.

"University Website" I xkcd.com

And given the tendency of most users to scan down the page just far enough to find an interesting link, the comparatively small amount of space "above the fold" on the Home page is the *choice* waterfront property, even more fiercely fought over.

- **Too many cooks.** Because the Home page is so important, it's the one page that everybody (even the CEO) has an opinion about.

- **One size fits all.** Unlike lower-level pages, the Home page has to appeal to everyone who visits the site, no matter how diverse their interests.

# The First Casualty of War

Given everything the Home page has to accomplish, if a site is at all complex even the best Home page design can't do it all. Designing a Home page inevitably involves compromise. And as the compromises are worked out and the pressure mounts to squeeze in just one more thing, some things inevitably get lost in the shuffle.

The one thing you can't afford to lose in the shuffle—and the thing that most often gets lost—is **conveying the big picture**. Whenever someone hands me a Home page design to look at, there's one thing I can almost always count on: They haven't made it clear enough *what the site is*.

As quickly and clearly as possible, the Home page needs to answer the four
questions I have in my head when I enter a new site for the first time:

What is this?

What can I
do here?

What do they
have here?

Why should I be
here—and not
somewhere else?

I need to be able to answer these questions at a glance, correctly and
unambiguously, with very little effort.

If it's not clear to me what I'm looking at in the first few seconds, interpreting
everything else on the page is harder, and the chances are greater that I'll
misinterpret something and get frustrated.

But if I do "get it," I'm much more likely to correctly interpret everything I see on
the page, which greatly improves my chances of having a satisfying, successful
experience.

This is what I call the Big Bang Theory of Web Design. Like *the* Big Bang Theory,
it's based on the idea that the first few seconds you spend on a new Web site or
Web page are critical.

We know now from a very elegant experiment (search for "Attention Web Designers: You Have 50 Milliseconds to Make a Good First Impression!") that a lot happens as soon as you open a page. For instance, you take a quick look around (in milliseconds) and form a number of general impressions: Does it look good? Is there a lot of content or a little? Are there clear regions of the page? Which ones attract you?

The most interesting thing about the experiment was that they showed that these initial impressions tended to be very similar to the impressions people had after they actually had a chance to spend time on the page. In other words, we make snap judgments, but they tend to be a pretty reliable predictor of our more reasoned assessments.

This is not to say that our initial understanding of things is always right. In fact, one of the things I've seen most often in usability tests is that people form ideas about what things are and how they work which are just wrong. Then they use these first bits of "knowledge" to help interpret everything they see.

If their first assumptions are wrong ("This is a site for ___"), they begin to try to force-fit that explanation on to everything they encounter. And if it's wrong, they'll end up creating more misinterpretations. If people are lost when they start out, they usually just keep getting...loster.

This is why it's so crucial that you get them off on the right foot, making sure that they're clear on the big picture.

Don't get me wrong: Everything else *is* important. You *do* need to impress me, entice me, direct me, and expose me to your deals. But these things won't slip through the cracks; there will always be plenty of people—inside and outside the development team—seeing to it that they get done. All too often, though, no one has a vested interest in getting the main point across.

½ then ½ again –
you end up hilighting everything

## THE TOP FOUR PLAUSIBLE EXCUSES FOR
## NOT SPELLING OUT THE BIG PICTURE ON THE HOME PAGE

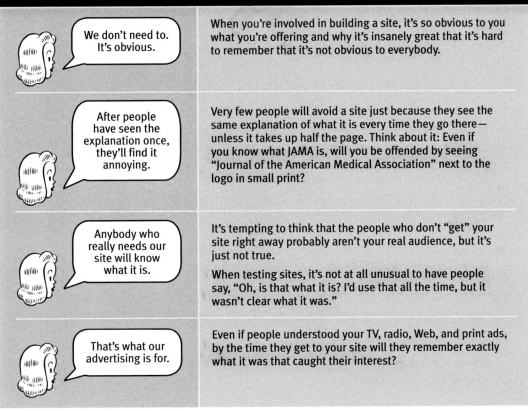

**We don't need to. It's obvious.**

When you're involved in building a site, it's so obvious to you what you're offering and why it's insanely great that it's hard to remember that it's not obvious to everybody.

**After people have seen the explanation once, they'll find it annoying.**

Very few people will avoid a site just because they see the same explanation of what it is every time they go there—unless it takes up half the page. Think about it: Even if you know what JAMA is, will you be offended by seeing "Journal of the American Medical Association" next to the logo in small print?

**Anybody who really needs our site will know what it is.**

It's tempting to think that the people who don't "get" your site right away probably aren't your real audience, but it's just not true.

When testing sites, it's not at all unusual to have people say, "Oh, is that what it is? I'd use that all the time, but it wasn't clear what it was."

**That's what our advertising is for.**

Even if people understood your TV, radio, Web, and print ads, by the time they get to your site will they remember exactly what it was that caught their interest?

# But...the *Home* page? Really?

I know what some of you are thinking:

"Nobody enters a site through the Home page anymore. That's so 2004."

And you're right, of course. Compared to the early days of the Web, the Home page has lost its preeminence. Now people are just as likely—or more likely—to enter your site by clicking on a link in an email, a blog, or something from a social network that takes them directly to a page deep in your site.

Because of this, every page of your site should do as much as it can to orient them properly: to give them the right idea about who you are, what you do, and what your site has to offer.

The problem is, though, there's not much space on most pages to do that well. As a result, many users have formed a new behavior.

People will teleport into the depths of a site and look at the page the link took them to. Very often, though, the next thing they'll do is visit the Home page to get their bearings. (I like to think of it as divers bobbing up to the surface to see where they are.) If the page they went to was interesting, they want to see what else is on the site. If it contained information they need to rely on, they may want to find out who publishes it, and how credible it is.

The Home page is still the place where this happens, and you need to do it well.

# How to get the message across

Everything on the Home page can contribute to our understanding of what the site is. But there are three important places on the page where we expect to find explicit statements of what the site is about.

- **The tagline.** One of the most valuable bits of real estate is the space right next to the Site ID. When we see a phrase that's visually connected to the ID, we know it's meant to be a tagline, and so we read it as a description of the whole site. We'll look at taglines in detail in the next section.

- **The Welcome blurb.** The Welcome blurb is a terse description of the site, displayed in a prominent block on the Home page, usually at the top left or center of the content space so it's the first thing that catches your eye.

- **The "Learn more."** Innovative products and business models tend to require a fair amount of explanation, often more than most people have the patience for. But people have become accustomed to watching short videos on their computers and mobile devices. As a result, people have now come to expect a short explanatory video on most sites and are often willing to watch them.

The point isn't that everyone will use these three elements—or even that everyone will notice them. Most users will probably try to guess what the site is first from the overall content of the Home page. But if they can't guess, you want to have someplace on the page where they can go to find out.

Here are a few guidelines for getting the message across:

- **Use as much space as necessary.** The temptation is to not want to use any space because (a) you can't imagine that anybody doesn't know what this site is, and (b) everyone's clamoring to use the Home page space for other purposes.

  Take Kickstarter.com, for example. Because of their novel proposition, Kickstarter has a lot of 'splainin' to do, so they wisely use a lot of Home page space to do it. Almost every element on the page helps explain or reinforce what the site is about.

*Ricky should have trademarked that*

Kickstarter may not have a tagline (unless it's "Bring creativity to life") but they do put an admirable amount of effort into making sure people understand what they do and how it works.

"What is Kickstarter?" is clearly the most prominent item in the primary navigation.

- **...but don't use any more space than necessary.** For most sites, there's no need to use a lot of space to convey the basic proposition, and messages that take up the entire Home page are usually too much for people to bother absorbing anyway. Keep it short—just long enough to get the point across, and no longer. Don't feel compelled to mention every great feature, just a few of the most important ones.

- **Don't use a mission statement as a Welcome blurb.** Many sites fill their Home page with their corporate mission statement that sounds like it was written by a Miss America finalist. "XYZCorp offers world-class solutions in the burgeoning field of blah blah blah blah blah...." Nobody reads them.

- **It's one of the most important things to test.** You can't trust your own judgment about this. You need to show the Home page to people from outside your organization to tell you whether the design is getting this job done because the "main point" is the one thing nobody inside the organization will notice is missing.

# Nothing beats a good tagline!™

A tagline is a pithy phrase that characterizes the whole enterprise, summing up what it is and what makes it great. Taglines have been around for a long time in advertising, entertainment, and publishing: "Thousands of cars at impossibly low prices," "More stars than there are in the heavens,"[1] and "All the News That's Fit to Print,"[2] for example.

On a Web site, the tagline appears right below, above, or next to the Site ID.

Taglines are a very efficient way to get your message across, because they're the one place on the page where users most expect to find a concise statement of the site's purpose.

*Just Do It*
*The Happiest Place on Earth*
*There are some things money can't buy. For everything else, there's MasterCard*
*The Greatest Casualty is being Forgotten - wounded warrior*
*Wander Wisely*

---

[1] *Metro-Goldwyn-Mayer studios, in the 1930s and '40s.*

[2] The New York Times. *I have to confess a personal preference for the* Mad *magazine parody version, though: "All the News That Fits, We Print."*

Some attributes to look for when choosing a tagline:

- Good taglines are **clear** and **informative** and explain exactly what your site or your organization does.

- Good taglines are **just long enough, but not too long**. Six to eight words seem to be long enough to convey a full thought, but short enough to absorb easily.

- Good taglines **convey differentiation** and a clear benefit. Jakob Nielsen has suggested that a really good tagline is one that no one else in the world could use except you, and I think it's an excellent way to look at it.

- Bad taglines sound **generic**.

NationalGrid can probably get away with using a motto instead of a differentiating tagline, because they're a public utility with a captive audience, so differentiation isn't an issue.

Don't confuse a tagline with a motto, like "We bring good things to life," "You're in good hands," or "To protect and to serve." A motto expresses a guiding principle, a goal, or an ideal, but a tagline conveys a value proposition. Mottoes are lofty and reassuring, but if I don't know what the thing is, a motto isn't going to tell me.

- Good taglines are **personable, lively,** and **sometimes clever**. Clever is good, but only if the cleverness helps convey—not obscure—the benefit.

# Tagline? We don't need no stinking tagline

Some sites can get by without a tagline. For instance:

- The relative handful of sites that have already achieved household word status.

- Sites that are very well known from their offline origins.

Personally, though, I'd argue that even *these* sites would benefit from a tagline. After all, no matter how well known you are, why pass up an unobtrusive chance to tell people why they're better off at your site? And even if a site comes from a strong offline brand, the mission online is never exactly the same and it's important to explain the difference.

# The fifth question

Once I know what I'm looking at, there's still one more important question that the Home page has to answer for me:

Where do I start?

When I enter a new site, after a quick look around the Home page I should be able to say with confidence:

- Here's where to start if I want to search.

- Here's where to start if I want to browse.

- Here's where to start if I want to sample their best stuff.

*or our app*

On sites that are built around a step-by-step process (applying for a mortgage, for instance), the entry point for the process should leap out at me. And on sites where I have to register if I'm a new user or sign in if I'm a returning user, the places where I register or sign in should be prominent.

Unfortunately, the need to promote *everything* (or at least everything that supports this week's business model) sometimes obscures these entry points. It can be hard to find them when the page is full of promos yelling "Start here!" and "No, click *me* first!"

The best way to keep this from happening is to make the entry points look like entry points (i.e., make the search box look like a search box and the list of sections look like a list of sections). It also helps to label them clearly, with labels like "Search," "Browse by Category," "Sign in," and "Start here" (for a step-by-step process).

# Why Golden Geese make such tempting targets

There's something about the Home page that seems to inspire shortsighted behavior. When I sit in on meetings about Home page design, I often find the phrase "killing the golden goose" running through my head.[3]

The worst of these behaviors, of course, is the tendency to try to promote everything.

The problem with promoting things on the Home page is that it works too well. Anything with a prominent Home page link is virtually guaranteed to get more traffic—usually a great deal more—leading all of the site's stakeholders to think, "Why don't I have one?"

---

[3]  *I always thought that the phrase came from the story of Jack and the Beanstalk. In fact, Jack's Giant did have a goose that laid golden eggs, but nobody tried to kill it. The senseless slaughter occurs in one of Aesop's fables, and there's not much to it, plot-wise: Man finds goose, man gets greedy, man kills goose, man gets no more eggs. Moral: "Greed often overreaches itself."*

The problem is, the rewards and the costs of adding more things to the Home page aren't shared equally. The section that's being promoted gets a huge gain in traffic, while the overall loss in effectiveness of the Home page as it gets more cluttered is shared by all sections.

It's a perfect example of the tragedy of the commons.[4] The premise is simple:

*Any shared resource (a "commons") will inevitably be destroyed by overuse.*

Take a town pasture, for example. For each animal a herdsman adds to the common pasture, he receives all proceeds from the sale of the animal—a positive benefit of +1. But the negative impact of adding an animal—its contribution to overgrazing—is shared by all, so the impact on the individual herdsman is less than –1.

The only sensible course for each herdsman is to add another animal to the herd. And another, and another—preferably before someone else does. And since each rational herdsman will reach the same conclusion, the commons is doomed.

Preserving the Home page from promotional overload requires constant vigilance, since it usually happens gradually, with the slow, inexorable addition of just... one...more...thing.

All the stakeholders need to be educated about the danger of overgrazing the Home page and offered other methods of driving traffic, like cross-promoting from other popular pages or taking turns using the same space on the Home page.

---

4  *The concept, originated by nineteenth-century amateur mathematician William Forster Lloyd, was popularized in a classic essay on overpopulation by biologist Garrett Hardin ("The Tragedy of the Commons," Science, December 1968).*

CHAPTER

# 8

# "The Farmer and the Cowman Should Be Friends"

WHY MOST ARGUMENTS ABOUT USABILITY ARE
A WASTE OF TIME, AND HOW TO AVOID THEM

*One man likes to push a plough*
*The other likes to chase a cow*
*But that's no reason why they can't be friends!*

—*OKLAHOMA!*, OSCAR HAMMERSTEIN II

L eft to their own devices, Web teams aren't notoriously successful at making decisions about usability questions. Most teams end up spending a lot of precious time rehashing the same issues over and over.

Consider this scene:

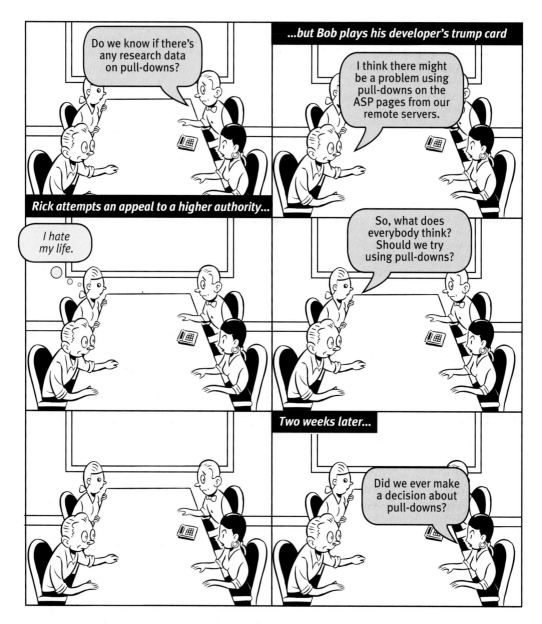

I usually call these endless discussions "religious debates," because they have a lot in common with most discussions of religion and politics: They consist largely of people expressing strongly held personal beliefs about things that can't be proven—supposedly in the interest of agreeing on the best way to do something important (whether it's attaining eternal peace, governing effectively, or just designing Web pages). And, like most religious debates, they rarely result in anyone involved changing his or her point of view.

Besides wasting time, these arguments create tension and erode respect among team members and can often prevent the team from making critical decisions.

Unfortunately, there are several forces at work in most Web teams that make these debates almost inevitable. In this chapter, I'll describe these forces and explain what I think is the best antidote.

## *"Everybody* likes _____."

All of us who work on Web sites have one thing in common—we're also Web users. And like all Web users, we tend to have strong feelings about what we like and don't like about Web sites.

As individuals, we love pages with main menus across the top and submenus down the left side because they're familiar and easy to use, or we hate them because they're so boring. We love pages with large evocative images because they're engaging, or we hate them because we just want to get to the content. We really enjoy using sites with ____, or we find ____ to be a royal pain.

And when we're working on a Web team, it turns out to be very hard to check those feelings at the door.

The result is usually a room full of individuals with strong personal convictions about what makes for a good Web site.

And given the strength of these convictions—and human nature—there's a natural tendency to project these likes and dislikes onto users in general: to think that most users like the same things we like. We tend to think that most users are like us.

It's not that we think that *everyone* is like us. We know there are *some* people out there who hate the things we love—after all, there are even some of them on our own Web team. But not *sensible* people. And there aren't many of them.

# Farmers vs. cowmen

On top of this layer of personal passion, there's another layer: professional passion. Like the farmers and the cowmen in *Oklahoma!,* the players on a Web team have very different perspectives on what constitutes good Web design based on what they do for a living.[1]

The ideal Web page as seen by someone whose job is...

CEO      Developer      Designer      Business Development

It's always seemed to me that these people probably have the jobs they do because of who they *are*. Designers, for instance, probably became designers because they enjoy pleasant visual experiences. They get visceral pleasure from looking at pages full of elegant type and subtle visual cues. There are endorphins involved.

*Disagree* And developers tend to like complexity. They enjoy figuring out how things work, reverse engineering them in their head, and looking for ideas they can use. Again, there are endorphins at work.

And because these reactions are happening at a brain-chemical level, it's very difficult for them to imagine that everybody doesn't feel exactly the same way.

The result is that designers want to build sites that look great, and developers want to build sites with interesting, original, ingenious features. I'm not sure

---

[1]   *In the play, the thrifty, God-fearing, family-oriented farmers are always at odds with the freewheeling, loose-living cowmen. Farmers love fences, cowmen love the open range.*

who's the farmer and who's the cowman in this picture, but I do know that their differences in perspective often lead to conflict—and hard feelings—when it comes time to establish design priorities.

*This is worst case scenario. Don't see it here.*

At the same time, designers and developers often find themselves siding together in another, larger clash between what Art Kleiner describes as the cultures of hype and craft.[2]

While the hype culture (upper management, marketing, and business development) is focused on making whatever promises are necessary to attract venture capital, revenue-generating deals, and users to the site, the burden of delivering on those promises lands on the shoulders of the craft culture artisans like the designers and developers.

This modern high-tech version of the perennial struggle between art and commerce (or perhaps farmers and cowmen vs. the railroad barons) adds another level of complexity to any discussions of usability issues—often in the form of apparently arbitrary edicts handed down from the hype side of the fence.[3]

---

[2]  *See "Corporate Culture in Internet Time" in* strategy+business *magazine at* strategy-business.com/press/article/10374.

[3]  *I once saw a particularly puzzling feature on the Home page of a prominent—and otherwise sensibly designed—site. When I asked about it, I was told, "Oh, that. It came to our CEO in a dream, so we had to add it." True story.*

# The myth of the Average User

The belief that most Web users are like us is enough to produce gridlock in the average Web design meeting. But behind that belief lies another one, even more insidious: the belief that most Web users are like *anything*.

As soon as the clash of personal and professional opinions results in a stalemate, the conversation usually turns to finding some way (whether it's the opinion of an outside expert, published research, a survey, or focus groups) to determine what *most* users like or don't like—to figure out what the Average Web User is really like. The only problem is, there is no Average User.

In fact, all of the time I've spent watching people use the Web has led me to the opposite conclusion:

ALL WEB USERS ARE UNIQUE
AND ALL WEB USE IS BASICALLY IDIOSYNCRATIC

The more you watch users carefully and listen to them articulate their intentions, motivations, and thought processes, the more you realize that their individual reactions to Web pages are based on so many variables that attempts to describe users in terms of one-dimensional likes and dislikes are futile—and counter-productive.

And the worst thing about the myth of the Average User is that it reinforces the idea that good Web design is largely a matter of figuring out what people like. It's an attractive notion: Either pull-downs are good (because most people like them), or they're bad (because most people don't). Stories should be on a single long page or they should be broken up into many shorter pages. Home page carousels, mega menus, rollovers, etc. are either good or bad, black or white.

The problem is there *are* no simple "right" answers for most Web design questions (at least not for the important ones). What works is good, integrated design that fills a need—carefully thought out, well executed, and tested.

That's not to say that there aren't some things you should *never* do, and some things you should *rarely* do. There are some ways to design Web pages that are clearly wrong. It's just that they aren't the things that Web teams usually argue about.

# The antidote for religious debates

The point is, it's not productive to ask questions like "Do most people like pull-down menus?" The right kind of question to ask is "Does *this* pull-down, with *these* items and *this* wording in *this* context on *this* page create a good experience for most people who are likely to use *this* site?"

And there's really only one way to answer that kind of question: testing. You have to use the collective skill, experience, creativity, and common sense of the team to build some version of the thing (even a crude version), then watch some people carefully as they try to figure out what it is and how to use it.

There's no substitute for it.

Where debates about what people like waste time and drain the team's energy, usability testing tends to defuse most arguments and break impasses by moving the discussion away from the realm of what's right or wrong and what people like or dislike and into the realm of what works or doesn't work. And by opening our eyes to just how varied users' motivations, perceptions, and responses are, testing makes it hard to keep thinking that all users are like us.

Can you tell that I think usability testing is a good thing?

The next chapter explains how to test your own site.

# 9

# Usability testing on 10 cents a day

## KEEPING TESTING SIMPLE—SO YOU DO ENOUGH OF IT

I used to get a lot of phone calls like this:

As soon as I'd hear "launching in two weeks" (or even "two months") and "usability testing" in the same sentence, I'd start to get that old fireman-headed-into-the-burning-chemical-factory feeling, because I had a pretty good idea of what was going on.

If it was two weeks, then it was almost certainly a request for a disaster check. The launch was fast approaching and everyone was getting nervous, and someone had finally said, "Maybe we better do some usability testing."

If it was two months, then odds were that what they wanted was to settle some ongoing internal debates—usually about something like aesthetics. Opinion around the office was split between two different designs; some people liked the sexy one, some liked the elegant one. Finally someone with enough clout to authorize the expense got tired of the arguing and said, "All right, let's get some testing done to settle this."

And while usability testing will sometimes settle these arguments, the main thing it usually ends up doing is revealing that the things they were arguing about weren't all that important. People often test to decide which color drapes are best, only to learn that they forgot to put windows in the room. For instance, they might discover that it doesn't make much difference whether you go with cascading menus or mega menus if nobody understands the value proposition of your site.

I don't get nearly as many of these calls these days, which I take as a good sign that there's more awareness of the need to make usability part of every project right from the beginning.

Sadly, though, this is still how a lot of usability testing gets done: too little, too late, and for all the wrong reasons.

## Repeat after me:
## Focus groups are not usability tests.

Sometimes that initial phone call is even scarier:

When the last-minute request is for a focus group, it's usually a sign that the request originated in Marketing. If the Marketing people feel that the site is headed in the wrong direction as the launch date approaches, they may feel that their only hope of averting potential disaster is to appeal to a higher authority: market research. And one of the types of research they know best is focus groups.

I've often had to work very hard to make clients understand that what they need is usability testing, not focus groups—so often that I finally made a short animated video about just how hard it can be (someslightlyirregular.com/2011/08/you-say-potato).

Here's the difference in a nutshell:

- In a **focus group**, a small group of people (usually 5 to 10) sit around a table and talk about things, like their opinions about products, their past experiences with them, or their reactions to new concepts. Focus groups are good for quickly getting a sampling of users' feelings and opinions about things.

- **Usability tests** are about watching one person at a time try to use something (whether it's a Web site, a prototype, or some sketches of a new design) to do typical tasks so you can detect and fix the things that confuse or frustrate them.

The main difference is that in usability tests, you watch people actually *use* things, instead of just listening to them talk about them.

Focus groups can be great for determining what your audience wants, needs, and likes—in the abstract. They're good for testing whether the idea behind your site makes sense and your value proposition is attractive, to learn more about how people currently solve the problems your site will help them with, and to find out how they feel about you and your competitors.

But they're *not* good for learning about whether your site works and how to improve it.

The kinds of things you learn from focus groups—like whether you're building the right product—are things you should know *before* you begin designing or building anything, so focus groups are best used in the planning stages of a project. Usability tests, on the other hand, should be used through the entire process.

# Several true things about usability testing

Here are the main things I know about usability tests:

- **If you want a great site, you've got to test.** After you've worked on a site for even a few weeks, you can't see it freshly anymore. You know too much. The only way to find out if it really works is to watch other people try to use it.

  Testing reminds you that not everyone thinks the way you do, knows what you know, and uses the Web the way you do.

  I used to say that the best way to think about testing is that it's like travel: a broadening experience. It reminds you how different—and the same—people are and gives you a fresh perspective on things.[1]

  But I finally realized that testing is really more like having friends visiting from out of town. Inevitably, as you make the rounds of the local tourist sites with them, you see things about your hometown that you usually don't notice because you're so used to them. And at the same time, you realize that a lot of things that you take for granted aren't obvious to everybody.

- **Testing one user is 100 percent better than testing none.** Testing always works, and even the worst test with the wrong user will show you important things you can do to improve your site.

  When I teach workshops, I make a point of always doing a live usability test at the beginning so that people can see that it's very easy to do and it always produces valuable insights.

  I ask for a volunteer to try to perform a task on a site belonging to one of the other attendees. These tests last less than fifteen minutes, but in that time the person whose site is being tested usually scribbles several pages of notes. And they always ask if they can have the recording of the test to show to their team back home. (One person told me that after his team saw the recording, they made one change to their site which they later calculated had resulted in $100,000 in savings.)

---

[1] *As the Lean Startup folks would say, it gets you out of the building.*

- **Testing one user early in the project is better than testing 50 near the end.** Most people assume that testing needs to be a big deal. But if you make it into a big deal, you won't do it early enough or often enough to get the most out of it. A simple test early—while you still have time to use what you learn from it—is almost always more valuable than an elaborate test later.

Part of the conventional wisdom about Web development is that it's very easy to go in and make changes. The truth is, it's often not that easy to make changes—especially major changes—to a site once it's in use. Some percentage of users will resist almost any kind of change, and even apparently simple changes often turn out to have far-reaching effects. Any mistakes you can correct early in the process will save you trouble down the line.

# Do-it-yourself usability testing

Usability testing has been around for a long time, and the basic idea is pretty simple: If you want to know whether something is easy enough to use, watch some people while they try to use it and note where they run into problems.

In the beginning, though, usability testing was a very expensive proposition. You had to have a usability lab with an observation room behind a one-way mirror and video cameras to record the users' reactions and the screen. You had to pay a usability professional to plan and facilitate the tests for you. And you had to recruit a lot of participants[2] so you could get results that were statistically significant. It was Science. It cost $20,000 to $50,000 a shot. It didn't happen very often.

Then in 1989 Jakob Nielsen wrote a paper titled "Usability Engineering at a Discount" and pointed out that it didn't have to be that way. You didn't need a usability lab, and you could achieve the same results with far fewer participants. The price tag dropped to $5,000 to $10,000 per round of testing.

---

[2] *We call them participants rather than "test subjects" to make it clear that we're not testing them; we're testing the site.*

The idea of discount usability testing was a huge step forward. The only problem is that every Web site (and app) needs testing and $5,000 to $10,000 is still a lot of money, so it doesn't happen nearly often enough.

What I'm going to commend to you in this chapter is something even simpler (and a lot less expensive): Do-it-yourself usability testing.

I'm going to explain how you can do your own testing when you have no time and no money.

Don't get me wrong: If you can afford to hire a professional to do your testing, do it. Odds are they'll be able to do a better job than you can. But if you can't hire someone, do it yourself.

I believe in the value of this kind of testing so much that I wrote an entire (short) book about how to do it. It's called *Rocket Surgery Made Easy: The Do-It-Yourself Guide to Finding and Fixing Usability Problems*.

It covers the topics in this chapter in a lot more detail and gives you step-by-step directions for the whole process.

| | TRADITIONAL TESTING | DO-IT-YOURSELF TESTING |
|---|---|---|
| TIME SPENT FOR EACH ROUND OF TESTING | 1–2 days of tests, then a week to prepare a briefing or report, followed by some process to decide what to fix | One morning a month includes testing, debriefing, and deciding what to fix<br><br>By early afternoon, you're done with usability testing for the month |
| WHEN DO YOU TEST? | When the site is nearly complete | Continually, throughout the development process |
| NUMBER OF ROUNDS OF TESTING | Typically only one or two per project, because of time and expense | One every month |
| NUMBER OF PARTICIPANTS IN EACH ROUND | Eight or more | Three |
| HOW DO YOU CHOOSE THE PARTICIPANTS? | Recruit carefully to find people who are like your target audience | Recruit loosely, if necessary<br><br>Doing frequent testing is more important than testing "actual" users |
| WHERE DO YOU TEST? | Off-site, in a rented facility with an observation room with a one-way mirror | On-site, with observers in a conference room using screen sharing software to watch |
| WHO WATCHES? | Full days of off-site testing means not many people will observe firsthand | Half day of on-site testing means more people can see the tests "live" |
| REPORTING | Someone takes at least a week to prepare a briefing or write a Big Honkin' Report (25–50 pages) | A 1–2 page email summarizes decisions made during the team's debriefing |
| WHO IDENTIFIES THE PROBLEMS? | The person running the tests usually analyzes the results and recommends changes | The entire development team and any interested stakeholders meet over lunch the same day to compare notes and decide what to fix |
| PRIMARY PURPOSE | Identify as many problems as possible (sometimes hundreds), then categorize them and prioritize them by severity | Identify the most serious problems and commit to fixing them before the next round of testing |
| OUT-OF-POCKET COSTS | $5,000 to $10,000 per round if you hire someone to do it | A few hundred dollars or less per round |

# How often should you test?

I think every Web development team should spend one morning a month doing usability testing.

In a morning, you can test three users, then debrief over lunch. That's it. When you leave the debriefing, the team will have decided what you're going to fix before the next round of testing, and you'll be done with testing for the month.[3]

Why a morning a month?

- **It keeps it simple so you'll keep doing it.** A morning a month is about as much time as most teams can afford to spend doing testing. If it's too complicated or time-consuming, it's much more likely that you won't make time for it when things get busy.

- **It gives you what you need.** Watching three participants, you'll identify enough problems to keep you busy fixing things for the next month.

- **It frees you from deciding when to test.** You should pick a day of the month—like the third Thursday—and make that your designated testing day.

  This is much better than basing your test schedule on milestones and deliverables ("We'll test when the beta's ready to release") because schedules often slip and testing slips along with them. Don't worry, there will always be *something* you can test each month.

- **It makes it more likely that people will attend.** Doing it all in a morning on a predictable schedule greatly increases the chances that team members will make time to come and watch at least some of the sessions, which is highly desirable.

---

[3] *If you're doing Agile development, you'll be doing testing more frequently, but the principles are still the same. For instance, you might be testing with two users every two weeks. Creating a fixed schedule and sticking to it is what's important.*

# How many users do you need?

I think the ideal number of participants for each round of do-it-yourself testing is three.

Some people will complain that three aren't enough. They'll say that it's too small a sample to prove anything and that it won't uncover all of the problems. Both of these are true but they just don't matter, and here's why:

- **The purpose of this kind of testing isn't to *prove* anything.** Proving things requires *quantitative* testing, with a large sample size, a clearly defined and rigorously followed test protocol, and lots of data gathering and analysis.

  Do-it-yourself tests are a qualitative method whose purpose is to *im*prove what you're building by identifying and fixing usability problems. The process isn't rigorous at all: You give them tasks to do, you observe, and you learn. The result is actionable insights, not proof.

- **You don't need to find all of the problems.** In fact, you'll *never* find *all* of the problems in anything you test. And it wouldn't help if you did, because of this fact:

  *You can find more problems in half a day than you can fix in a month.*

  You'll always find more problems than you have the resources to fix, so it's very important that you focus on fixing the most serious ones first. And three users are very likely to encounter many of the most significant problems related to the tasks that you're testing.

Problems you have the resources to fix

Problems you can find with just a few test participants

Also, you're going to be doing another round each month. It's much more important to do more rounds of testing than to wring everything you can out of each round.

# How do you choose the participants?

When people decide to test, they often spend a lot of time trying to recruit users who they think will precisely reflect their target audience—for instance, "male accountants between the ages of 25 and 30 with one to three years of computer experience who have recently purchased expensive shoes."

It's good to do your testing with participants who are like the people who will use your site, but the truth is that recruiting people who are from your target audience isn't quite as important as it may seem. For many sites, you can do a lot of your testing with almost anybody. And if you're just starting to do testing, your site probably has a number of usability flaws that will cause real problems for almost anyone you recruit.

Recruiting people who fit a narrow profile usually requires more work (to find them) and often more money (for their stipend). If you have plenty of time to spend on recruiting or you can afford to hire someone to do it for you, then by all means be as specific as you want. But if finding the ideal users means you're going to do less testing, I recommend a different approach:

## RECRUIT LOOSELY AND GRADE ON A CURVE

In other words, try to find users who reflect your audience, but don't get hung up about it. Instead, loosen up your requirements and then make allowances for the differences between your participants and your audience. When somebody has a problem, ask yourself "Would our users have that problem, or was it only a problem because they didn't know what our users know?"

If using your site requires specific domain knowledge (e.g., a currency exchange site for money management professionals), then you'll need to recruit *some* people with that knowledge. But they don't all have to have it, since many of the most serious usability problems are things that anybody will encounter.

In fact, I'm in favor of always using some participants who *aren't* from your target audience, for three reasons:

- **It's usually not a good idea to design a site so that only your target audience can use it.** Domain knowledge is a tricky thing, and if you design a site for money managers using terminology that you think all money managers will understand, what you'll discover is that a small but not insignificant number of them won't know what you're talking about. And in most cases, you need to be supporting novices as well as experts anyway.

- **We're all beginners under the skin.** Scratch an expert and you'll often find someone who's muddling through—just at a higher level.

- **Experts are rarely insulted by something that is clear enough for beginners.** Everybody appreciates clarity. (True clarity, that is, and not just something that's been "dumbed down.") If "almost anybody" can use it, your experts will be able to use it, too.

# How do you find participants?

There are many places and ways to recruit test participants, like user groups, trade shows, Craigslist, Facebook, Twitter, customer forums, a pop-up on your site, or even asking friends and neighbors.

If you're going to do your own recruiting, I recommend that you download the Nielsen Norman Group's free 147-page report *How to Recruit Participants for Usability Studies*.[4] You don't have to read it all, but it's an excellent source of advice.

Typical participant incentives for a one-hour test session range from $50 to $100 for "average" Web users to several hundred dollars for busy, highly paid professionals, like cardiologists for instance.

I like to offer people a little more than the going rate, since it makes it clear that I value their time and improves the chances that they'll show up. Remember that even if the session is only an hour, people usually have to spend another hour traveling.

---

[4] *...at nngroup.com/reports/tips/recruiting. It's from 2003, but if you factor in 20% inflation for the dollar amounts, it's all still valid. And did I mention that it's free?*

# Where do you test?

To conduct the test, you need a quiet space where you won't be interrupted (usually either an office or a conference room) with a table or desk and two chairs. And you'll need a computer with Internet access, a mouse, a keyboard, and a microphone.

You'll be using screen sharing software (like GoToMeeting or WebEx) to allow the team members, stakeholders, and anyone else who's interested to observe the tests from another room.

You should also run screen recording software (like Camtasia from Techsmith) to capture a record of what happens on the screen and what the facilitator and the participant say. You may never refer to it, but it's good to have in case you want to check something or use a few brief clips as part of a presentation.

# Who should do the testing?

The person who sits with the participant and leads them through the test is called the facilitator. Almost anyone can facilitate a usability test; all it really takes is the courage to try it, and with a little practice, most people can get quite good at it.

I'm assuming that you're going to facilitate the tests yourself, but if you're not, try to choose someone who tends to be patient, calm, empathetic, and a good listener. Don't choose someone whom you would describe as "definitely not a people person" or "the office crank."

Other than keeping the participants comfortable and focused on doing the tasks, the facilitator's main job is to encourage them to think out loud as much as possible. The combination of watching what the participants do and hearing what they're thinking while they do it is what enables the observers to see the site through someone else's eyes and understand why some things that are obvious to them are confusing or frustrating to users.

# Who should observe?

As many people as possible!

One of the most valuable things about doing usability testing is the effect it can have on the observers. For many people, it's a transformative experience that dramatically changes the way they think about users: They suddenly "get it" that users aren't all like them.

You should try to do whatever you can to encourage everyone—team members, stakeholders, managers, and even executives—to come and watch the test sessions. In fact, if you have any money for testing, I recommend using it to buy the best snacks you can to lure people in. (Chocolate croissants seem to work particularly well.)

You'll need an observation room (usually a conference room), a computer with Internet access and screen sharing software, and a large screen monitor or projector and a pair of external speakers so everyone can see and hear what's happening in the test room.

During the break after each test session, observers need to write down the three most serious usability problems they noticed during that session so they can share them in the debriefing. You can download a form I created for this purpose from my Web site. They can take as many notes as they want, but it's important that they make this short list because, as you'll see, the purpose of the debriefing is to identify the most serious problems so they get fixed first.

# What do you test, and when do you test it?

As any usability professional will tell you, it's important to start testing as early as possible and to keep testing through the entire development process.

In fact, it's never *too* early to start. Even before you begin designing your site, for instance, it's a good idea to do a test of competitive sites. They may be actual competitors, or they may just be sites that have the same style, organization, or features that you plan on using. Bring in three participants and watch them try to do some typical tasks on one or two competitive sites and you'll learn a lot about what works and doesn't work without having to design or build anything.

If you're redesigning an existing site, you'll also want to test it before you start, so you'll know what's not working (and needs to be changed) and what is working (so you don't break it).

Then throughout the project, continue to test everything the team produces, beginning with your first rough sketches and continuing on with wireframes, page comps, prototypes, and finally actual pages.

# How do you choose the tasks to test?

For each round of testing, you need to come up with tasks: the things the participants will try to do.

The tasks you test in a given round will depend partly on what you have available to test. If all you have is a rough sketch, for instance, the task may consist of simply asking them to look at it and tell you what they think it is.

If you have more than a sketch to show them, though, start by making a list of the tasks people need to be able to do with whatever you're testing. For instance, if you're testing a prototype of a login process, the tasks might be

Create an account
Log in using an existing username and password
Retrieve a forgotten password
Retrieve a forgotten username
Change answer to a security question

Choose enough tasks to fill the available time (about 35 minutes in a one-hour test), keeping in mind that some people will finish them faster than you expect.

Then word each task carefully, so the participants will understand exactly what you want them to do. Include any information that they'll need but won't have, like login information if you're having them use a demo account. For example:

> You have an existing account with the username delphi21 and the password correcthorsebatterystaple. You've always used the same answers to security questions on every site, and you just read that this is a bad idea. Change your answer for this account.

You can often get more revealing results if you allow the participants to choose some of the details of the task. It's much better, for instance, to say "Find a book you want to buy, or a book you bought recently" than "Find a cookbook for under $14." It increases their emotional investment and allows them to use more of their personal knowledge of the content.

# What happens during the test?

You can download the script that I use for testing Web sites (or the slightly different version for testing apps) at rocketsurgerymadeeasy.com. I recommend that you read your "lines" exactly as written, since the wording has been carefully chosen.

A typical one-hour test would be broken down something like this:

- **Welcome** (4 minutes). You begin by explaining how the test will work so the participant knows what to expect.

- **The questions** (2 minutes). Next you ask the participant a few questions about themselves. This helps put them at ease and gives you an idea of how computer-savvy and Web-savvy they are.

- **The Home page tour** (3 minutes). Then you open the Home page of the site you're testing and ask the participant to look around and tell you what they make of it. This will give you an idea of how easy it is to understand your Home page and how much the participant already knows your domain.

- **The tasks** (35 minutes). This is the heart of the test: watching the participant try to perform a series of tasks (or in some cases, just one long task). Again, your job is to make sure the participant stays focused on the tasks and keeps thinking aloud.

  If the participant stops saying what they're thinking, prompt them by saying—wait for it—"What are you thinking?" (For variety, you can also say things like "What are you looking at?" and "What are you doing now?")

  During this part of the test, it's crucial that you let them work on their own and don't do or say anything to influence them. Don't ask them leading questions, and don't give them any clues or assistance unless they're hopelessly stuck or extremely frustrated. If they ask for help, just say something like "What would you do if I wasn't here?"

- **Probing** (5 minutes). After the tasks, you can ask the participant questions about anything that happened during the test and any questions that the people in the observation room would like you to ask.

- **Wrapping up** (5 minutes). Finally, you thank them for their help, pay them, and show them to the door.

# A sample test session

Here's an annotated excerpt from a typical—but imaginary—test session. The participant's name is Janice, and she's about 25 years old.

## INTRODUCTION

Hi, Janice. My name is Steve Krug, and I'm going to be walking you through this session. Before we begin, I have some information for you, and I'm going to read it to make sure I cover everything.

> I'm reading from the script that I use when I do usability tests.
>
> You can download this script at rocketsurgerymadeeasy.com.

You probably already have a good idea of why we've asked you to come here today, but let me go over it again briefly. We're testing a Web site that we're working on so we can see what it's like for people to use it. The session should take about an hour.

I want to make it clear right away that we're testing the *site*, not you. You can't do anything wrong here. In fact, this is probably the one place today where you don't have to worry about making mistakes.

We want to hear exactly what you think, so please don't worry that you're going to hurt our feelings. We want to improve it, so we need to know honestly what you think.

As we go along, I'm going to ask you to think out loud, to tell me what's going through your mind. This will help us.

If you have questions, just ask. I may not be able to answer them right away, since we're interested in how people do when they don't have someone sitting next to them to help, but I will try to answer any questions you still have when we're done.

And if you need to take a break at any point, just let me know.

You may have noticed the microphone. With your permission, we're going to record what happens on the screen and what you say. The recording will be used only to help us figure out how to improve the site, and it won't be seen by anyone except the people working on the project. It also helps me, because I don't have to take as many notes.

Also, there are a few people from the Web design team observing the session in another room. (They can't see us, just the screen.)

If you would, I'm going to ask you to sign a simple permission form for us. It just says that we have your permission to record you, but that it will only be seen by the people working on the project.

Do you have any questions before we begin?

No. I don't think so.

It's important to mention this, because it will seem rude not to answer their questions as you go along. You have to make it clear before you start that (a) it's nothing personal and (b) you'll try to answer them at the end if they still want to know.

At this point, most people will say something like, "I'm not going to end up on *America's Funniest Home Videos*, am I?"

Give them the recording permission form to sign.

You'll find a sample form and some other useful forms and checklists at rocketsurgerymadeeasy.com.

## BACKGROUND QUESTIONS

Before we look at the site, I'd like to ask you just a few quick questions. First, what's your occupation? What do you do all day?

 I'm a router.

I've never heard of that before. What does a router do, exactly?

 I take orders as they come in and send them to the right office. We're a big multinational company, so there's a lot to sort out.

OK. Now, roughly how many hours a week would you say you spend using the Internet, including Web browsing *and* email? Just a ballpark estimate.

 Oh, I don't know. Probably four hours a day at work, and maybe eight hours a week at home. Mostly that's on the weekend. I'm too tired at night to bother. But I like playing games sometimes.

What's the split between email and browsing—a rough percentage?

 Well, at the office I spend most of my time checking email. I get a lot of email, and a lot of it's junk but I have to go through it anyway. Maybe two-thirds of my time is on email and one-third is browsing.

I find it's good to start with a few questions to get a feel for who they are and how they use the Internet. It gives them a chance to loosen up a little and gives you a chance to show that you're going to be listening attentively to what they say—and that there are no wrong or right answers.

Don't hesitate to admit your ignorance about anything. Your role here is not to come across as an expert, but as a good listener.

Notice that she's not sure how much time she really spends on the Internet. Most people aren't. Don't worry. Accurate answers aren't important here. The main point here is just to get her talking and thinking about how she uses the Internet and to give you a chance to gauge what kind of user she is.

What kinds of sites are you looking at when you browse the Web?

> At work, mostly our corporate intranet. And some competitors' sites. At home, game sites and some shopping.

Do you have any favorite Web sites?

> Well, Google, of course. I use it all the time. And something called Snakes.com, because I have a pet snake.

*mlbtraderumors.com*
*pirateball*
*news.google*

Really? What kind of snake?

> A python. He's about four feet long, but he should get to be eight or nine when he's fully grown.

OK, great. We're done with the questions, and we can start looking at things.

> OK, I guess.

Don't be afraid to digress and find out a little more about the user, as long as you come back to the topic before long.

# THE HOME PAGE TOUR

First, I'm just going to ask you to look at this page and tell me what you make of it: what strikes you about it, whose site you think it is, what you can do here, and what it's for. Just look around and do a little narrative.

You can scroll if you want to, but don't click on anything yet.

Until now, the browser has been opened to Google so there's nothing distracting to look at.

At this point, I reach over and open a tab with the site we're testing and give the mouse to the participant.

Well, I guess the first thing I notice is that I like the color. I like the shade of orange, and I like the little picture of the sun [at the top of the page, in the eLance logo].

Let's see. [Reads.] "The global services market." "Where the world competes to get your job done."

In an average test, it's just as likely that the next user will say that she hates this shade of orange and that the drawing is too simplistic. Don't get too excited by individual reactions to site aesthetics.

I don't know what that means. I have no idea.

"Animate your logo: free." [Looking at the Cool Stuff section on the left.] "Graphic design marketplace." "View the RFP marketplace." "eLance marketplaces."

There's a lot going on here. But I have no idea what any of it is.

*you will get conflicting opinions*

If you had to take a guess, what do you think it might be?

> Well, it seems to have something to do with buying and selling...something.

> [Looks around the page again.] Now that I look at the list down here [the category list halfway down the page], I guess maybe it must be services. Legal, financial, creative... they all sound like services.

> So I guess that's what it is. Buying and selling services.

OK. Now, if you were at home, what would you click on first?

> I guess I'd click on that graphic design thing. I'm interested in graphic design.

This user has been doing a good job of thinking out loud on her own. If she wasn't, this is where I'd start asking her, "What are you thinking?"

## THE TASKS

OK, now we're going to try doing some specific tasks.

And again, as much as possible, it will help us if you can try to think out loud as you go along.

Can you think of some service that you need that you could use this site to get help with?

> Hmm. Let me think. I think I saw "Home Improvement" there somewhere. We're thinking of building a deck. Maybe I could find somebody to do that.

So if you were going to look for somebody to build your deck, what would you do first?

> I guess I'd click on one of the categories down here. I think I saw home improvement. [Looks.] There it is, under "Family and Household."

So what would you do?

> Well, I'd click…. [Hesitates, looking at the two links under "Family and Household."]

**Family & Household**
Food & Cooking, Gardening, Genealogy, Home Improvement, Interior Design, Parenting, Pets, Real Estate…
RFPs | Fixed-Price

Now I give her a task to perform so we can see whether she can use the site for its intended purpose.

Whenever possible, it's good to let the user have some say in choosing the task.

Well, now I'm not sure what to do. I can't click on Home Improvement, so it looks like I have to click on either "RFPs" or "Fixed-Price." But I don't know what the difference is.

Fixed-price I sort of understand; they'll give me a quote, and then they have to stick to it. But I'm not sure what RFPs is.

Well, which one do you think you'd click on?

Fixed-price, I guess.

Why don't you go ahead and do it?

As it turns out, she's mistaken. Fixed-price (in this case) means services available for a fixed hourly rate, while an RFP (or Request for Proposal) is actually the choice that will get her the kind of quote she's looking for. This is the kind of misunderstanding that often surprises the people who built the site.

From here on, I just watch while she tries to post a project, letting her continue until either (a) she finishes the task, (b) she gets really frustrated, or (c) we're not learning anything new by watching her try to muddle through.

I'd give her three or four more tasks to do, which should take not more than 45 minutes altogether.

## PROBING

Now that we're done with the tasks, I have a few questions.

What about these pictures near the top of the page—the ones with the numbers? What did you make of them?

I noticed them, but I really didn't try to figure them out. I guess I thought they were telling me what the steps in the process would be.

Any reason why you didn't pay much attention to them?

No. I guess I just wasn't ready to start the process yet. I didn't know if I wanted to use it yet. I just wanted to look around first.

OK. Great.

While the participant is doing the tasks, I'm careful not to ask leading questions because I don't want to bias her.

But I always save some time at the end specifically to ask probing questions so I can understand more about what happened and why it happened.

In this case, I ask this question because the site's designers think most users are going to start by clicking on the pictures of the five steps and that everyone will at least look at them.

That's really all there is to it.

If you'd like to see a more complete test, you'll find a twenty-minute video on my site. Just go to rocketsurgerymadeeasy.com and click on "Demo test video."

# Typical problems

Here are some of the types of problems you're going to see most often:

- **Users are unclear on the concept.** They just don't get it. They look at the site or a page and either they don't know what to make of it or they think they do but they're wrong.

- **The words they're looking for aren't there.** This usually means that either you failed to anticipate what they'd be looking for or the words you're using to describe things aren't the words they'd use.

- **There's too much going on.** Sometimes what they're looking for is right there on the page, but they're just not seeing it. In this case, you need to either reduce the overall noise on the page or turn up the volume on the things they need to see so they "pop" out of the visual hierarchy more.

# The debriefing: Deciding what to fix

After each round of tests, you should make time as soon as possible for the team to share their observations and decide which problems to fix and what you're going to do to fix them.

I recommend that you debrief over lunch right after you do the tests, while everything is still fresh in the observers' minds. (Order the really good pizza from the expensive pizza place to encourage attendance.)

Whenever you test, you're almost always going to find some serious usability problems. Unfortunately, they aren't always the ones that get fixed. Often, for instance, people will say, "Yes, that's a real problem. But that functionality is all going to change soon, and we can live with it until then." Or faced with a choice between trying to fix one serious problem or a lot of simple problems, they opt for the low-hanging fruit.

This is one reason why you can so often run into serious usability problems even on large, well-funded Web sites, and it's why one of my maxims in *Rocket Surgery* is

FOCUS RUTHLESSLY ON FIXING
THE MOST SERIOUS PROBLEMS FIRST

Here's the method I like to use to make sure this happens, but you can do it any way that works for your team:

- **Make a collective list.** Go around the room giving everyone a chance to say what they thought were the three most serious problems they observed (of the nine they wrote down; three for each session). Write them down on a whiteboard or sheets of easel pad paper. Typically, a lot of people will say "Me, too" to some of them, which you can keep track of by adding checkmarks.

    There's no discussion at this point; you're just listing the problems. And they have to be *observed* problems; things that actually happened during one of the test sessions.

- **Choose the ten most serious problems.** You can do informal voting, but you can usually start with the ones that got the most checkmarks.

- **Rate them.** Number them from 1 to 10, 1 being the worst. Then copy them to a new list with the worst at the top, leaving some room between them.

- **Create an ordered list.** Starting at the top, write down a rough idea of how you're going to fix each one in the next month, who's going to do it, and any resources it will require.

    You don't have to fix each problem perfectly or completely. You just have to do something—often just a tweak—that will take it out of the category of "serious problem."

    When you feel like you've allocated all of the time and resources you have available in the next month for fixing usability problems, STOP. You've got what you came for. The group has now decided what needs to be fixed and made a commitment to fixing it.

Here are some tips about deciding what to fix—and what not to.

- **Keep a separate list of low-hanging fruit.** You can also keep a list of things that aren't serious problems but are very easy to fix. And by very easy, I mean things that one person can fix in less than an hour, *without* getting permission from anyone who isn't at the debriefing.

- **Resist the impulse to add things.** When it's obvious in testing that users aren't getting something, the team's first reaction is usually to add something, like an explanation or some instructions. But very often the right solution is to take something (or some *things*) away that are obscuring the meaning, rather than adding yet another distraction.

- **Take "new feature" requests with a grain of salt.** Participants will often say, "I'd like it better if it could do x." It pays to be suspicious of these requests for new features. I find that if you ask them to describe how that feature would work—during the probing time at the end of the test—it almost always turns out that by the time they finish describing it they say something like "But now that I think of it, I probably wouldn't use that." Participants aren't designers. They may occasionally come up with a great idea, but when they do you'll know it immediately, because your first thought will be "Why didn't we think of that?!"

- **Ignore "kayak" problems.** In any test, you're likely to see several cases where users will go astray momentarily but manage to get back on track almost immediately without any help. It's kind of like rolling over in a kayak; as long as the kayak rights itself quickly enough, it's all part of the so-called fun. In basketball terms, no harm, no foul.

  As long as (a) everyone who has the problem notices that they're no longer headed in the right direction quickly, and (b) they manage to recover without help, and (c) it doesn't seem to faze them, you can ignore the problem. In general, if the user's second guess about where to find things is always right, that's good enough.

# Alternative lifestyles

Here are two other ways to do testing that have distinct advantages:

- **Remote testing.** The difference here is that instead of coming to your office, participants do the test from the comfort of their own home or office, using screen sharing. Eliminating the need to travel can make it much easier to recruit busy people and, even more significantly, it expands your recruiting pool from "people who live near your office" to "almost anyone." All they need is high-speed Internet access and a microphone.

- **Unmoderated remote testing.** Services like UserTesting.com provide people who will record themselves doing a usability test. You simply send in your tasks and a link to your site, prototype, or mobile app. Within an hour (on average), you can watch a video of someone doing your tasks while thinking aloud.[5] You don't get to interact with the participant in real time, but it's relatively inexpensive and requires almost no effort (especially recruiting) on your part. All you have to do is watch the video.

# Try it, you'll like it

Whatever method you use, try doing it. I can almost guarantee that if you do, you'll want to keep doing it.

Here are some suggestions for fending off any objections you might encounter:

---

[5] *Full disclosure: I receive some compensation from UserTesting.com for letting them use my name. But I only do that because I've always thought they have a great product—which is why I'm mentioning them here.*

# THE TOP FIVE PLAUSIBLE REASONS FOR NOT TESTING WEB SITES

| | |
|---|---|
| **We don't have the time.** | It's true that most Web development schedules seem to be based on the punchline from a Dilbert cartoon. If testing is going to add to everybody's to-do list, then it won't get done. That's why you have to make testing as simple as possible.<br><br>Done right, it will save time because you won't have to (a) argue endlessly and (b) redo things at the end. |
| **We don't have the money.** | Forget $5,000 to $10,000. You should only have to spend a few hundred dollars for each round of testing—even less if your participants are volunteers. |
| **We don't have the expertise.** | The least-known fact about usability testing is that it's incredibly easy to do. Yes, some people will be better at it than others, but I've rarely seen a usability test fail to produce useful results, no matter how poorly it was conducted. |
| **We don't have a usability lab.** | You don't need one.<br><br>All you really need is a room with a desk, a computer, and two chairs where you won't be interrupted and another room where the observers can watch on a large screen. |
| **We wouldn't know how to interpret the results.** | One of the nicest things about usability testing is that the important lessons tend to be obvious to everyone who's watching. The most serious problems are hard to miss. |

# 10

# Mobile: It's not just a city in Alabama anymore

WELCOME TO THE 21ST CENTURY —
YOU MAY EXPERIENCE A SLIGHT SENSE OF VERTIGO

Ahh, the smartphone.

Phones had been getting gradually smarter for years, gathering in desk drawers and plotting amongst themselves. But it wasn't until the Great Leap Forward[1] that they finally achieved consciousness.

I, for one, was glad to welcome our tiny, time-wasting overlords. I know there was a time when I didn't have a powerful touch screen computer with Internet access in my pocket, but it's getting harder and harder to remember what life was like then.

And of course it was about this same time that the Mobile Web finally came into its own. There *had* been Web browsers on phones before, but they—to use the technical term—sucked.

The problem had always been—as the Genie aptly put it—the itty-bitty living space. Mobile devices meant cramped devices, squeezing Web pages the size of a sheet of paper into a screen the size of a postage stamp. There were various attempts at solutions, even some profoundly debased "mobile" versions of sites (remember pressing numbers to select numbered menu items?) and, as usual, the early adopters and the people who really needed the data muddled through.

But Apple married more computer horsepower (in an emotionally pleasing, thin, aesthetic package—why are thin watches so desirable?) with a carefully wrought browser interface. One of Apple's great inventions was the ability to scroll (swiping up and down) and zoom in and out (pinching and...unpinching) very quickly. (It was the *very quickly* part—the responsiveness of the hardware—that finally made it useful.)

---

[1]  *Introduction of the iPhone June 2007.*

For the first time, the Web was fun to use on a device that you could carry with you at all times. With a battery that lasted all day. You could look up anything anywhere anytime.

It's hard to overestimate what a sea change this was.

Of course, it wasn't only about the Web. Just consider how many things the smartphone allowed you to carry in your pocket or purse at all times: a camera (still *and* video, and, for many people, the best one they'd ever owned), a GPS with maps of the whole world, a watch, an alarm clock, all of your photos and music, etc., etc.

It's true: The best camera really is the one you have with you.

And think about the fact that for most people in emerging countries, in the same way they bypassed landlines and went straight to cellphones, the smartphone is their first—and only—computer.

There's not much denying that mobile devices are the wave of the future, except for things where you need enormous horsepower (professional video editing, for example, at least for now) or a big playing surface (Photoshop or CAD).

# What's the difference?

So, what's different about usability when you're designing for use on a mobile device?

In one sense, the answer is: Not much. The basic principles are still the same. If anything, people are moving faster and reading even less on small screens.

But there are *some* significant differences about mobile that make for challenging new usability problems.

As I write this, Web and app design for mobile devices is still in its formative "Wild West" days in many ways. It's going to take another few years for things to shake out, probably just in time for innovations that will force the whole cycle to start over again.

I'm not going to talk very much about specific best practices because many of the bright interface design ideas that will eventually become the prevailing conventions probably haven't emerged yet. And of course the technology is going to keep changing under our feet faster than we can run.

"App" | xkcd.com

What I *will* do is tell you a few things that I'm sure will continue to be true. And the first one is...

# It's all about tradeoffs

One way to look at design—any kind of design—is that it's essentially about constraints (things you *have to* do and things you *can't* do) and tradeoffs (the less-than-ideal choices you make to live within the constraints).

To paraphrase Lincoln, the best you can do is please some of the people some of the time.[2]

There's a well-established meme that suggests that rather than being the negative force that they often feel like, constraints actually make design easier and foster innovation.

And it's true that constraints are often helpful. If a sofa has to fit in *this* space and match *this* color scheme, it's sometimes easier to find one than if you just go shopping for any sofa. Having *something* pinned down can have a focusing effect,

---

[2]  *...if, in fact, he ever actually said "You can fool some of the people all of the time, and all of the people some of the time, but you cannot fool all of the people all of the time." One of the things I've learned from the Internet is that when it comes to memorable sayings attributed to famous people, 92% of the time they never said them. See en.wikiquote.org/wiki/Abraham_Lincoln.*

where a blank canvas with its unlimited options—while it sounds liberating—can have a paralyzing effect.

You may not buy the idea that constraints are a positive influence, but it really doesn't matter: Whenever you're designing, you're dealing with constraints. And where there are constraints, there are tradeoffs to be made.

In my experience, many—if not most—serious usability problems are the result of a poor decision about a tradeoff.

For example, I don't use CBS News on my iPhone.

I've learned over time that their stories are broken up into too-small (for me) chunks, and each one takes a long time to load. (If the pages loaded faster, I might not mind.) And to add insult to injury, on each new page you have to scroll down past the same photo to get to the next tiny morsel of text.

Here's what the experience looks like:

Tap to open the story, then wait. And wait. And wait.

When the page finally loads, swipe to scroll down past the photo.

Read the two paragraphs of text, then tap Next and wait. And wait.

Repeat 8 times to read the whole story.

It's so annoying that when I'm scanning Google News (which I do several times a day) and notice that the story I'm about to tap is linked to CBS News, I always click on Google's "More stories" link to choose another source.

When I run into a problem like this, I know that it's not there because the people who designed it didn't think about it. In fact, I'm sure it was the subject of some intense debate that resulted in a compromise.

I don't know what constraints were at work in this particular tradeoff. Since there are ads on the pages, it may have been a need to generate more page views. Or it could have something to do with the way the content is segmented for other purposes in their content management system. I have no idea. All I do know is that the choice they made didn't place enough weight on creating a good experience for the user.

Most of the challenges in creating good mobile usability boil down to making good tradeoffs.

# The tyranny of the itty-bitty living space

The most obvious thing about mobile screens is that they're small. For decades, we've been designing for screens which, while they may have felt small to Web designers at the time, were luxurious by today's standards. And even then, designers were working overtime trying to squeeze everything into view.

But if you thought Home page real estate was precious before, try accomplishing the same things on a mobile site. So there are definitely many new tradeoffs to be made.

One way to deal with a smaller living space is to leave things out: Create a mobile site that is a subset of the full site. Which, of course, raises a tricky question: Which parts do you leave out?

One approach was Mobile First. Instead of designing a full-featured (and perhaps bloated) version of your Web site first and then paring it down to create the mobile version, you design the mobile version first based on the features and content that are most important to your users. Then you add on more features and content to create the desktop/full version.

It was a great idea. For one thing, Mobile First meant that you would work hard to determine what was really essential, what people needed most. Always a good thing to do.

But some people interpreted it to mean that you should choose what to include based on what people want to do when they're mobile. This assumed that when people accessed the mobile version they were "on the move," not sitting at their desk, so they'd only need the kinds of features you'd use on the move. For example, you might want to check your bank balances while out shopping, but you wouldn't be likely to reconcile your checkbook or set up a new account.

Of course, it turned out this was wrong. People are just as likely to be using their mobile devices while sitting on the couch at home, and they want (and expect) to be able to do everything. Or at least, everybody wants to do *some* things, and if you add them all up it amounts to everything.

If you're going to include everything, you have to pay even more attention to prioritizing.

Things I want to use in a hurry or frequently should be close at hand. Everything else can be a few taps away, but there should be an obvious path to get to them.

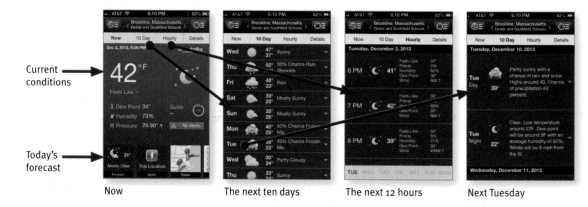

Current conditions

Today's forecast

Now      The next ten days      The next 12 hours      Next Tuesday

In some cases, the lack of space on each screen means that mobile sites become much deeper than their full-size cousins, so you might have to tap down three, four, or five "levels" to get to some features or content.

This means that people will be tapping more, but that's OK. With small screens it's inevitable: To see the same amount of information, you're going to be either tapping or scrolling a lot more. As long as the user continues to feel confident that what they want is further down the screen or behind that link or button, they'll keep going.

Here's the main thing to remember, though:

MANAGING REAL ESTATE CHALLENGES SHOULDN'T
BE DONE AT THE COST OF USABILITY[3]

# Breeding chameleons

The siren song of one-design-fits-all-screen-sizes has a long history of bright hopes, broken promises, and weary designers and developers.

If there are two things I can tell you about scalable design (a/k/a dynamic layout, fluid design, adaptive design, and responsive design), they're these:

- It tends to be a lot of work.

- It's very hard to do it well.

In the past, scalable design—creating one version of a site that would look good on many different size screens—was optional. It *seemed* like a good idea, but very few people actually cared about it. Now that small screens are taking over, everybody cares: If you have a Web site, you have to make it usable on any size screen.

Developers learned long ago that trying to create separate versions of anything—keeping two sets of books, so to speak—is a surefire path to madness. It doubles the effort (at least) and guarantees that either things won't be updated as frequently or the versions will be out of sync.

It's still getting sorted out. This time, the problem has real revenue implications, so there will be technical solutions, but it will take time.

---

[3] *Thanks to Manikandan Baluchamy for this maxim.*

In the meantime, here are three suggestions:

- **Allow zooming.** If you don't have the resources to "mobilize" your site at all and you're not using responsive design, you should at least make sure that your site doesn't *resist* efforts to view it on a mobile device. There are few things more annoying than opening up a site on your phone and discovering that you can't zoom in on the tiny text at all. (Well, all right. Actually there are a lot of things more annoying. But it's pretty annoying.)

- **Don't leave me standing at the front door.** Another real nuisance: You tap on a link in an email or a social media site and instead of taking you to the article in question it takes you to the mobile Home page, leaving you to hunt for the thing yourself.

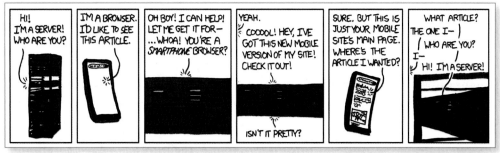

"Server Attention Span" | xkcd.com

- Always provide a link to the "full" Web site. No matter how fabulous and complete your mobile site is, you do need to give users the option of viewing the non-mobile version, especially if it has features and information that aren't available in your mobile version. (The current convention is to put a Mobile Site/Full Site toggle at the bottom of every page.)

There are many situations where people will be willing to zoom in and out through the small viewport of a mobile device in return for access on the go to features they've become accustomed to using or need at that moment. Also, some people will prefer to see the desktop pages when using 7" tablets with high-resolution screens in landscape mode.

# Don't hide your affordances under a bushel

Affordances are visual clues in an object's design that suggest how we can use it. (I mentioned them back in Chapter 3. Remember the doorknobs and the book by Don Norman? He popularized the term in the first edition of *The Design of Everyday Things* in 1988 and the design world quickly adopted it.[4])

Affordances are the meat and potatoes of a visual user interface. For instance, the three-dimensional style of some buttons makes it clear they're meant to be clicked. The same as with the scent of information for links, the clearer the visual cues, the more unambiguous the signal.

Strong affordance ⟶ Not so much

In the same way, a rectangular box with a border around it suggests that you can click in it and type something. If you had an editable text box without a border, the user could still click on it and type in it if he knew it was there. But it's the affordance—the border—that makes its function clear.

Name

Name     John Smi|

Name

Name     John Smi|

---

4   *Unfortunately, the way they used it wasn't exactly what he intended. He's clarified it in the new edition of* Everyday Things *by proposing to call the clues "signifiers" instead, but it may be too late to put that genie back in the bottle. With apologies to Don, I'm going to keep calling them affordances here because (a) it's still the prevailing usage, and (b) it makes my head hurt too much otherwise.*

For affordances to work, they need to be noticeable, and some characteristics of mobile devices have made them less noticeable or, worse, invisible. And by definition, affordances are the *last* thing you should hide.

This is not to say that all affordances need to hit you in the face. They just have to be visible enough that people can notice the ones they need to get their tasks done.

# No cursor = no hover = no clue

Before touch screens arrived, Web design had come to rely heavily on a feature called hover—the ability of screen elements to change in some way when the user points the cursor at them without clicking.

But a capacitive touch screen (used on almost all mobile devices) can't accurately sense that a finger is hovering above the glass, only when the finger has touched it. This is why they don't have a cursor.[5]

As a result, many useful interface features that depended on hover are no longer available, like tool tips, buttons that change shape or color to indicate that they're clickable, and menus that drop down to reveal their contents without forcing you to make a choice.

As a designer, you need to be aware that these elements don't exist for mobile users and try to find ways to replace them.

# Flat design: Friend or foe?

Affordances require visual distinctions. But the recent trend in interface design (which may have waned by the time you read this) has moved in exactly the opposite direction: removing visual distinctions and "flattening" the appearance of interface elements.

---

[5]  *Did you ever notice that the cursor was missing? I have to admit that I used my first iPhone for several months before it dawned on me that there was no cursor.*

It looks darned good (to some people, anyway), and it can make screens less cluttered-looking. But at what price?

In this case the tradeoff is between a clean, uncluttered look on one hand and providing sufficient visual information so people can perceive affordances on the other.

Unfortunately, Flat design has a tendency to take along with it not just the potentially distracting decoration but also the useful information that the more textured elements were conveying.

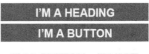

The distinctions required to draw attention to an affordance often need to be multi-dimensional: It's the position of something (e.g., in the navigation bar) *and* its formatting (e.g., reversed type, all caps) that tell you it's a menu item.

By removing a number of these distinctions from the design palette, Flat design makes it harder to differentiate things.

Flat design has sucked the air out of the room. It reminds me of the pre-color world in my favorite *Calvin and Hobbes* cartoon/comic/comic strip. (The rest of the cartoon is at the end of Chapter 13.)

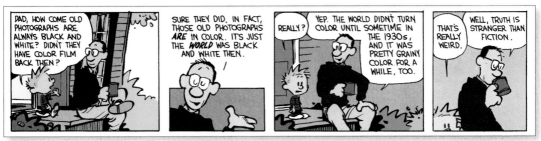

You can do all the Flat design you want (you may have to, it may be forced on you), but make sure you're using all of the remaining dimensions to compensate for what you lose.

# You actually can be too rich or too thin

...but computers can never be too fast. Particularly on mobile devices, speed just makes everything feel better. Slow performance equals frustration for users and loss of goodwill for publishers.

For instance, I prize the breaking news alerts from the AP (Associated Press) mobile app. They're always the first hint I get of major news stories.

Unfortunately for AP, though, whenever I tap on one of their alerts, the app insists on loading a huge chunk of photos for all the other current top stories before showing me any details about the alert.

As a result, I've formed a new habit: When an AP alert arrives, I immediately open the *New York Times* site or Google News to see if they've picked up the story yet.

We're all used to very fast connections nowadays, but we have to remember that mobile download speeds are unreliable. If people are at home or sitting at Starbucks, download speeds are probably good, but once they leave the comfort of Wi-Fi and revert to 4G or 3G or worse, performance can vary widely.

Be careful that your responsive design solutions aren't loading up pages with huge amounts of code and images that are larger than necessary for the user's screen.

# Mobile apps, usability attributes of

You may remember that way back on page 9 I mentioned that I'd talk later about attributes that some people include in their definitions of usability: useful, learnable, memorable, effective, efficient, desirable, and delightful. Well, that time has arrived.

Personally, my focus has always been on the three that are central to my definition of usability:

> A person of average (or even below average) ability and experience can figure out how to use the thing [i.e., it's *learnable*] to accomplish something [*effective*] without it being more trouble than it's worth [*efficient*].

I don't spend much time thinking about whether things are *useful* because it strikes me as more of a marketing question, something that should be established before any project starts, using methods like interviews, focus groups, and surveys. Whether something is *desirable* seems like a marketing question too, and I'll have more to say about that in the final chapter.

For now let's talk about *delight, learnability,* and *memorability* and how they apply to mobile apps.

# Delightful is the new black

What is this "delight" stuff, anyway?

Delight is a bit hard to pin down; it's more one of those "I'll know it when I feel it" kind of things. Rather than a definition, it's probably easier to identify some of the words people use when describing delightful products: fun, surprising, impressive, captivating, clever, and even magical.[6]

---

[6] *My personal standard for a delightful app tends to be "does something you would have been burned at the stake for a few hundred years ago."*

Delightful apps usually come from marrying an idea about something people would really enjoy being able to do, but don't imagine is possible, with a bright idea about how to use some new technology to accomplish it.

SoundHound is a perfect example.

Not only can it identify that song that you hear playing wherever you happen to be, but it can display the lyrics and scroll them in sync with the song.

And Paper is not your average drawing app. Instead of dozens of tools with thousands of options, you get five tools with no options. And each one is optimized to create things that look good.

Building delight into mobile apps has become increasingly important because the app market is so competitive. Just doing something well isn't good enough to create a hit; you have to do something incredibly well. Delight is sort of like the extra credit assignment of user experience design.

Making your app delightful is a fine objective. Just don't focus so much attention on it that you forget to make it usable, too.

# Apps need to be learnable

One of the biggest problems with apps is that if they have more than a few features they may not be very easy to learn.

Take Clear, for example. It's an app for making lists, like to-do lists. It's brilliant, innovative, beautiful, useful, and fun to use, with a clean minimalist interface. All of the interactions are elegantly animated, with sophisticated sound effects. One reviewer said, "It's almost like I'm playing a pinball machine while I'm staying productive."

The problem is that one reason it's so much fun to use is that they've come up with innovative interactions, gestures, and navigation, but there's a lot to learn.

With most apps, if you get any instructions at all it's usually one or two screens when you first launch the app that give a few essential hints about how the thing works. But it's often difficult or impossible to find them again to read later.

And if help exists at all (and you can find it), it's often one short page of text or a link to the developer's site with no help to be found or a customer support page that gives you the email address where you can send your questions.

This can work for apps that are only doing a very few things, but as soon as you try to create something that has a lot of functionality—and particularly any functions that don't follow familiar conventions or interface guidelines—it's often not enough.

The people who made Clear have actually done a very good job with training compared to most apps. The first time you use it, you tap your way through a nicely illustrated ten-screen quick tour of the main features.

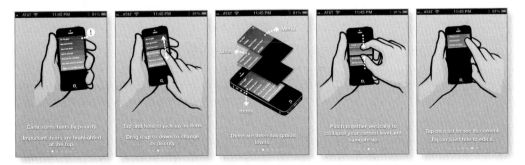

This is followed by an ingenious tutorial that's actually just one of their lists.

Each item in the list tells you something to try, and by the time you're done you've practiced using almost all of the features.

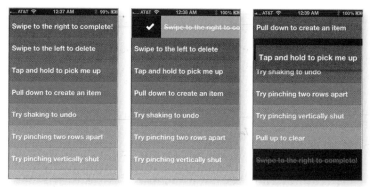

But when I've used it to do demo usability tests during my presentations, it hasn't fared so well.

I give the participant/volunteer a chance to learn about the app by reading the description in the app store, viewing the quick tour, and trying the actions in the tutorial. Then I ask them to do the type of primary task the app is designed for: create a new list called "Chicago trip" with three items in it — Book hotel, Rent car, and Choose flight.

So far, no one has succeeded.

Even though it's shown in the slide show on the way in, people don't seem to get the concept that there are levels: the level of lists, the level of items in lists, and the level of settings. And even if they remember seeing it, they still can't figure out how to navigate between levels. And if you can't figure that out, you can't get to the Help screens. Catch-22.

That's not to say that no one in the real world learns how to use it. It gets great reviews and is consistently a best seller. But I have to wonder how many people who bought it have never mastered it, or how many more sales they could make if it were easier to learn.

And this is a company that's put a lot of effort into training and help. Most don't.

You need to do better than most, and usability testing will help you figure out how.

# Apps need to be memorable, too

There's one more attribute that's important: memorability. Once you've figured out how to use an app, will you remember how to use it the next time you try or will you have to start over again from scratch?

I don't usually talk much about memorability because I think the best way to make things easy to *relearn* is to make them incredibly clear and easy to *learn* in the first place. If it's easy to learn the first time, it's easy to learn the second time.

But it's certainly a serious problem with some apps.

One of my favorite drawing apps is ASketch. I *love* this app because no matter what you try to draw and how crudely you draw it, it ends up looking interesting.

But for months, each time I opened it I couldn't remember how to start a new drawing.

In fact, I couldn't remember how to get to *any* of the controls. To maximize the drawing space there weren't any icons on the screen.

I'd try all the usual suspects: double tap, triple tap, tap near the middle at the top or bottom of the screen, various swipes and multi-finger taps, and finally I'd hit on it. But by the next time I went to use it I'd forgotten what the trick was again.

Memorability can be a big factor in whether people adopt an app for regular use. Usually when you purchase one, you'll be willing to spend some time right away figuring out how to use it. But if you have to invest the same effort the next time, it's unlikely to feel like a satisfying experience. Unless you're very impressed by what it does, there's a good chance you'll abandon it—which is the fate of most apps.

Life is cheap (99 cents) on mobile devices.

# Usability testing on mobile devices

For the most part, doing usability testing on mobile devices is exactly the same as the testing I described in Chapter 9.

You're still making up tasks for people to do and watching them try to do them. You still prompt them to say what they're thinking while they work. You still need to keep quiet most of the time and save your probing questions for the end. And you should still try to get as many stakeholders as possible to come and observe the tests in person.

Almost everything that's different when you're doing mobile testing isn't about the process; it's about logistics.

# The logistics of mobile testing

When you're doing testing on a personal computer, the setup is pretty simple:

- The facilitator looks at the same screen as the participant.
- Screen sharing software allows the observers to see what's happening.
- Screen recording software creates a video of the session.

But if you've ever tried doing tests on mobile devices, you know that the setup can get very complicated: document cameras, Webcams, hardware signal processors, physical restraints (well, maybe not physical restraints, but "Don't move the device beyond this point" markers to keep the participant within view of a camera), and even things called sleds and goosenecks.

Here are some of the issues you have to deal with:

- Do you need to let the participants use their own devices?
- Do they need to hold the device naturally, or can it be sitting on a table or propped up on a stand?
- What do the observers need to see (e.g., just the screen, or both the screen and the participant's fingers so they can see their gestures)? And how do you display it in the observation room?
- How do you create a recording?

One of the main reasons why mobile testing is complicated is that some of the tools we rely on for desktop testing don't exist yet for mobile devices. As of this writing, robust mobile screen recording and screen sharing apps aren't available, mainly because the mobile operating systems tend to prohibit background processes. And the devices don't really have quite enough horsepower to run them anyway.

I expect this to change before long. With so many mobile sites and apps to test, there are already a lot of companies trying to come up with solutions.

# My recommendations

Until better technology-based solutions come along, here's what I'd lean toward:

- **Use a camera pointed at the screen instead of mirroring.** Mirroring is the same as screen sharing: It displays what's on the screen. You can do it with software (like Apple's Airplay) or hardware (using the same kind of cable you use to play a video from your phone or tablet on a monitor or TV).

  But mirroring isn't a good way to watch tests done on touch screen devices, because you can't see the gestures and taps the participant is making. Watching a test without seeing the participant's fingers is a little like watching a player piano: It moves very fast and can be hard to follow. Seeing the hand and the screen is much more engaging.

  If you're going to capture fingers, there's going to be a camera involved. (Some mirroring software will shows dots and streaks on the screen, but it's not the same thing.)

- **Attach the camera to the device so the user can hold it naturally.** In some setups, the device sits on a table or desk and can't be moved. In others, the participant can hold the device, but they're told to keep it inside an area marked with tape. The only reason for restricting movement of the device is to make it easier to point a camera at it and keep it in view.

  If you attach the camera to the device, the participant can move it freely and the screen will stay in view and in focus.

- **Don't bother with a camera pointed at the participant.** I'm really not a fan of the face camera. Some observers like seeing the participant's face, but I think it's actually a distraction. I'd much rather have observers focus on what's happening on the screen, and they can almost always tell what the user is feeling from their tone of voice anyway.

Adding a second camera inevitably makes the configuration much more complicated, and I don't think it's worth the extra complexity. Of course, if your boss insists on seeing faces, show faces.

# Proof of concept: My Brundleyfly[7] camera

Out of curiosity, I built myself a camera rig by merging a clip from a book light with a Webcam. It weighs almost nothing and captures the audio with its built-in microphone. Mine cost about $30 in parts and took about an hour to make. I'm sure somebody will manufacture something similar—only much better—before long. I'll put instructions for building one yourself online at rocketsurgerymadeeasy.com.

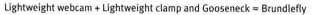

Lightweight webcam + Lightweight clamp and Gooseneck = Brundlefly

Attaching a camera to the device creates a very easy-to-follow view. The observers get a stable view of the screen even if the participant is waving it around.

I think it solves most of the objections to other mounted-camera solutions:

- **They're heavy and awkward.** It weighs almost nothing and barely changes the way the phone feels in your hand.

---

7 *Brundlefly is the word Jeff Goldblum's character (Seth Brundle) in* The Fly *uses to describe himself after his experiment with a teleportation device accidentally merges his DNA with that of a fly.*

- **They're distracting.** It's very small (smaller than it looks in the photo) and is positioned out of the participant's line of sight, which is focused on the phone.

- **Nobody wants to attach anything to their phone.** Sleds are usually attached to phones with Velcro or double-sided tape. This uses a padded clamp that can't scratch or mar anything but still grips the device firmly.

  One limitation of this kind of solution is that it is tethered: It requires a USB extension cable running from the camera to your laptop. But you can buy a long extension inexpensively.

The rest of the setup is very straightforward:

- Connect the Brundlefly to the facilitator's laptop via USB.

- Open something like AmCap (on a PC) or QuickTime Player (on a Mac) to display the view from the Brundlefly. The facilitator will watch this view.

- Share the laptop screen with the observers using screen sharing (GoToMeeting, WebEx, etc.)

- Run a screen recorder (e.g., Camtasia) on the computer in the observation room. This reduces the burden on the facilitator's laptop.

That's it.

# Finally...

In one form or another, it seems clear that mobile is where we're going to live in the future, and it provides enormous opportunities to create great user experiences and usable things. New technologies and form factors are going to be introduced all the time, some of them involving dramatically different ways of interacting.[8]

Just make sure that usability isn't being lost in the shuffle. And the best way to do this is by testing.

---

[8] *Personally, I think talking to your computer is going to be one of the next big things. Recognition accuracy is already amazing; we just need to find ways for people to talk to their devices without looking, sounding, and feeling foolish. Someone who's seriously working on the problems should give me a call; I've been using speech recognition software for 15 years, and I have a lot of thoughts about why it hasn't caught on.*

# 11

# Usability as common courtesy

## WHY YOUR WEB SITE SHOULD BE A MENSCH[1]

---

[1] *Mensch: a German-derived Yiddish word originally meaning "human being." A person of integrity and honor; "a stand-up guy"; someone who does the right thing.*

*Sincerity: that's the hard part.*
*If you can fake that, the rest is easy.*

—OLD JOKE ABOUT A HOLLYWOOD AGENT

Some time ago, I was booked on a flight to Denver. As it happened, the date of my flight also turned out to be the deadline for collective bargaining between the airline I was booked on and one of its unions.

Concerned, I did what anyone would do: (a) Start checking Google News every hour to see if a deal had been reached, and (b) visit the airline's Web site to see what *they* were saying about it.

I was shocked to discover that not only was there nothing about the impending strike on the airline's Home page, but there wasn't a word about it to be found anywhere on the entire site. I searched. I browsed. I scrolled through all of their FAQ lists. Nothing but business as usual. "Strike? What strike?"

Now, on the morning of a potential airline strike, you have to know that there's really only one frequently asked question related to the site, and it's being asked by hundreds of thousands of people who hold tickets for the coming week: What's going to happen to me?

I might have expected to find an entire FAQ list dedicated to the topic:

> Is there really going to be a strike?
> What's the current status of the talks?
> If there is a strike, what will happen?
> How will I be able to rebook my flight?
> What will you do to help me?

Nothing.

What was I to take away from this?

Either (a) the airline had no procedure for updating their Home page for special circumstances, (b) for some legal or business reason they didn't want to admit that there might be a strike, (c) it hadn't occurred to them that people might be interested, or (d) they just couldn't be bothered.

[ 165 ]

No matter what the real reason was, they did an outstanding job of depleting my goodwill towards both the airline and their Web site. Their brand—which they spend hundreds of millions of dollars a year polishing—had definitely lost some of its luster for me.

Most of this book has been about building *clarity* into Web sites: making sure that users can understand what it is they're looking at—and how to use it—without undue effort. Is it clear to people? Do they "get it"?

But there's another important component to usability: doing the right thing—being considerate of the user. Besides "Is my site clear?" you also need to be asking, "Does my site behave like a mensch?"

# The reservoir of goodwill

I've always found it useful to imagine that every time we enter a Web site, we start out with a reservoir of goodwill. Each problem we encounter on the site lowers the level of that reservoir. Here, for example, is what my visit to the airline site might have looked like:

I enter the site.

My goodwill is a little low, because I'm not happy that their negotiations may seriously inconvenience me.

I glance around the Home page.

It feels well organized, so I relax a little. I'm confident that if the information is here, I'll be able to find it.

There's no mention of the strike on the Home page.

I don't like the fact that it feels like business as usual.

There's a list of five links to News stories on the Home page but none are relevant.

I click on the Press Releases link at the bottom of the list.

Latest press release is five days old.

I go to the About Us page.

No promising links, but plenty of promotions, which is very annoying. Why are they trying to sell me more tickets when I'm not sure they're going to fly me tomorrow?

I search for "strike" and find two press releases about a strike a year ago and pages from the corporate history about a strike in the 1950s.

At this point, I would like to leave, but they're the sole source for this information.

I look through their FAQ lists, then leave.

The reservoir is limited, and if you treat users badly enough and exhaust it there's a good chance that they'll leave. But leaving isn't the only possible negative outcome; they may not be as eager to use your site in the future, or they may think less of your organization and savage you on Facebook or Twitter. For those of you in marketing, your NPS (Net Promoter Score) probably goes down.

There are a few things worth noting about this reservoir:

- **It's idiosyncratic.** Some people have a large reservoir, some small. Some people are more suspicious by nature, or more ornery; others are inherently more patient, trusting, or optimistic. The point is, you can't count on a very large reserve.

- **It's situational.** If I'm in a huge hurry, or have just come from a bad experience on another site, my expendable goodwill may already be low when I enter your site, even if I naturally have a large reserve.

- **You can refill it.** Even if you've made mistakes that have diminished my goodwill, you can replenish it by doing things that make me feel like you're looking out for my best interests.

- **Sometimes a single mistake can empty it.** For instance, just opening up a registration form with tons of fields may be enough to cause some people's reserve to plunge instantly to zero.

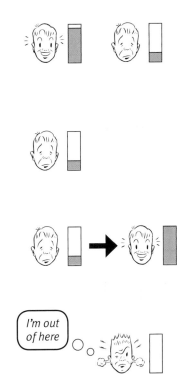

# Things that diminish goodwill

Here are a few of the things that tend to make users feel like the people publishing a site don't have their best interests at heart:

 **Hiding information that I want.** The most common things to hide are customer support phone numbers, shipping rates, and prices.

The whole point of hiding support phone numbers is to try to keep users from calling, because each call costs money. The usual effect is to diminish goodwill and ensure that they'll be even more annoyed when they do find the number and call. On the other hand, if the 800 number is in plain sight—perhaps even on every page—somehow knowing that they *can* call if they want to is often enough to keep people looking for the information on the site longer, increasing the chances that they'll solve the problem themselves.

Some sites hide pricing information in hopes of getting users so far into the process that they'll feel vested in it by the time they experience the sticker shock. My favorite example is Web sites for wireless access in public places like airports. Having seen a "Wireless access available!" sign and knowing that it's free at some airports, you open up your laptop, find a signal, and try to connect. But then you have to scan, read, and click your way through three pages, following links like "Wireless Access" and "Click here to connect" before you get to a page that even hints at what it might cost you. It feels like an old phone sales tactic: If they can just keep you on the line long enough and keep throwing more of their marketing pitch at you, maybe they can convince you along the way.

**Punishing me for not doing things your way.** I should *never* have to think about formatting data: whether or not to put dashes in my Social Security number, spaces in my credit card number, or parentheses in my phone number. Many sites perversely insist on no spaces in credit card numbers, when the spaces actually make it much easier to type the number correctly. Don't make me jump through hoops just because you don't want to write a little bit of code.

**Asking me for information you don't really need.** Most users are very skeptical of requests for personal information and find it annoying if a site asks for more than what's needed for the task at hand.

**Shucking and jiving me.** We're always on the lookout for faux sincerity, and disingenuous attempts to convince me that you care about me can be particularly annoying. Think about what goes through your head every time you hear "Your call is important to us."

> Right. That's why your "unusually high call volume" is keeping me on hold for 20 minutes: because my call is important to you, but my time isn't.

**Putting sizzle in my way.** Having to wade through pages bloated with feel-good marketing photos makes it clear that you don't understand— or care—that I'm in a hurry.

**Your site looks amateurish.** You can lose goodwill if your site looks sloppy, disorganized, or unprofessional, like *no* effort has gone into making it presentable.

*error messages should be presentable too - clear & concise*

Note that while people love to make comments about the appearance of sites—especially about whether they like the colors—almost no one is going to leave a site just because it doesn't look *great*. (I tell people to ignore all comments that users make about colors during a user test, unless three out of four people use a word like "puke" to describe the color scheme. Then it's worth rethinking.[2])

There may be times when you'll choose to have your site do some of these user-unfriendly things deliberately. Sometimes it makes business sense not to do exactly what the customer wants. For instance, uninvited pop-ups almost always annoy people to some extent. But if your statistics show you can get 10 percent more revenue by using pop-ups and you think it's worth annoying your users, you can do it. It's a business decision. Just be sure you do it in an informed way, rather than inadvertently.

---

[2] *This actually happened once during a round of testing I facilitated. We changed the color.*

# Things that increase goodwill

The good news is that even if you make mistakes, it's possible to restore my goodwill by doing things that convince me that you *do* have my interests at heart. Most of these are just the flip side of the other list:

⬛ **Know the main things that people want to do on your site and make them obvious and easy.** It's usually not hard to figure out what people want to do on a given Web site. I find that even people who disagree about everything else about their organization's site almost always give me the same answer when I ask them, "What are the three main things your users want to do?" The problem is, making those things easy doesn't always become the top priority it should be. (If most people are coming to your site to apply for a mortgage, nothing should get in the way of making it dead easy to apply for a mortgage.)

⬛ **Tell me what I want to know.** Be upfront about things like shipping costs, hotel daily parking fees, service outages—anything you'd rather *not* be upfront about. You may lose points if your shipping rates are higher than I'd like, but you'll often gain enough points for candor and for making it easy for me to compensate for the price difference.

⬛ **Save me steps wherever you can.** For instance, instead of giving me the shipping company's tracking number for my purchase, put a link in my email receipt that opens their site and submits my tracking number when I click it. *pretty much standard now* (As usual, Amazon was the first site to do this for me.)

⬛ **Put effort into it.** My favorite example is the HP technical support site, where it seems like an enormous amount of work has gone into (a) generating the information I need to solve my problems, (b) making sure that it's accurate and useful, (c) presenting it clearly, and (d) organizing it so I can find it. I've had a lot of HP printers, and in almost every case where I've had a problem I've been able to solve it on my own. As a result, I keep buying HP printers.

**Know what questions I'm likely to have, and answer them.** Frequently Asked Questions lists are enormously valuable, especially if

*Are we considering this?*

- They really are FAQs, not marketing pitches masquerading as FAQs (also known as QWWPWAs: Questions We *Wish* People Would Ask).

- You keep them up to date. Customer Service and Technical Support can easily give you a list of this week's five most frequently asked questions. I would always put this list at the top of any site's Support page.

- They're candid. Often people are looking in the FAQs for the answer to a question you'd rather they hadn't asked. Candor in these situations goes a *long* way to increasing goodwill.

**Provide me with creature comforts like printer-friendly pages.** Some people love being able to print stories that span multiple pages with a single click, and CSS makes it relatively easy to create printer-friendly pages with little additional effort. Drop the ads (the possibility of a banner ad having any impact other than being annoying is even greater when it's just taking up space on paper), but *don't* drop the illustrations, photos, and figures.

**Make it easy to recover from errors.** If you actually do enough user testing, you'll be able to spare me from many errors before they happen. But where the potential for errors is unavoidable, always provide a graceful, obvious way for me to recover.

**When in doubt, apologize.** Sometimes you can't help it: You just don't have the ability or resources to do what the user wants (for instance, your university's library system requires separate passwords for each of your catalog databases, so you can't give users the single login they'd like). If you can't do what they want, at least let them know that *you* know you're inconveniencing them.

# 12

# Accessibility and you

JUST WHEN YOU THINK YOU'RE DONE, A CAT FLOATS
BY WITH BUTTERED TOAST STRAPPED TO ITS BACK

*When a cat is dropped, it always lands on its feet, and when toast is dropped, it always lands with the buttered side facing down. I propose to strap buttered toast to the back of a cat; the two will hover, spinning, inches above the ground. With a giant buttered-cat array, a high-speed monorail could easily link New York with Chicago.*

—JOHN FRAZEE, IN *THE JOURNAL OF IRREPRODUCIBLE RESULTS*

P eople sometimes ask me, "What about accessibility? Isn't that part of usability?"

And they're right, of course. Unless you're going to make a blanket decision that people with disabilities aren't part of your audience, you really can't say your site is usable unless it's accessible.

At this point, everyone involved in Web design knows at least a little bit about Web accessibility. And yet almost every site I go to still fails my three-second accessibility test—increasing the size of the type.[1]

Change browser "Text Size" to "Largest"

Before                     After (no difference)

Why is that?

---

[1] *If you're about to send me email reminding me that Zoom has replaced Text Size in most browsers, thanks, but you can save those keystrokes. Every site gets larger if you use Zoom, but only sites that have moved beyond fixed-size fonts (usually a good indicator of effort to make things accessible) respond to Text Size.*

# What developers and designers hear

In most organizations, the people who end up being responsible for doing something about accessibility are the people who actually build the thing: the designers and the developers.

When they try to learn about what they should do, whatever books or articles they pick up inevitably list the same set of reasons why they need to make their sites accessible:

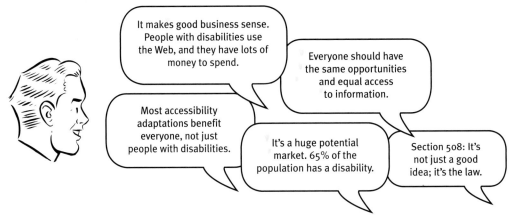

There's a lot of truth in all of these. Unfortunately, there's also a lot that's unlikely to convince 22-year-old developers and designers that they should be "doing accessibility." Two arguments in particular tend to make them skeptical:

- **__% of the population has a disability.** Since their world consists largely of able-bodied 22-year-olds, it's very hard for them to believe that a large percentage of the population actually needs help accessing the Web. They're willing to write it off as the kind of exaggeration that people make when they're advocating for a worthy cause, but there's also a natural inclination to think, "If one of their claims is so clearly untrue, I'm entitled to be skeptical about the rest."

- **Making things more accessible benefits everyone.** They know that some adaptations do, like the classic example, closed captioning, which does often come in handy for people who can hear.[2] But since this always seems to

---

[2] *Melanie and I often use it when watching British films, for instance.*

be the only example cited, it feels a little like arguing that the space program was worthwhile because it gave us Tang.[3] It's much easier for developers and designers to imagine cases where accessibility adaptations are likely to make things worse for "everyone else."

The worst thing about this skepticism is that it obscures the fact that there's really only one reason that's important:

- **It's the right thing to do.** And not just the right thing; it's *profoundly* the right thing to do, because the one argument for accessibility that doesn't get made nearly often enough is how extraordinarily better it makes some people's lives. Personally, I don't think anyone should need more than this one example: Blind people with access to a computer can now read almost any newspaper or magazine on their own. Imagine that.

How many opportunities do we have to dramatically improve people's lives just by doing our job a little better?

And for those of you who don't find this argument compelling, be aware that even if you haven't already encountered it, there will be a legislative stick coming sooner or later. Count on it.

# What designers and developers fear

As they learn more about accessibility, two fears tend to emerge:

- **More work.** For developers in particular, accessibility can seem like just one more complicated new thing to fit into an already impossible project schedule. In the worst case, it gets handed down as an "initiative" from above, complete with time-consuming reports, reviews, and task force meetings.

---

[3]  *A powdered orange-flavored breakfast drink, invented for the astronauts (see also: freeze-dried food).*

- **Compromised design.** What designers fear most is what I refer to as buttered cats: places where good design for people with disabilities and good design for everyone else are going to be in direct opposition. They're worried that they're going to be forced to design sites that are less appealing—and less useful—for the majority of their audience.

In an ideal world, accessibility would work like a sign I saw in the back of a Chicago taxi. At first it looked like an ordinary sign. But something about the way it caught the light made me take a closer look, and when I did, I realized that it was ingenious.

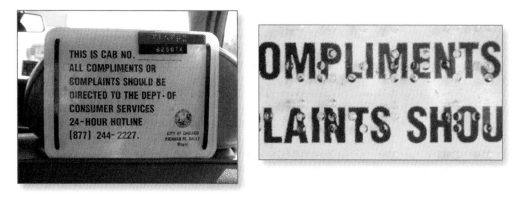

The sign was overlaid with a thin piece of Plexiglas, and the message was embossed in Braille on the Plexiglas. Ordinarily, both the print and the Braille would have been half as large so they could both fit on the sign, but with this design each audience got the best possible experience. It was an elegant solution.

I think for some designers, though, accessibility conjures up an image something like the Vonnegut short story where the government creates equality by handicapping everyone.[4]

---

[4] In "Harrison Bergeron," the main character, whose intelligence is "way above normal," is required by law to wear a "mental handicap radio" in his ear that blasts various loud noises every 20 seconds "to keep people like George from taking unfair advantage of their brains."

# The truth is, it *can* be complicated

When people start reading about accessibility, they usually come across one piece of advice that sounds very promising:

The problem is, when they run their site through a validator, it turns out to be more like a grammar checker than a spell checker. Yes, it does find some obvious mistakes and oversights that are easy to fix, like missing alt text.[5] But it also inevitably turns up a series of vague warnings that you *may* be doing something wrong and a long list of recommendations of things for you to check that it admits may *not* be problems at all.

This can be very discouraging for people who are just learning about accessibility, because the long lists and ambiguous advice suggest that there's an awful lot to learn.

And the truth is, it's a lot harder than it ought to be to make a site accessible.

After all, most designers and developers are not going to become accessibility experts. If Web accessibility is going to become ubiquitous, it's going to have to be easier to do. Screen readers and other adaptive technologies have to get smarter, the tools for building sites (like Dreamweaver) have to make it easier to code correctly for accessibility, and our design processes need to be updated to include thinking about accessibility from the beginning.

---

[5]  *Alt text provides a text description of an image ("Picture of two men on a sailboat," for example), which is essential for people using screen readers or browsing with images turned off.*

# The four things you can do right now

The fact that it's not a perfect world at the moment doesn't let any of us off the hook, though.

Even with current technology and standards, it's possible to make any site very accessible without an awful lot of effort by focusing on a few things that will have the most impact. And they don't involve getting anywhere near a buttered cat.

# #1. Fix the usability problems that confuse everyone

One of the things that I find annoying about the Tang argument ("making sites accessible makes them more usable for everyone") is that it obscures the fact that the reverse actually *is* true: Making sites more usable for "the rest of us" is one of the most effective ways to make them more effective for people with disabilities.

If something confuses most people who use your site, it's almost certain to confuse users who have accessibility issues. (After all, people don't suddenly become remarkably smarter just because they have a disability.) And it's very likely that they're going to have a harder time recovering from their confusion.

For instance, think of the last time you had trouble using a Web site (running into a confusing error message when you submitted a form, for example). Now imagine trying to solve that problem without being able to see the page.

The single best thing you can do to improve your site's accessibility is to test it often, and continually smooth out the parts that confuse everyone. In fact, if you don't do this first, no matter how rigorously you apply accessibility guidelines, people with disabilities still won't be able to use your site. If it's not clear to begin with, just fixing code problems is like [insert your favorite putting-lipstick-on-a-pig metaphor here].

# #2. Read an article

As I hope you've seen by now, the best way to learn how to make anything more usable is to watch people actually try to use it. But most of us have no experience at using adaptive technology, let alone watching other people use it.

If you have the time and the motivation, I'd highly recommend locating one or two blind Web users and spending a few hours with them observing how they actually use their screen reader software.

Fortunately, someone has done the heavy lifting for you. Mary Theofanos and Janice (Ginny) Redish watched 16 blind users using screen readers to do a number of tasks on a variety of sites and reported what they observed in an article titled "Guidelines for Accessible and Usable Web Sites: Observing Users Who Work with Screen Readers."[6]

As with any kind of user testing, it produced invaluable insights. Here's one example of the kinds of things they learned:

> **Screen-reader users scan with their ears.** Most blind users are just as impatient as most sighted users. They want to get the information they need as quickly as possible. They do not listen to every word on the page—just as sighted users do not read every word. They "scan with their ears," listening to just enough to decide whether to listen further. Many set the voice to speak at an amazingly rapid rate.
>
> They listen to the first few words of a link or line of text. If it does not seem relevant, they move quickly to the next link, next line, next heading, next paragraph. Where a sighted user might find a keyword by scanning over the entire page, a blind user may not hear that keyword if it is not at the beginning of a link or a line of text.

I recommend that you read this article before you read anything else about accessibility. In 20 minutes, it will give you an appreciation for the problems you're trying to solve that you won't get from any other articles or books.

---

6  Published in the ACM magazine Interactions (November-December 2003). With permission from ACM, Ginny has made it available for personal use at redish.net/images/stories/PDF/InteractionsPaperAuthorsVer.pdf. Yes, it's ten years old, but it's still relevant.

# #3. Read a book

After you've read Ginny and Mary's article, you're ready to spend a weekend reading a book about Web accessibility. These two are particularly good:

- *A Web for Everyone: Designing Accessible User Experiences* by Sarah Horton and Whitney Quesenbery. (Their approach: "Good UX equals good accessibility. Here's how to do both.")

- *Web Accessibility: Web Standards and Regulatory Compliance* by Jim Thatcher et al. ("Here are the laws and regulations, and we'll help you understand how to meet them.")

These books cover a lot of ground, so don't worry about absorbing all of it. For now, you just need to get the big picture.

# #4. Go for the low-hanging fruit

Now you're ready to do what most people think of as Web accessibility: implementing specific changes in your pages.

As of right now, these are probably the most important things to do:

- **Add appropriate alt text to every image.** Add an empty (or "null") alt attribute (`<alt="">`) for images that screen readers should ignore, and add helpful, descriptive text for the rest.

To learn how to write good alt text—and in fact to learn how to do any of the things in this list—head over to webaim.org. The folks at WebAIM have written excellent practical articles covering the nuts-and-bolts details of almost every accessibility technique.

- **Use headings correctly.** The standard HTML heading elements convey useful information about the logical organization of your content to people using screen readers and make it easier for them to navigate via the keyboard. Use `<h1>` for the page title or main content heading, `<h2>` for the major section headings, `<h3>` for subheadings, and so on, and then use CSS to redefine the visual appearance of each level.

- **Make your forms work with screen readers.** This largely boils down to using the HTML `<label>` element to associate the fields with their text labels, so people know what they're supposed to enter.

- **Put a "Skip to Main Content" link at the beginning of each page.** Imagine having to spend 20 seconds (or a minute, or two) listening to the global navigation at the top of every page before you could look at the content, and you'll understand why this is important.

- **Make all content accessible by keyboard.** Remember, not everyone can use a mouse.

- **Create significant contrast between your text and background.** Don't ever use light grey text on a dark grey background, for instance.

- **Use an accessible template.** If you're using WordPress, for example, make sure that the theme you choose has been designed to be accessible.

That's it. You'll probably learn how to do a lot more as you go along, but even if you do only what I've covered here, you'll have made a really good start.

When I wrote this chapter seven years ago, it ended with this:

> Hopefully in five years I'll be able to just remove this chapter and use the space for something else because the developer tools, browsers, screen readers, and guidelines will all have matured and will be integrated to the point where people can build accessible sites without thinking about it.

Sigh.

Hopefully we'll have better luck this time.

# 13

# Guide for the perplexed[1]

## MAKING USABILITY HAPPEN WHERE YOU LIVE

---

[1]  The Guide for the Perplexed *(the real one) is a seminal commentary on the meaning of the Talmud written in the 12th century by Rabbi Moshe ben Maimon (better known as Maimonides). I've just always thought it was the best title I've ever heard.*

I get a lot of email from people asking me some variation of this question:

> OK, I get it. This usability stuff is important, and I really want to work on it myself. How do I convince my boss—and his boss—that they should be taking users seriously and allow me to spend time making it happen?

What *can* you do if you find yourself in an environment where your desire to "do usability" isn't supported?

## Ya gotta know the territory

First, a little background about how the place of usability in the world has changed.

Back in the late 1990s, Usability and User Centered Design (UCD) were the terms most people used to describe any efforts to design with the user in mind. And there were essentially two "professions" that focused on making Web sites more usable: Usability (making sure things are designed in a way that enables people to use them successfully) and Information Architecture (making sure the content is organized in a way that allows people to find what they need).

Now the term you hear most often is User Experience Design, or just User Experience (UXD or UX, for short), and there are probably a dozen specialties involved, like Interaction Design, Interface Design, Visual Design, and Content Management—and, of course, Usability and Information Architecture—all under the UX umbrella.

One difference between User Centered Design and User Experience Design is their scope. UCD focused on designing the right product and making sure that it was usable. UX sees its role as taking the users' needs into account at every stage of the product life cycle, from the time they see an ad on TV, through purchasing it and tracking its delivery online, and even returning it to a local branch store.

The good news is that there's a lot more awareness now of the importance of focusing on the user. Steve Jobs (and Jonathan Ive) made a very compelling business case for UX, and as a result usability is an easier sell than it was even a few years ago.

The bad news is that where usability used to be the standard bearer for user-friendly design, now it's got a lot of siblings looking for seats at the table, each convinced that their set of tools are the best ones for the job. The worse news is that not many people understand the differences between the specialties or the unique contributions they can make.

This is the field you're playing on. So when someone tells you: "I'm in UX" or "Usability is so 2002—it's all UX now," smile graciously and ask them a few questions about how they're learning about users, how they're testing whether people can use what they're building, and how they get changes to happen. If they don't do any of those things, they need your help. If they do, learn from them. It's not what we call ourselves that matters, it's the attitude we bring and the skills we can contribute.

# The usual advice

Here are the two suggestions I've always heard for convincing management to support (and fund) usability work:

- **Demonstrate ROI.** In this approach, you gather and analyze data to prove that a usability change you've made resulted in cost savings or additional revenue ("Changing the label on this button increased sales by 0.25%"). There's an excellent book about it: *Cost-justifying Usability: An Update for the Internet Age*, edited by Randolph Bias and Deborah Mayhew.

- **Speak their language.** Instead of talking about the benefits for users, learn what the current vexing corporate problems are and describe your efforts in a way that makes it clear that they're part of the solution: Talk about things like pain points, touch points, KPIs, and CSI, or whatever management buzzwords are trending in your organization.

These are both fine ideas and worth doing if you can manage it. But making an ROI case tied to costs and revenues can be a lot of work, and unless it's rigorously implemented there'll always be someone who'll claim that the added value was caused by something else. And learning to speak "business" can be challenging, too. That's what MBA degrees are for.

# If I were you...

...I'd last about a week at your job. Every time I go to a client's office I spend most of my time marveling at the fact that so many people can survive in the corporate world. I'm just not equipped for dealing with the office politics in a large (i.e., more than two people) organization and sitting in meetings all day.

But I have spent a fair amount of time *visiting* corporate offices and getting managers to take usability seriously. So I do have some ideas about tactics that work, and people who have tried them tell me they've had some success. So here's what I'd do if I were you:

- **Get your boss (and her boss) to watch a usability test.** The tactic that I think works best is getting people from higher up the food chain to come and observe even one usability test. Tell them that you're going to be doing some testing and it would be great for the Web team's morale if they could just poke their head in for a few minutes.

  In my experience, executives often become fascinated and stay longer than they'd planned, because it's the first time they've seen anyone try to use the company's site and it's often not nearly as pretty a picture as they'd imagined.

  It's important to get them to come in person. The difference between watching a usability test live and hearing a presentation about it is like the difference between watching a sporting event while it's happening versus listening to a recap of it on the evening news. Live games create memorable experiences; the evening news not so much.

If you can't get them to come, then settle for second best: include clips of high-lights from tests in your presentations. If you don't get to do a presentation, post a short clip (less than 3 minutes) on your intranet and send out email with an intriguing description and a link to the video. Even executives like watching short videos.

- **Do the first one on your own time.** When you do your first test, don't ask for permission; just keep it incredibly simple and informal, and find volunteers for participants so it doesn't cost anything.

  And try to make sure that something improves as a result. Pick an easy target to test—something that you know has at least one serious usability problem that can be fixed quickly without having to get a lot of people to sign off on the change—renaming a poorly labeled button, for instance. Then test it, fix it, and publicize it.

  If you can find a simple way to measure the improvement, do so. For instance, you might test something that's been causing a lot of support calls and then show how much the calls on that issue decreased after you fixed the problem.

- **Do a test of the competition.** I mentioned in Chapter 9 that it's a good idea to test some competitive sites at the start of any project. But it's also a great way to drum up support for testing. Everybody loves learning about the competition, and because it's not your site being tested, no one has anything personally on the line. It makes a great brown bag lunch event.

- **Empathize with management.** A few years ago at the UXPA annual conference, I looked around and thought "What a nice group of people!" Then it dawned on me: of course they're nice. Empathy is virtually a professional requirement for usability work. And if you're interested in doing it, you're probably empathetic too. I recommend that you apply that empathy to your bosses. Not in the "how can I figure out what motivates these people so I can get them to do what I want" way, but more in the "understand the position they find themselves in" way, having real, emotional empathy for them. You may be surprised by the effect.

- **Know your place in the grand scheme of things.** Personally, in the situation you're in, I think a little bit of humility goes a long way. The reality is that in the business world almost everyone is just a very small cog in a huge collection of cogs.[2]

  You want your enthusiasm for usability to be infectious, but it just doesn't work to go around with the attitude that you're bringing the truth—about usability, or anything else—to the unwashed masses. Your primary role should be to share what you know, not to tell people how things should be done.

I'd also recommend two books that can help.

First there's Tomer Sharon's *It's Our Research: Getting Stakeholder Buy-In for User Experience Research Projects.* Tomer is a UX Researcher at Google, and I've never heard him say anything that wasn't true, pithy, and actionable.

Any book with section titles like "Become the voice of reason" and "Accept the fact that it might not work and that it's okay" is obviously worth reading.

Leah Buley's *The User Experience Team of One: A Research and Design Survival Guide* is written specifically for people who are "the only person in your company practicing (or aspiring to practice) user centered design" or who "regularly work on a team where you are the *only* UX person." Chapters 3 (Building Support for Your Work) and 4 (Growing Yourself and Your Career) are full of good advice and useful resources.

---

2 *Sorry. Try not to take it personally. Do good work. Enjoy your home life. Be happy.*

# Resist the dark forces

Usability is, at its heart, a user advocate job: Like the Lorax, you speak for the trees. Well, the users, actually. Usability is about serving people better by building better products.

But there's a trend—which I first noticed about five years ago—for some people[3] to try to get usability practitioners to help them figure out how to manipulate users rather than serve their needs.[4]

I have no problem with the idea of people asking for our help influencing users.

If you want to know how to influence people, just read Robert Cialdini's classic book on the subject, *Influence: The Psychology of Persuasion*. It's brilliant and effective, full of time-proven ideas.

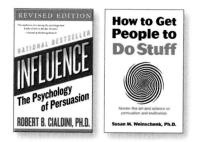

Or read any of Susan Weinschenk's books about the useful lessons that neuropsychology research can teach us about human motivation and decision making.

I don't have a problem with helping to *persuade* people to do things, either, as long as it's not deceptive. The think-aloud protocol in usability tests can often produce valuable insights into why attempts at persuasion succeed or fail.

But I get anxious whenever I hear people talk about using usability tests to help determine whether something is *desirable*, because it's just not something usability tests are good for measuring. You may get a sense during a test session that the participant finds something desirable, but it's just that: a sense. Whether something is desirable is a market research question, best answered by using market research tools and instruments.

---

[3] *[cough] marketing [cough]*

[4] *There's even a book called* Evil by Design: Interaction Design to Lead Us into Temptation *by Chris Nodder that explains how an understanding of human frailties can guide your design decisions. Each chapter deals with one of the Seven Deadly Sins (Gluttony, Pride, Sloth, and so on).*

The real problem is that these people often aren't actually asking for our help determining whether something is desirable, or even for help in figuring out how to make what they produce *more* desirable. Instead, they're looking to usability to tell them how to make people *think* it's desirable, i.e., to manipulate them.

Sometimes the intended manipulation is relatively benign, like using a slightly hidden checkbox checked by default to automatically sign you up for a newsletter.

Sometimes it inches closer to the darkness, doing things like tricking people into installing an unwanted browser toolbar[5] and changing their default search and Home page settings while they're not looking. We've all been on the receiving end of this kind of deception.

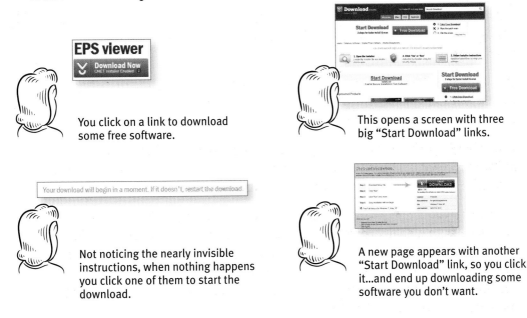

You click on a link to download some free software.

This opens a screen with three big "Start Download" links.

Not noticing the nearly invisible instructions, when nothing happens you click one of them to start the download.

A new page appears with another "Start Download" link, so you click it...and end up downloading some software you don't want.

At its extreme, though, it can cross the line into true black hat practices, like phishing, scamming, and identity theft.

Just be aware that if people ask you to do any of this, it's not part of your job.

The users are counting on you.

---

5   *[cough] Yahoo [cough]*

# A few definitive answers

Before I wrap up, a little bonus for hanging in this far.

Almost everything in this book has been about how much the answer to usability questions depends on the context and that the answer to most usability questions is "It depends."

But I know that we all love to have definitive answers, so here's a tiny collection of things that you should always do or never do.

- **Don't use small, low-contrast type.** You can use large, low-contrast type, or small (well, smallish) high-contrast type. But *never* use small, low-contrast type. (And try to stay away from the other two, too.) Unless you're designing your own design portfolio site, and you really, truly don't care whether anybody can read the text or not.

- **Don't put labels inside form fields.** Yes, it can be very tempting, especially on cramped mobile screens. But don't do it unless all of these are true: The form is exceptionally simple, the labels disappear when you start typing and reappear if you empty the field, the labels can never be confused with answers, and there's no possibility that you'll end up submitting the labels along with what you type ("Job TiAssistant Managertle"). *And* you've made sure they're completely accessible.

    If you don't agree, before you send me email please search for "Don't Put Labels Inside Text Boxes (Unless You're Luke W)" and read it.

- **Preserve the distinction between visited and unvisited text links.** By default, Web browsers display links to pages that you've already opened in a different color so you can see which options you've already tried. This turns out to be very useful information, especially since it's tracked by URL, not by the wording of the link. So if you clicked on Book a trip, when you see Book a flight later you know that it would take you to the same page.

    You can choose any colors you want, as long as they're noticeably different.

- **Don't float headings between paragraphs.** Headings should be closer to the text that follows them than the text that precedes them. (Yes, I know I mentioned this is Chapter 3, but it's so important it's worth repeating.)

That's all, folks.

As Bob and Ray used to say, "Hang by your thumbs, and write if you get work."

I hope you'll check in at my Web site stevekrug.com from time to time, and always feel free to send me email at stevekrug@gmail.com. I can promise you I will read it and appreciate it, even if I can't always find enough time to reply.

But above all, be of good cheer. As I said at the beginning, building a great Web site or app is an enormous challenge, and anyone who gets it even half right has my admiration.

And please don't take anything I've said as being against breaking "the rules" — or at least bending them. I know there are even sites where you *do* want the interface to make people think, to puzzle or challenge them. Just be sure you know which rules you're bending and that you at least *think* you have a good reason for bending them.

Oh, by the way, here's the rest of *Calvin and Hobbes.*

CALVIN AND HOBBES © 1989 Watterson. Reprinted with permission of UNIVERSAL UCLICK. All rights reserved.

# Acknowledgments

...AND ALL I GOT WAS THIS LOUSY T-SHIRT

*...and the men of the U.S.S.* Forrestal, *without whose cooperation this film would never have been made.*

—CONVENTIONAL MOVIE ACKNOWLEDGMENT

[Insert some variation of the "It takes a village" meme here.]

But it's true. Not only *couldn't I* have done this alone—I wouldn't have wanted to. Again, I was fortunate enough to be able to round up the usual suspects who got me through the earlier editions and *Rocket Surgery*.

I have relied deeply on their kindness and their extraordinary goodwill in the face of my writing habits.

As usual, my peculiar relationship to time has made life difficult for everyone involved. (Have you ever heard the expression "If it weren't for the last minute, I wouldn't get anything done at all"?) Honestly, it's just that someone keeps setting my clock ahead every time I'm not looking.

Thanks—and in most cases apologies—are due to

**Elisabeth Bayle**, who has been my interlocutor, sounding board, and friend for some years now, and—even though she doesn't want to admit it—editor of this edition. If you're ever going to write a book, my best advice is to find someone who's smart, funny, and knows as much about the subject matter as you do, and then convince them to spend long hours listening, making great suggestions, and editing your work.

It's not so much that this book wouldn't have happened without her (although it wouldn't). It's that I wouldn't have considered doing it unless I knew she'd be involved. My thanks also go out to **Elliott** for always renewing her spirits after another long day working with me had drained them.

**Barbara Flanagan**, copy editor and dear old friend. To paraphrase an old joke, "Barbara has never been wrong about a point of grammar in her life. Well, there was that one time when she *thought* she was wrong, but she wasn't." Before you write me about some error in usage, be aware that Barbara long ago beat you to it, and then said, "But it's your voice. Your book. Your call." That's generosity of spirit.

**Nancy Davis**, editor-in-chief at Peachpit, who stepped away from that desk just far enough to be my *consigliere* and champion. She's one of those rare people whose praise means about ten times as much as normal praise. I will deeply miss having an excuse to chat with her about her ornithology-lovin' boys.

**Nancy Ruenzel, Lisa Brazieal, Romney Lange, Mimi Heft, Aren Straiger, Glenn Bisignani**, and all the other smart, nice, talented, hardworking people at Peachpit who have been so supportive (often while biting their tongues, I'm sure).

My reviewers—**Caroline Jarrett** and **Whitney Quesenbery**—who volunteered some of their precious time to keep me from appearing foolish. In another time, the right description for them would have been "fellow travelers." We see eye to eye on many things, and I'm just shallow enough to enjoy the company of people who agree with me. To protect the innocent, however, I feel compelled to note that inclusion in this list does not imply agreement with everything in this book.

**Randall Munroe** for his generous attitude about reprinting his work, and for giving my son and me a lot to laugh about over the years at xkcd.com. [1]

Smart and funny colleagues like **Ginny Redish, Randolph Bias, Carol Barnum, Jennifer McGinn, Nicole Burden, Heather O'Neill, Bruno Figuereido,** and **Luca Salvino**.

People who contributed specific bits of their knowledge, like **Hal Shubin, Joshua Porter, Wayne Pau, Jacqueline Ritacco**, and the folks at the **Bayard Institute** in Copenhagen.

**Lou Rosenfeld** for moral support, good counsel, and for just being Lou.

**Karen Whitehouse** and **Roger Black**, the spiritual godmother and godfather of the book, who got me into this mess in the first place by giving me the opportunity to write the first edition 14 years ago.

---

[1] *If you don't "get" some of them, there's a cottage industry of sites that will explain them to you, in the same way that Rex Parker does with each day's crossword puzzle in* The New York Times.

The large **community of usability professionals**, who tend to be a very nice bunch of folks. Go to an annual UXPA conference and find out for yourself.

The friendly **baristas** at the Putterham Circle Starbucks, often the only people I see during the day other than my wife. (It's not *their* fault that when corporate redesigned the place recently they decided that good lighting wasn't something people really needed.)

My son, **Harry,** now finishing his degree at RPI, whose company I treasure more than he knows. I exhaust his patience regularly by asking him to explain to me just one more time the difference between a meme and a trope.

If anyone has a job opening for a Cognitive Science major with a minor in Game Design, I'll be happy to pass it on.

And finally, **Melanie**, who has only one known failing: an inherited lack of superstition that leads her to say things like "Well, I haven't had a cold all Winter." Apart from that, I am, as I say so often, among the most fortunate of husbands.

If you'd like your life to be good, marry well.

# Index

## N

names, importance of, 14
navigation
    conventions, 64
    designing, 58
    lower-level, 72
    persistent, 66
    revealing content, 63
needless words, omitting, 48–52
new feature requests, 139
Nielsen, Jakob, xi, 54, 58–59, 96, 115, 121
noise. *See* visual noise
Norman, Don, 151

## P

page name
    importance of, 74–76
    matching what user clicked, 76
    position on page, 75
persistent navigation, 66
primary navigation. *See* Sections
*Prince and the Pauper, The,* 26
printer-friendly pages, 171
promos
    content promos, 86
    feature promos, 86
pull-down menus, limitations of, 108–09

## R

recruiting test participants, 120–21
Redish, Janice (Ginny), 40, 41, 46, 179, 194
registration, 87, 99
reinventing the wheel, 31
religious debates, 103, 104, 109
reservoir of goodwill, 166–71
responsive design, 149, 150
"right" way to design Web sites, 7
Rosenfeld, Louis, 194

## S

satisficing, 24–25
scanning pages, 22–23
scent of information, 43,
script for usability test, 125, 127–36
search box, 16–17, 30, 58, 71–72, 86, 99
    on Home page, 86
    options, 71
    wording, 71
search-dominant users, 58
secondary navigation. *See* subsections
section fronts, 50
Sections, 69–70
signifiers, 151
Site ID, 67–68
sizzle, 169
slow-loading pages, 59
stop signs, 29

street signs, 64, 74
subsections, 68–69

## T

tabs, 80–81
   color coding, 81
   importance of drawing correctly, 81
tagline, 93, 95–98
Talking Heads, 55
teleportation, 62, 67, 92
Theofanos, Mary, 179
tradeoffs, 145–47
tragedy of the commons, 100
trunk test, 82–83

## U

usability
   attributes of, 155
   defined, 9
usability lab, 115
usability testing, 3, 110
   do-it-yourself, 115
   vs. focus groups, 112–13
   of mobile devices, 160–63
   number of users to test, 119
   observers, 124
   recruiting participants, 120–21
   remote, 140
   reviewing results, 137–39
   sample session, 127

   unmoderated, 140
   value of starting early, 115
   what to test, 124
User Experience Design (UXD, UX), x, 183
UserTesting.com, 140
Utilities, 65, 69–70

## V–Z

validator, accessibility, 177
visual hierarchy, 33–36
visual noise, 38
Welcome blurb, 93
White, E. B., 49
xkcd, 194
Zuckerberg, Mark, 26

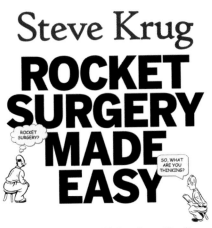

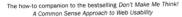The how-to companion to the bestselling *Don't Make Me Think!*
*A Common Sense Approach to Web Usability*

# Steve Krug

# ROCKET SURGERY MADE EASY

The Do-It-Yourself Guide to Finding
and Fixing Usability Problems

# Also Available

It's been known for years that usability testing can dramatically improve products. But with a typical price tag of $5,000 to $10,000 for a usability consultant to conduct each round of tests, it rarely happens.

In this how-to companion to *Don't Make Me Think: A Common Sense Approach to Web Usability*, Steve Krug spells out a streamlined approach to usability testing that anyone can easily apply to their own Web site, application, or other product. (As he said in *Don't Make Me Think*, "It's not rocket surgery".)

Using practical advice, plenty of illustrations, and his trademark humor, Steve explains how to:

- Test any design, from a sketch on a napkin to a fully functioning Web site or application
- Keep your focus on finding the most important problems (because no one has the time or resources to fix them all)
- Fix the problems that you find, using his "The least you can do" approach

By paring the process of testing and fixing products down to its essentials ("A morning a month, that's all we ask"), *Rocket Surgery* makes it realistic for teams to test early and often, catching problems while it's still easy to fix them. *Rocket Surgery Made Easy* uses the same proven mix of clear writing, before-and-after examples, witty illustrations, and practical advice that made *Don't Make Me Think* an instant classic.

**Steve Krug** (pronounced "kroog") is best known as the author of *Don't Make Me Think: A Common Sense Approach to Web Usability*, now in its third edition with over 350,000 copies in print. Ten years later, he finally gathered enough energy to write another one: the usability testing handbook *Rocket Surgery Made Easy*. The books were based on the 20+ years he's spent as a usability consultant for a wide variety of clients like Apple, Bloomberg.com, Lexus.com, NPR, the International Monetary Fund, and many others.

His consulting firm, Advanced Common Sense is based in Chestnut Hill, MA. Steve currently spends most of his time teaching usability workshops, consulting, and watching black-and-white movies from the '30s and '40s.

Rocket Surgery Made Easy: The Do-It-Yourself Guide to Finding and Fixing Usability Problems
Steve Krug, ISBN: 9780321657299
www.newriders.com